IMAGES
of America

AFRICAN AMERICANS IN SPOKANE

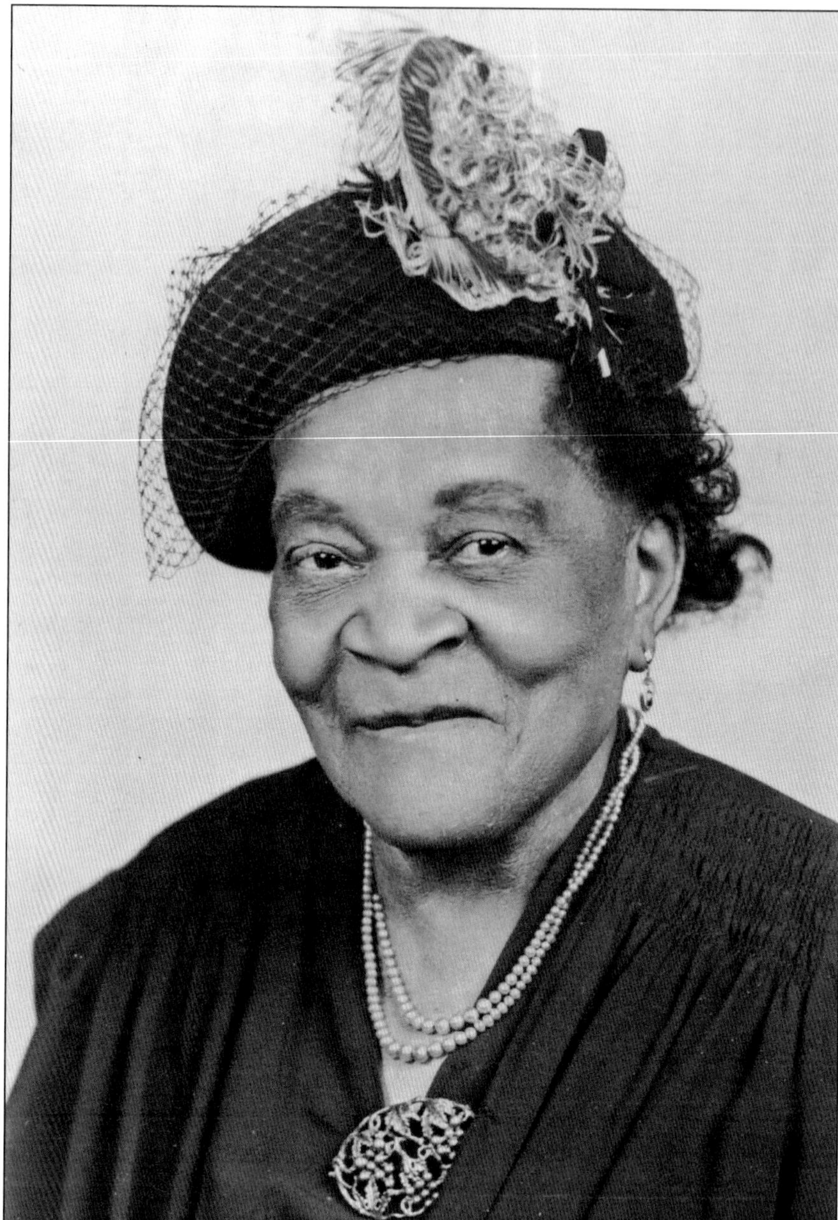

Dora Alice Freeman came to Spokane, Washington, from Durham, North Carolina, in 1904. In 1908, she became the first black sales clerk for Miller, Mower, and Flynn department store at Riverside Avenue and Monroe Street. Discharged because of white customers' complaints, she became a maid at the Auditorium Theatre and the Spokane Athletic Club. She reared six sons alone and died in 1964 at age 84. (Courtesy of Spokane Northwest Black Pioneers.)

On the Cover: This band is from the Pirates' Den, later called the Harlem Club. The truck carried band members around downtown Spokane to advertise the club. E. J. Brown, club owner, is standing at right. Buck Pierce Campbell is seated on the truck bed, third from right. The photograph, taken at the Masonic Temple on Riverside Avenue, is from about 1931. (Courtesy of Spokane Northwest Black Pioneers.)

IMAGES
of America

AFRICAN AMERICANS IN SPOKANE

Jerrelene Williamson,
Spokane Northwest Black Pioneers

ARCADIA
PUBLISHING

ISBN 978-0-7385-7011-2

Published by Arcadia Publishing
Charleston SC, Chicago IL, Portsmouth NH, San Francisco CA

Printed in the United States of America

Library of Congress Control Number: 2009922880

For all general information contact Arcadia Publishing at:
Telephone 843-853-2070
Fax 843-853-0044
E-mail sales@arcadiapublishing.com
For customer service and orders:
Toll-Free 1-888-313-2665

Visit us on the Internet at www.arcadiapublishing.com

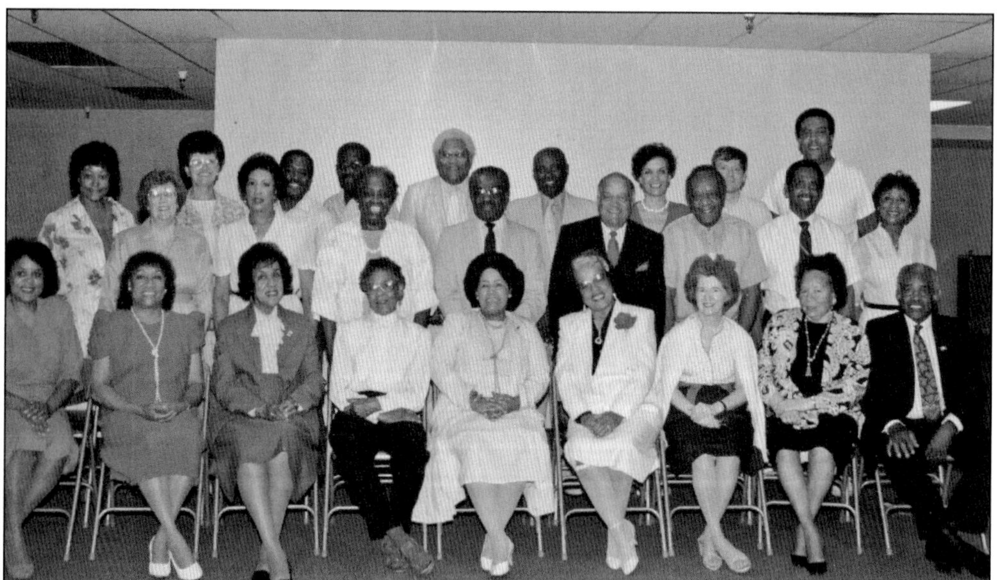

This book is dedicated to the brave African Americans who first traveled to the Spokane area and to the black pioneers who put together the photograph exhibit for the Centennial Tribute to Northwest Black Pioneers in 1989 to commemorate the centennial of Washington State. This is the group that produced the Centennial Tribute to Northwest Black Pioneers, pictured from left to right: (first row) Jeanne A. Baynes, Jerrelene Williamson, Eleanor E. Chase, Ruth N. Nichols, Juanita Leslie, Frances Z. Freeman, Gwen Hill, Pauline Lake, and Sylvester J. Lake; (second row) Nancy Compau, Kathy Smith, Amy L. Carter, Bill Gaskins Sr., Clarence T. Freeman, Alfonse H. Hill, Billy V. Morris, and Gloria Morris; (third row) Jennifer E. Roseman, Gloria S. Murphy, Rev. Percy ("Happy") Watkins, Charles L. Bridges, Carl Maxey, Elmo Dalbert, Char Cooper, Gerry Riddle, and Roland Chase.

CONTENTS

Acknowledgments

I would like to thank all of those who helped me with this book: The Northwest Museum of Arts and Culture, Spokane, Washington; Marsha Rooney, Rose Krause, Jane Davey, and Richard Bruce (sponsored by the Kalispel Tribe of Indians); the Eastern Washington State Historical Society; Riva Dean of Spokane Public Library; the Spokane Northwest Black Pioneers organization, especially Ruth N. Nichols and William Gaskins, the remaining board members I am honored to serve alongside; and my daughter Jennifer Roseman and Nancy Compau, formerly of Spokane Public Library, who compiled all the data for the Spokane Northwest Black Pioneers Collection.

A special thank-you goes to the former Bon Marche (Macy's) department stores and staff in Spokane for helping to organize the Centennial Tribute to Northwest Black Pioneers in 1989.

Many thanks go to the *Spokesman Review* and the *Spokane Chronicle* for their diligence in reporting such uplifting stories about the African American community in Spokane through the years.

Last, but not least, a very special thanks to Gwen Hill and my dear husband, Sam.

Unless otherwise noted, all photographs appear courtesy of Spokane Northwest Black Pioneers.

INTRODUCTION

This book is about African Americans in Spokane, Washington. It begins in the late 1890s, when a great migration of blacks came from Roslyn, Washington, after the mines closed. These blacks, along with others who came directly to Spokane from the southern United States, came to the Pacific Northwest for a better life. This book offers a glimpse of their lives in the city of Spokane. It tells about their families, their lifestyle, the discrimination they encountered, their churches and businesses, the employment situation, their triumphs, and their defeats. It is the story of a people and their everyday existence in a city that was not always welcoming to them. It is a story of African Americans determined to persevere against all odds.

The black settlers who came to Spokane from Roslyn were surprised to find a completely new way of life. In Spokane, there were no black-owned enterprises or stores that they could frequent. Roslyn, before the mines closed, was a thriving community. People of all nationalities worked in the mines and also had businesses. There were tailors, dressmakers, a general store, barbershops, and many other businesses, some of them owned by blacks. Mary Perkins, this author's great-aunt, owned one of these stores. There were many places to eat, according to her relatives who had lived in Roslyn. This book gives a little-known account of Roslyn's history.

In Spokane, most of the black men worked as laborers or porters in some hotels and did construction work on the roads to keep up Spokane's streets. They also worked as barbers in white-owned shops where black men were not serviced. There were a very few black men who had barbershops of their own. Black women did domestic work, cared for white children, cooked for white families, and worked as hotel maids. This book is about their story.

A black man who came to Spokane Falls (later called Spokane) was appointed deputy county commissioner in 1904. He and his family have quite a history in Spokane. He sued the Washington Water Power Company because he and his family were refused service at a restaurant in Natatorium Park, which the company owned. In another lawsuit, a black man sued the Pantages Theater for trying to make him sit in the balcony. These two court cases turned out very differently.

The National Association for the Advancement of Colored People (NAACP) has a place in this story, too. Its chapter in Spokane was started by a black businessman who owned a transfer and storage company and was president of the Negro Businessmen's League. He also was an active church member and Sunday school teacher in addition to being a community leader.

Included in this story are two black churches, established in Spokane at around the same time: Calvary Baptist Church and Bethel African Methodist Episcopal Church. Calvary was started in 1890, and Bethel began soon afterward. This book gives an account of the early ministers, the choirs, and the congregations of both of these great churches. The photographs show how much these first churches meant to Spokane's African American community

The African American churches in Spokane were the lifeblood of their people. There was always something going on at the church. There were plays, dinners, ice cream socials, contests, picnics, and ball games at the park, and many things to keep all ages busy. Blacks were refused service at restaurants and other places, so the churches provided their own entertainment.

This book covers the story of two women, one of whom came to Spokane with the Works Progress Administration (WPA) and opened a day care center for young black children and also a USO for black military men and women. The other woman was the first president of the Colored Women's Federation of Washington Jurisdiction in 1907.

There is the story of the Pirates' Den (later called the Harlem Club) that catered to both black and white; the Willow Inn, a black restaurant; and also Virgil's Chicken Shack, which customers said served some of the best food in the region. These restaurants were owned by entrepreneurs who made a living at what they were efficient at doing. Also included in this story is the Poodle Dog Restaurant, located near Howard Street and First Avenue, which was owned by Ollie Williams around 1912.

There were many black social clubs in the Spokane area. Their purpose was to entertain and to teach the young people about the social graces, such as the correct way to set a table or greet someone or how to act in public. Some of these clubs were the Pierian Club, the Wednesday Art Club, the Dunbar Reading Club, the Crest Club, the Phillis Wheatley Club, and others.

This book tells about discrimination in Spokane, not only against its own black citizens, but also against famous people who visited here. It describes subtle and not-so-subtle discrimination in all of its ugliness. Included are accounts of when notables like the Harlem Globetrotters, Sammy Davis Jr., and Louis Armstrong came to entertain in Spokane. It also gives an account of a lesser known story of when the great singer Marian Anderson came to Spokane.

There have been triumphs and tragedies on the national scene that affected African Americans in Spokane. One triumph was the passing of the Civil Rights Bill. A major tragedy was the assassination of the Rev. Dr. Martin Luther King Jr.

This is the story of black men and women who, despite the lowliest of circumstances in some cases, pushed forward to "make it work." It is a story of triumph, including the tale of a black man who came to this city on a freight train with a friend, found work, married a young lady from a prominent black family, opened his own business with his friend, and later was elected the first black mayor of Spokane.

There is also a story in this book about a black orphan who was born in Spokane, raised here, attended law school at Gonzaga University, and became a well-known attorney who "kicked against the bricks" of discrimination until the walls fell down.

Another account in this book is about a young man who went into the military service in World War II, became a captain, returned to Spokane, and became a leader in the community, establishing his own business. Today in downtown Spokane, a building is named after him.

Then there is the account of a man who, though born in Montana, came to Spokane as a child. When he grew to manhood, he tried many different occupations: playing in bands, studying to be a mortician, and taking flying lessons. Because of his ability in the latter endeavor, he became the first licensed African American pilot in Washington state. This man also learned the art of photography. He was always somewhere in the African American community taking photographs of different functions: parties, Masonic Lodge events, family gatherings, reunions, and church activities including contests, plays, and picnics. He also took countless photographs of individuals. Wherever there was something going on in the African American community, he was there with his camera. He finally opened a studio, where he continued to photograph African Americans in the Spokane community. He is gone now, but he will not be forgotten because his extensive collection is housed at the Northwest Museum of Arts and Culture (MAC) in Spokane.

One

Roslyn, Washington

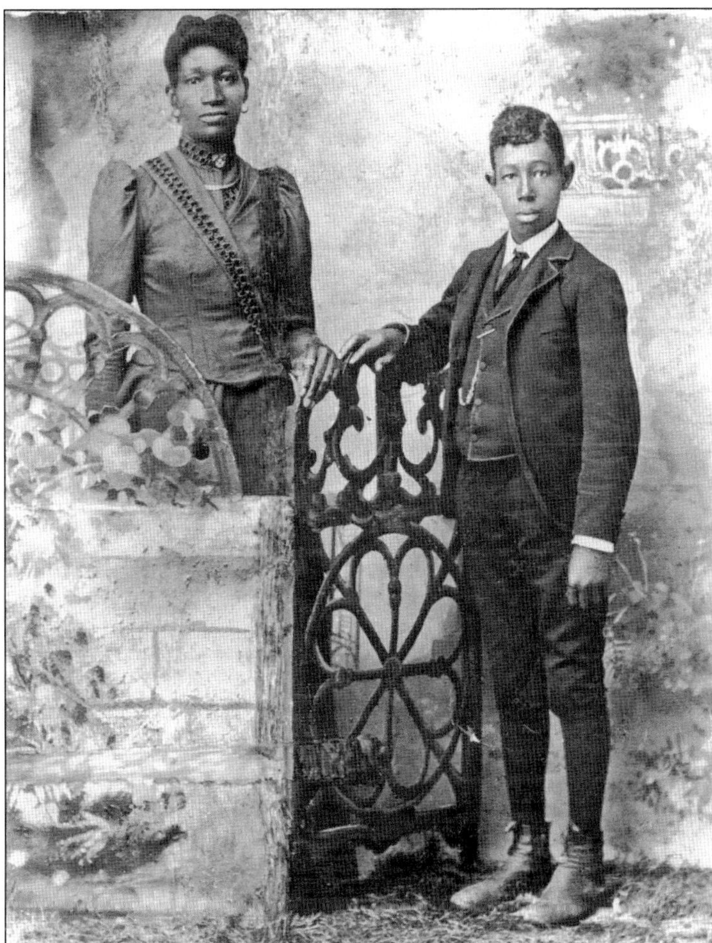

In 1888, the Northern Pacific Coal Company recruited black men, including Henry Breckenridge, to come to Roslyn, Washington, to work, but they discovered they were hired to break the white miners' strike. After much fighting and bloodshed, the strike was settled and the workers—black and white—returned to the mines. Henry's wife, Lucy, their son John, and Henry's sister, Mary, came to Roslyn on the second train.

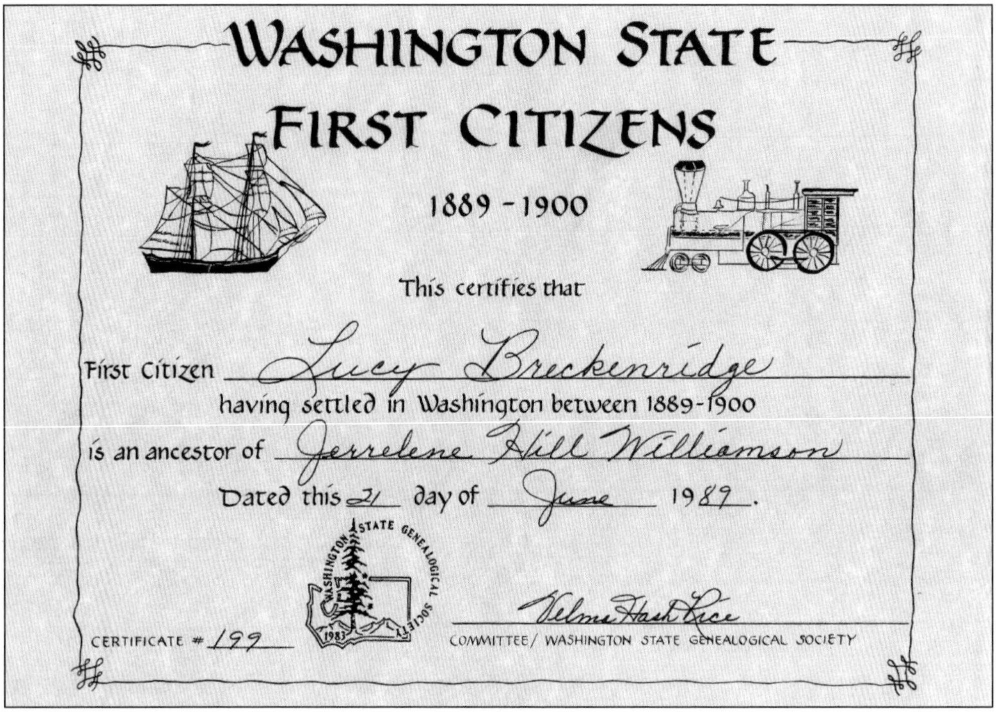

WASHINGTON STATE
FIRST CITIZENS
1889 - 1900

This certifies that

First Citizen Lucy Breckenridge
having settled in Washington between 1889-1900
is an ancestor of Jerrelene Hill Williamson
Dated this 21 day of June 1989.

WASHINGTON STATE GENEALOGICAL SOCIETY 1983

CERTIFICATE # 199

Velma Hash Rice
COMMITTEE/ WASHINGTON STATE GENEALOGICAL SOCIETY

Lucy Breckenridge was given this certificate for being one of the first citizens to arrive before Washington became a state in 1899. She was given this honor because of the documentation through census records, photographs, and other certified proof that she was in Washington in 1888. She was happy in the home that her daughter Mary bought for her in Spokane. Lucy Breckenridge passed away April 15, 1940.

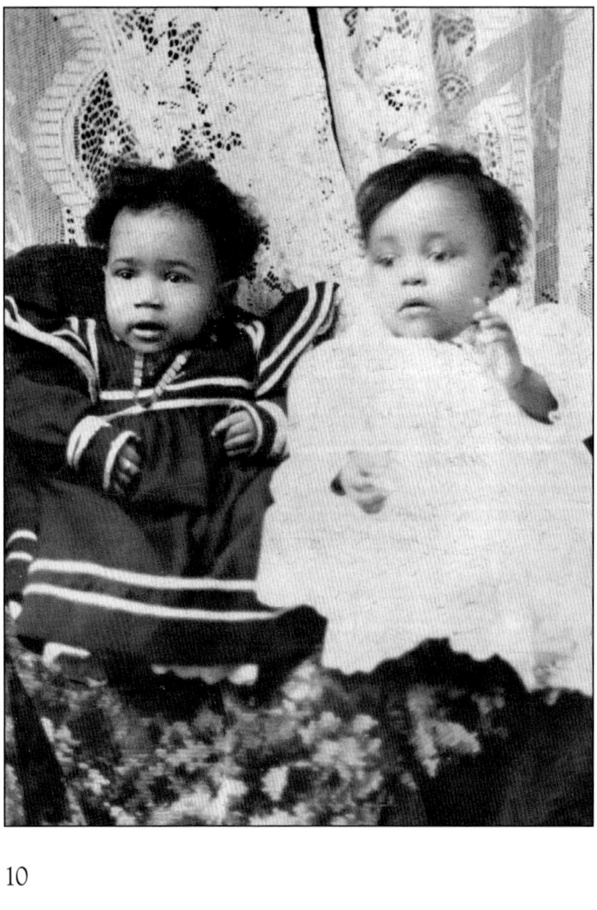

Emma Breckenridge, left, born in 1897, and Mary Breckenridge, born in 1898 in Roslyn, were niece and aunt, respectively. Emma was the daughter of Alice and John Breckenridge. Mary was the second child of Henry and Lucy Breckenridge. Emma and Mary grew up together in Spokane, attended the same school, and were very close. As adults, they worked as maids in Spokane hotels until Mary opened a restaurant in Tacoma, Washington.

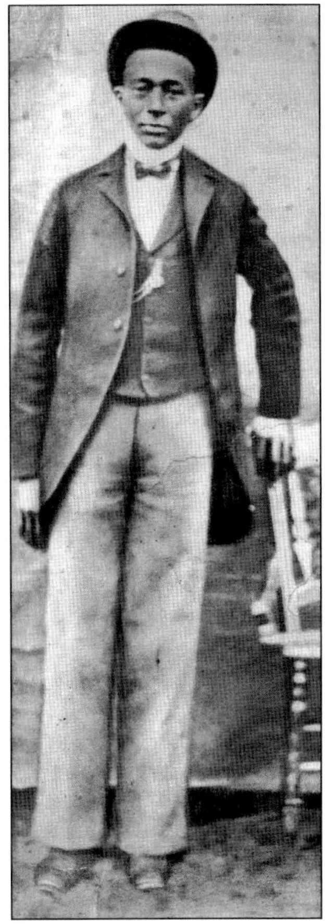

This is an early photograph of Emmett Brennan Reed, a Virginia native who was a coal miner in Virginia and Roslyn, Washington, before being ordained in the ministry in 1905. Reverend Reed had held pastorates in California, Kansas, and Montana before going to Spokane and serving at Calvary Baptist Church. He was a good friend of Henry and Lucy Breckenridge. There is much more about Reverend Reed in this book.

This picnic postcard was given to Lucy Breckenridge and sent back to Mary Perkins in Roslyn, Washington. The postcard is dated August 6, 1909. Mary Perkins was the sister of Henry, Lucy's husband. They came to Roslyn together from Staunton, Virginia. When Lucy and Henry moved to Spokane, along with their son John and his family, Mary stayed in Roslyn and opened a general store.

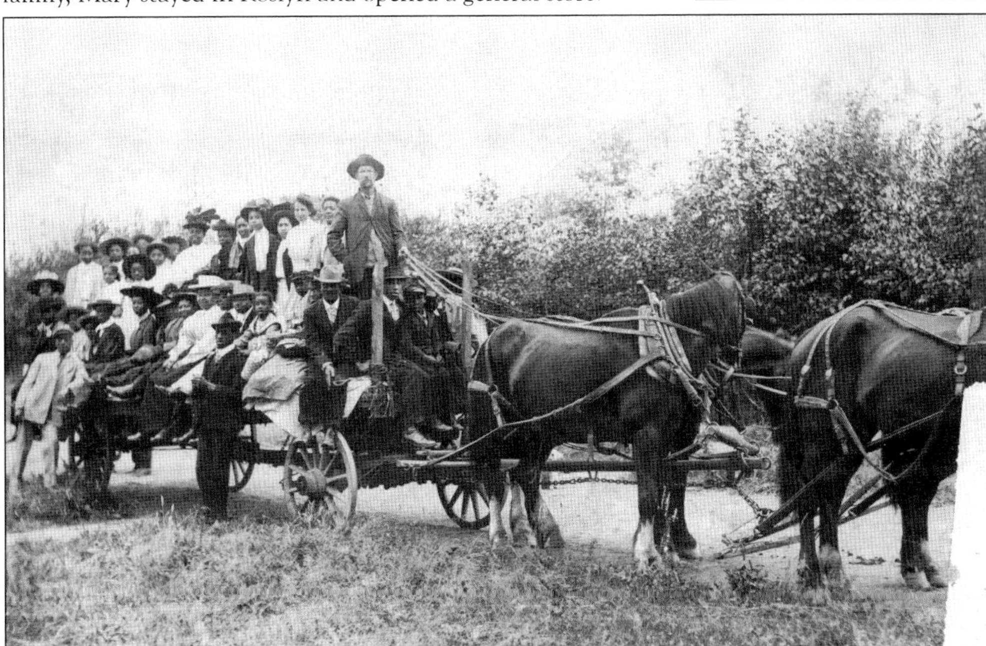

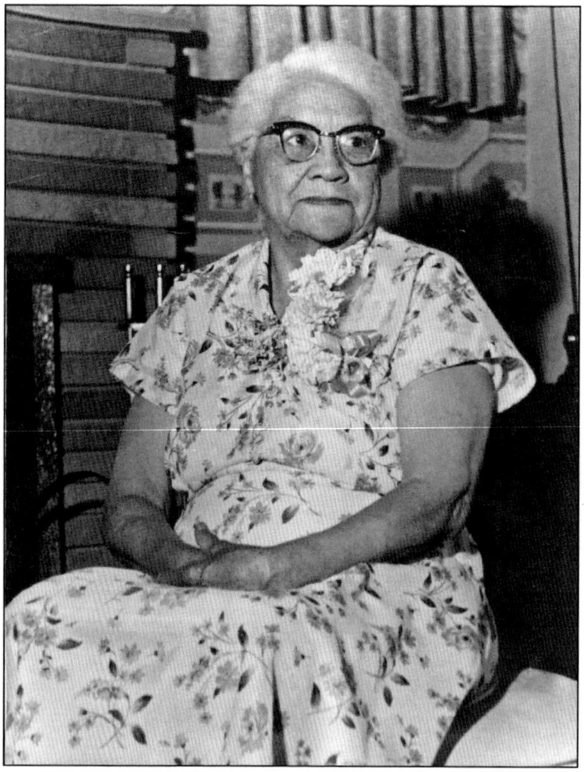

Mary Ann Jones, with her husband and three children, Anna, Adrian, and Bernice, lived in Roslyn, Washington. They moved to Spokane on June 25, 1926. This is a later photograph of her taken when she lived in Spokane. The family lived close to Calvary Baptist Church on Second Avenue when Reverend Reed was its pastor. Today the church is located at 203 East Third Avenue.

This Certificate of Marriage for Alice Ackerman and John Breckenridge was signed when they married in Roslyn, Washington, on June 30, 1896. Notice that on the certificate, "Territory" is crossed out and "State" is stamped on the document. Washington was declared a state in 1899. This is a rare document because the description on a legal document had not even been changed officially from territory to state.

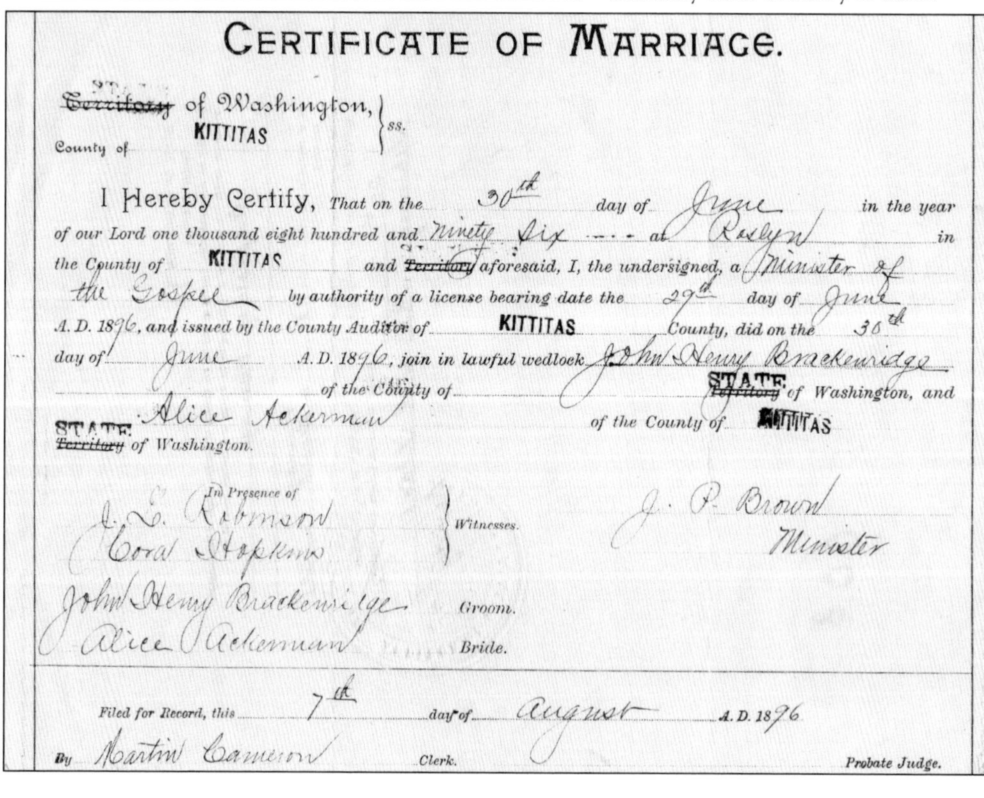

CERTIFICATE OF MARRIAGE.

STATE ~~Territory~~ of Washington, } ss.
County of KITTITAS

I Hereby Certify, That on the 30th day of June in the year of our Lord one thousand eight hundred and ninety six at Roslyn in the County of KITTITAS and STATE ~~Territory~~ aforesaid, I, the undersigned, a Minister of the Gospel by authority of a license bearing date the 29th day of June A. D. 1896, and issued by the County Auditor of KITTITAS County, did on the 30th day of June A. D. 1896, join in lawful wedlock John Henry Brackenridge of the County of STATE ~~Territory~~ of Washington, and Alice Ackerman of the County of KITTITAS STATE ~~Territory~~ of Washington.

In Presence of
J. E. Robinson
Coral Hopkins } Witnesses.

J. P. Brown
Minister

John Henry Brackenridge Groom.
Alice Ackerman Bride.

Filed for Record, this 7th day of August A. D. 1896

By Martin Cameron Clerk. Probate Judge.

Two

SPOKANE, WASHINGTON

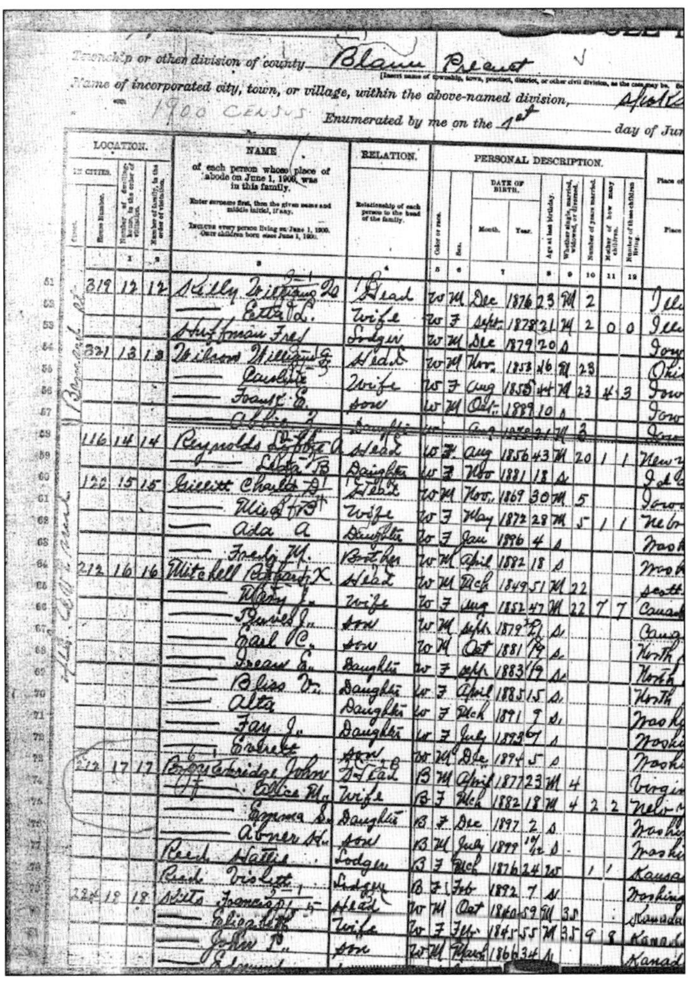

In the 1900 census, the African American influence in Spokane was just beginning to grow because of the influx from Roslyn. There were approximately 376 blacks in Spokane then, according to Joseph Franklin in *All Through the Night*. The Breckenridge family is listed as Henry and Lucy, John and Alice, and their small children. Abner, Alice and John's youngest son, is listed as 6 months old. He was born in Spokane in 1899.

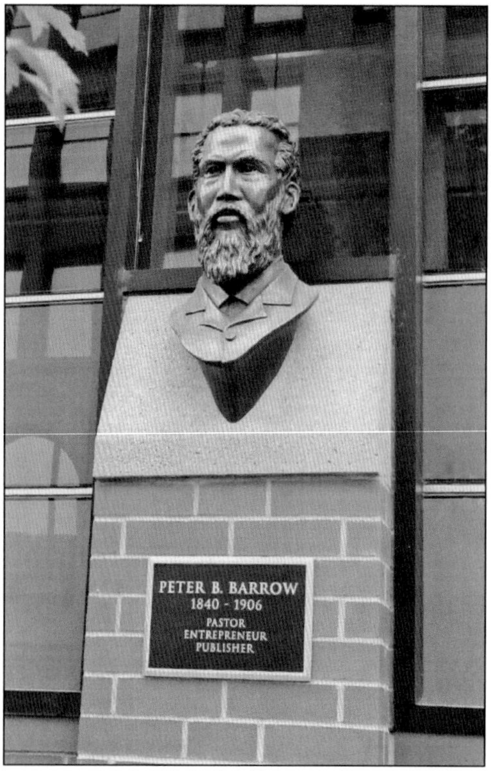

Rev. Peter Barnabas Barrow brought his family from Mississippi to Spokane in 1889 and became influential in religion and politics. In 1890, he helped establish Calvary Baptist Church, the oldest historically black church in Spokane, and was pastor from 1895 to 1906. This bust of Barrow is on the Wall of Recognition on the east side of the *Spokesman-Review* printing building in downtown Spokane.

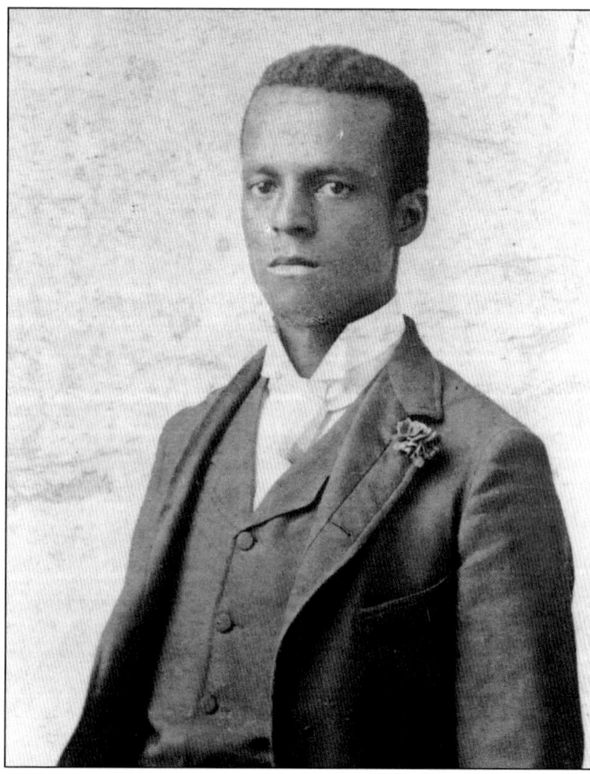

Emmett Hercules Holmes (1872–1948) was born in Mississippi and came to Spokane Falls in 1888. He was a butler for Austin Corbin, a founding father of Spokane. In 1890, the Holmes family helped found Calvary Baptist Church and Bethel African Methodist Episcopal Church. Holmes was the first black to be a deputy treasurer of Spokane County (1901–1909). He and his wife, Beatrice, had one son, Emmett Jr.

Henry W. Sample arrived in Spokane in 1891. He first worked as a waiter and then became one of the city's first black policemen, serving from 1892 to 1894. This photograph shows him on patrol with his horse. The photograph seems to have been taken on the outskirts of downtown Spokane, near the Spokane River. (Courtesy of Spokane Public Library.)

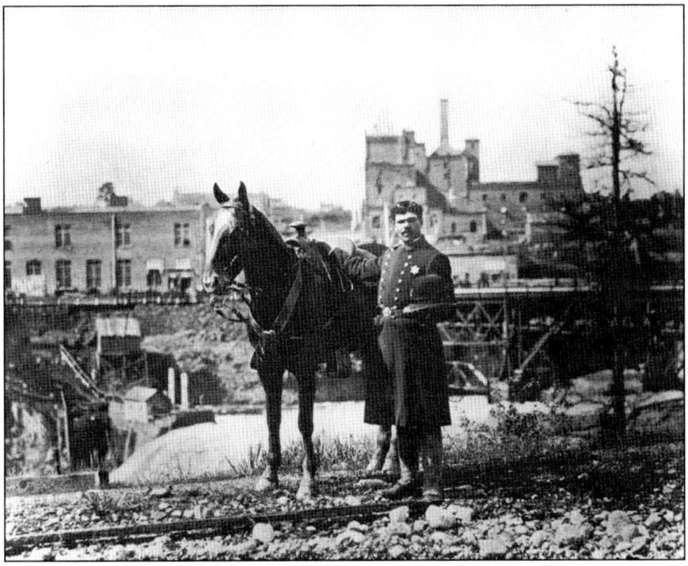

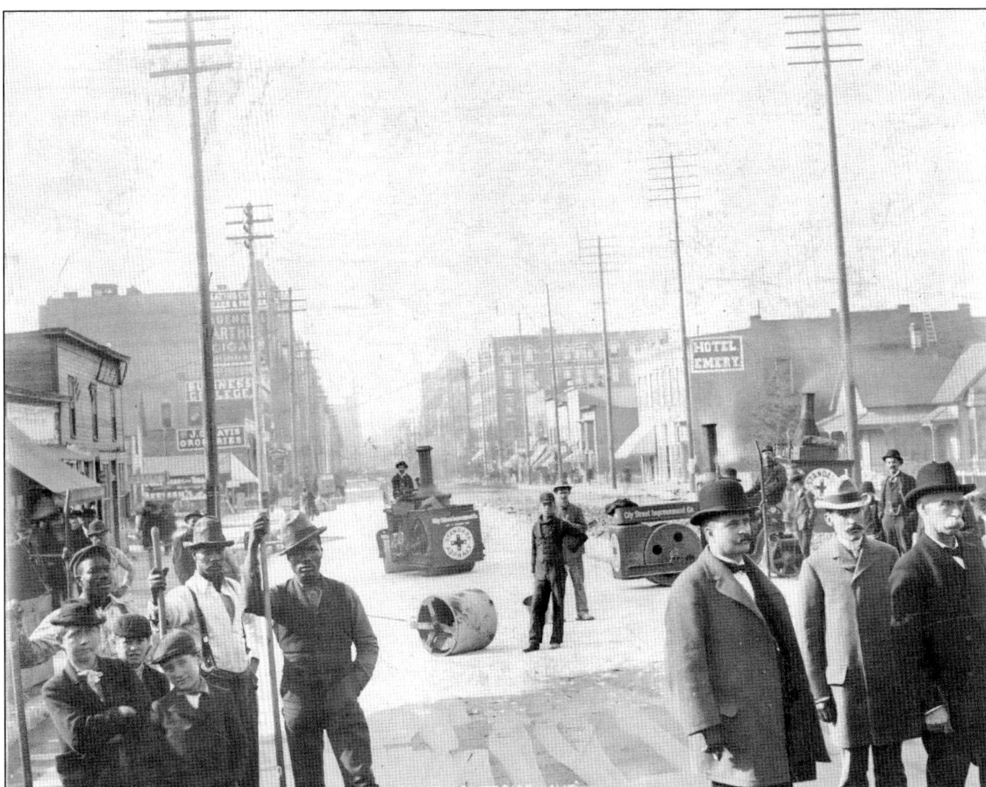

This rare photograph shows black men paving Riverside Avenue downtown on November 25, 1898. Black men generally worked as laborers, construction workers (although they were not allowed to join the unions), hotel porters, and janitors. Black women mostly did domestic work and were hotel maids. Clarence Freeman said the foundations under the downtown buildings were laid by black stonemasons from Virginia, some of whom were his relatives. (Courtesy of MAC/EWHS L85-224.)

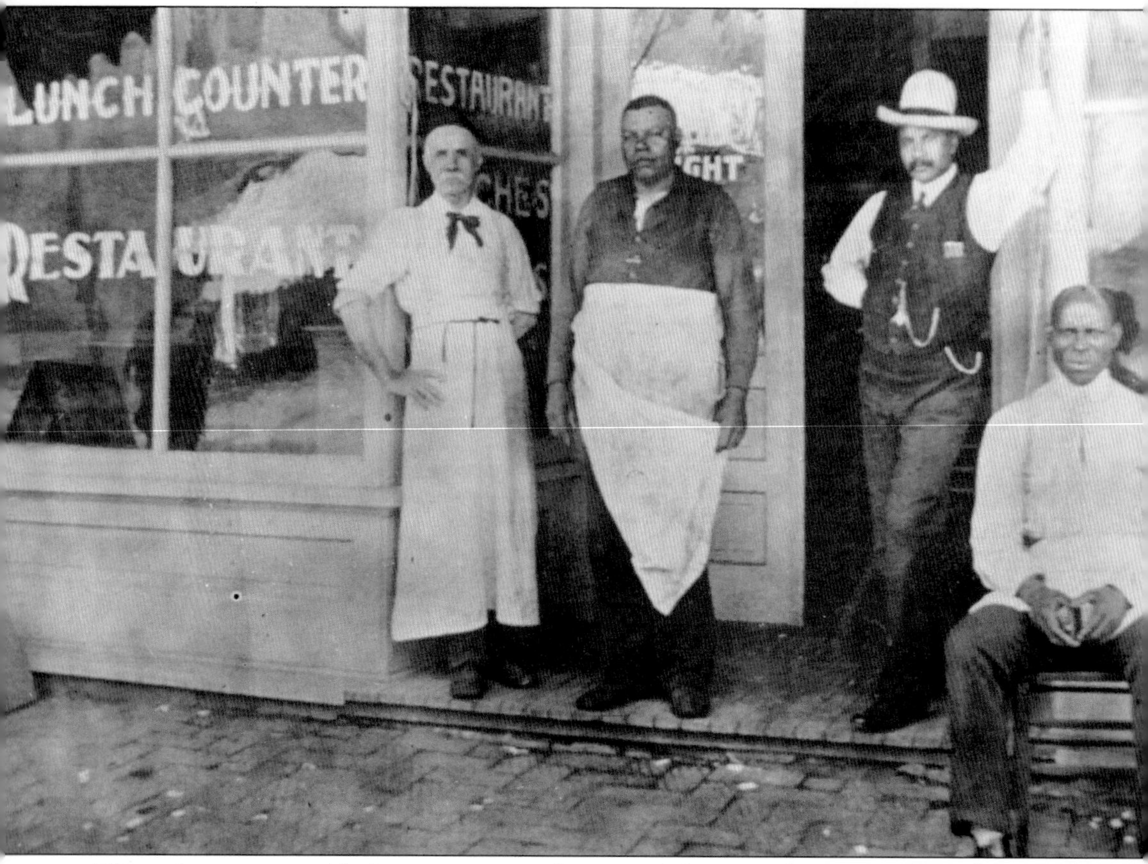

There also were some black entrepreneurs who opened their own businesses. One of these was the Poodle Dog Café restaurant. It was owned by Oliver ("Ollie") Williams and was located at 514 Front Avenue (now Spokane Falls Boulevard). This restaurant had been in this location since 1883, under the ownership of D. D. Squire, before Williams purchased it. It was a popular establishment in downtown Spokane. This photograph looks typically Western, with the gentleman in the cowboy hat and the chains hanging from his pockets. The way they are dressed is like something from an Old West movie. The Poodle Dog was a unique name for a restaurant for that time. This photograph drew a lot of attention at the Centennial Tribute to Northwest Black Pioneers. To have a black man own a restaurant in downtown Spokane was truly rare at that time. (Courtesy of MAC/EWHS L93-18.165.)

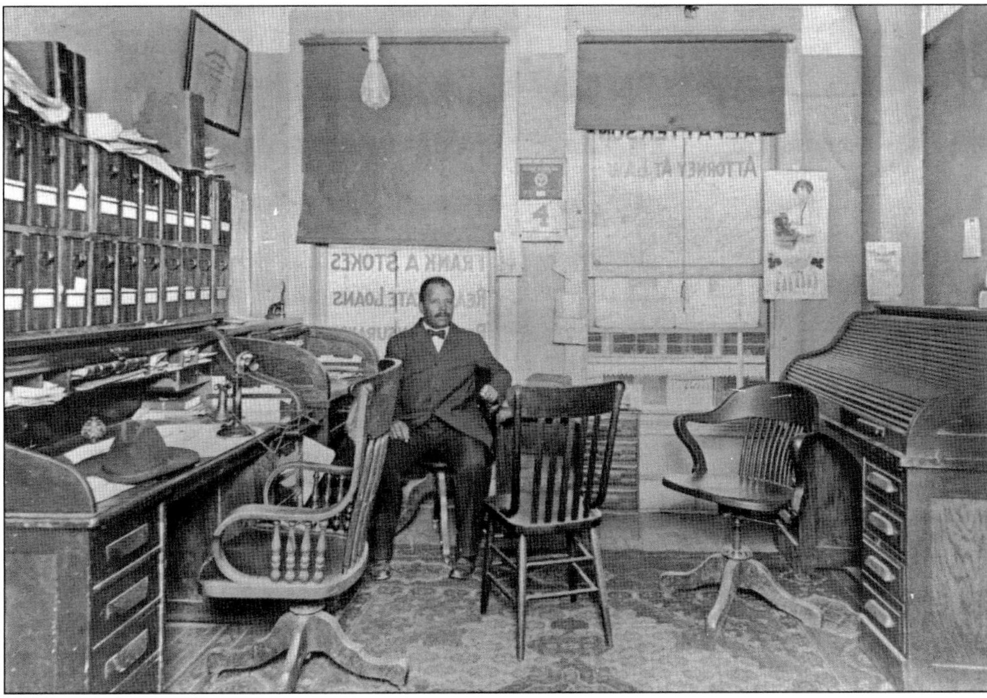

This *c.* 1900 photograph was taken in the office of Frank A. Stokes, a businessman in downtown Spokane. As noted on the window, he dealt in real estate, loans, and other enterprises. Stokes was a true black pioneer in Spokane. He was a member of the Bethel African Methodist Episcopal Church, one of the first black churches in Spokane.

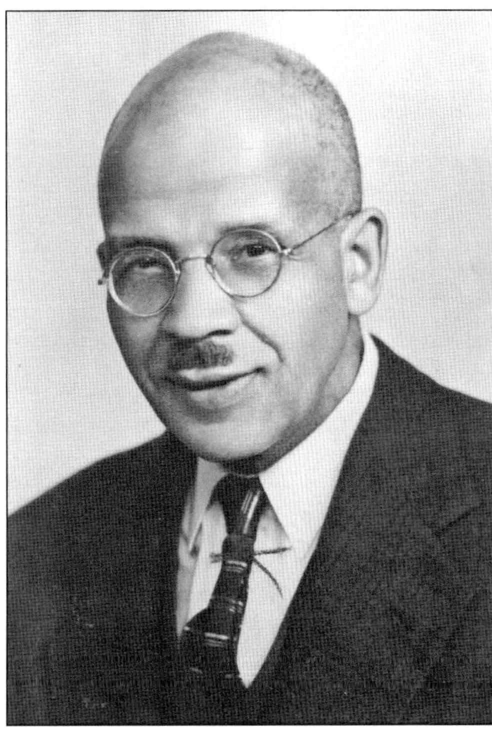

This is a later, 1940s photograph of Frank A. Stokes. In 1919, he helped organize the Spokane branch of the National Association for the Advancement of Colored People (NAACP), which was instrumental in making progress in race relations. Stokes, his wife Lillian, and their children were longtime members of Bethel AME Church. The Stokeses are the grandparents of Brian Stokes Mitchell, actor, singer, and Broadway star.

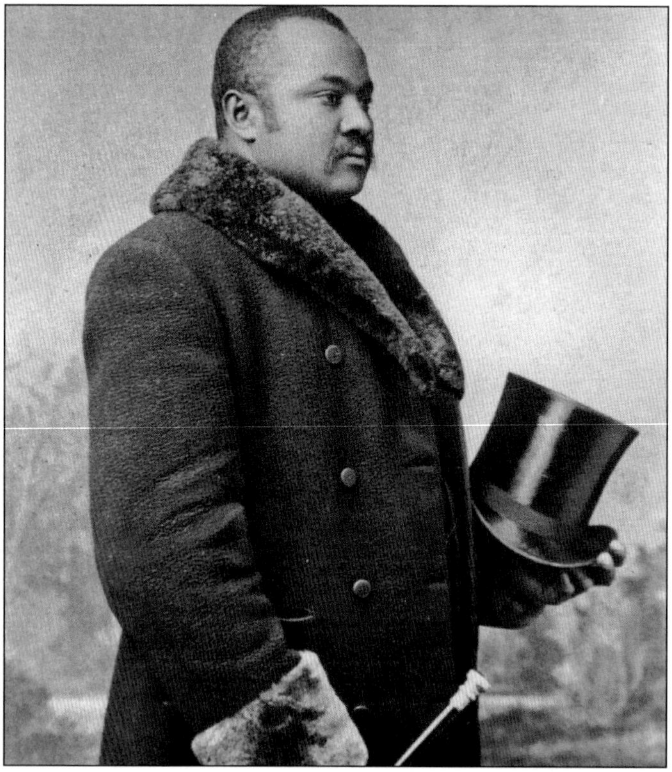

Jeremiah ("Jerry") Flowers, a Spokane black pioneer, was born in Mississippi and came to Spokane Falls in 1888. He was married to Cornelia Holmes, the daughter of Spokane pioneers John and Helen Holmes. Flowers worked as a hotel cook and later was a porter at the Oregon Railroad and Navigation Company depot. The Flowers family resided on East Hartson Street in Spokane. This photograph is from about 1890.

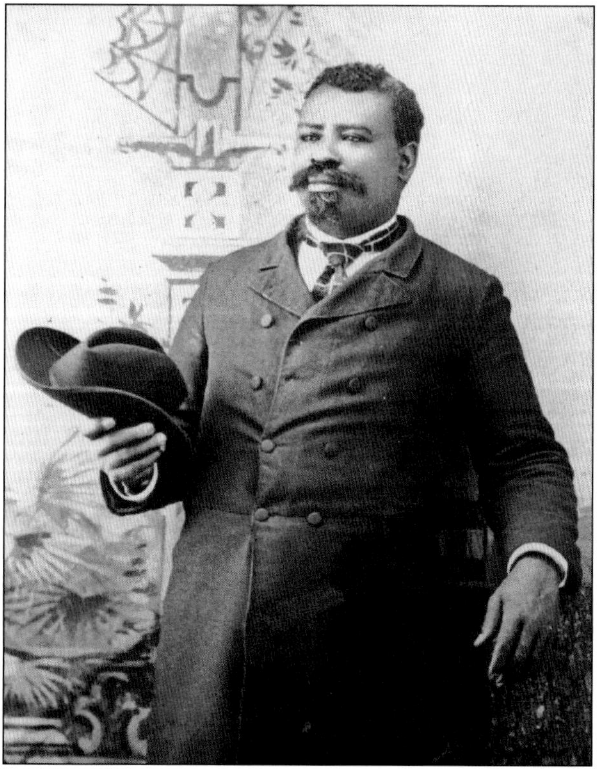

Rev. A. O. Augustus was the presiding elder of the Missionary District of the Bethel AME Church. He was sent from California to Spokane to help organize St. Paul's African Methodist Episcopal Church (later called Bethel African Methodist Episcopal Church) in 1890. Bethel AME was located then at Fifth Avenue and Pine Street. Its present location is at 605 Richard Allen Court.

Before the collection of items for the exhibits for the Centennial Tribute to Northwest Black Pioneers, many were not aware that there had been a black policeman in Spokane's early days. This photograph in the Spokane Public Library (from the former Cheney Cowles Museum) shows this policeman, Walter Lawson, in his patrol uniform. Needless to say, this find was prominently displayed in the exhibits. (Courtesy of MAC/EWHS L84-36.49.)

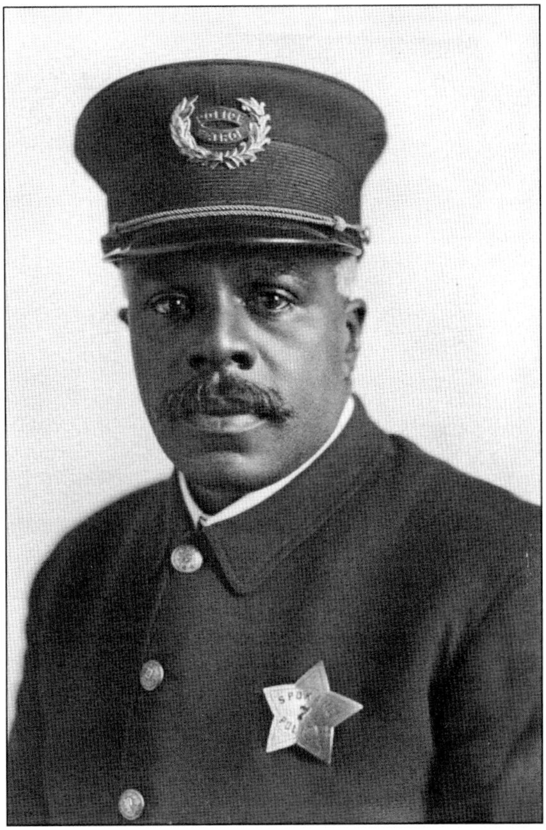

This photograph is another one taken of Walter Lawson, with the Spokane Police Department. He arrived in Spokane in 1894 and held other jobs in the city before becoming a policeman in 1900. He was the police chauffeur from 1914 to 1917. Not much else is recorded pertaining to this man, but the photograph is enough to tell his story. (Courtesy of MAC/EWHS L97-56.174.)

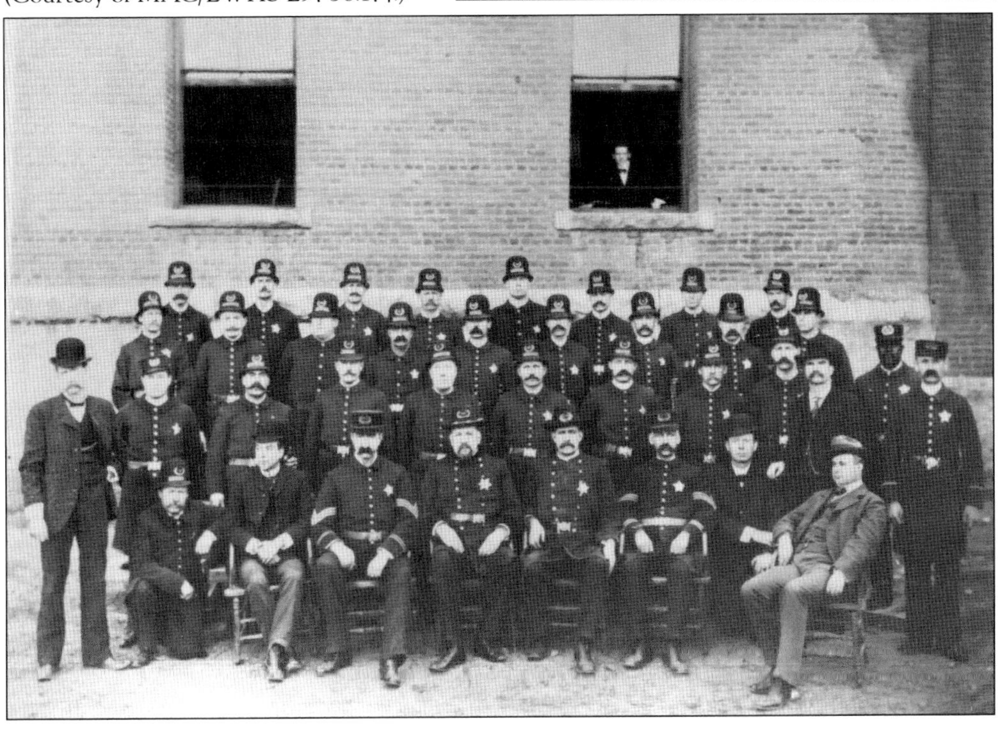

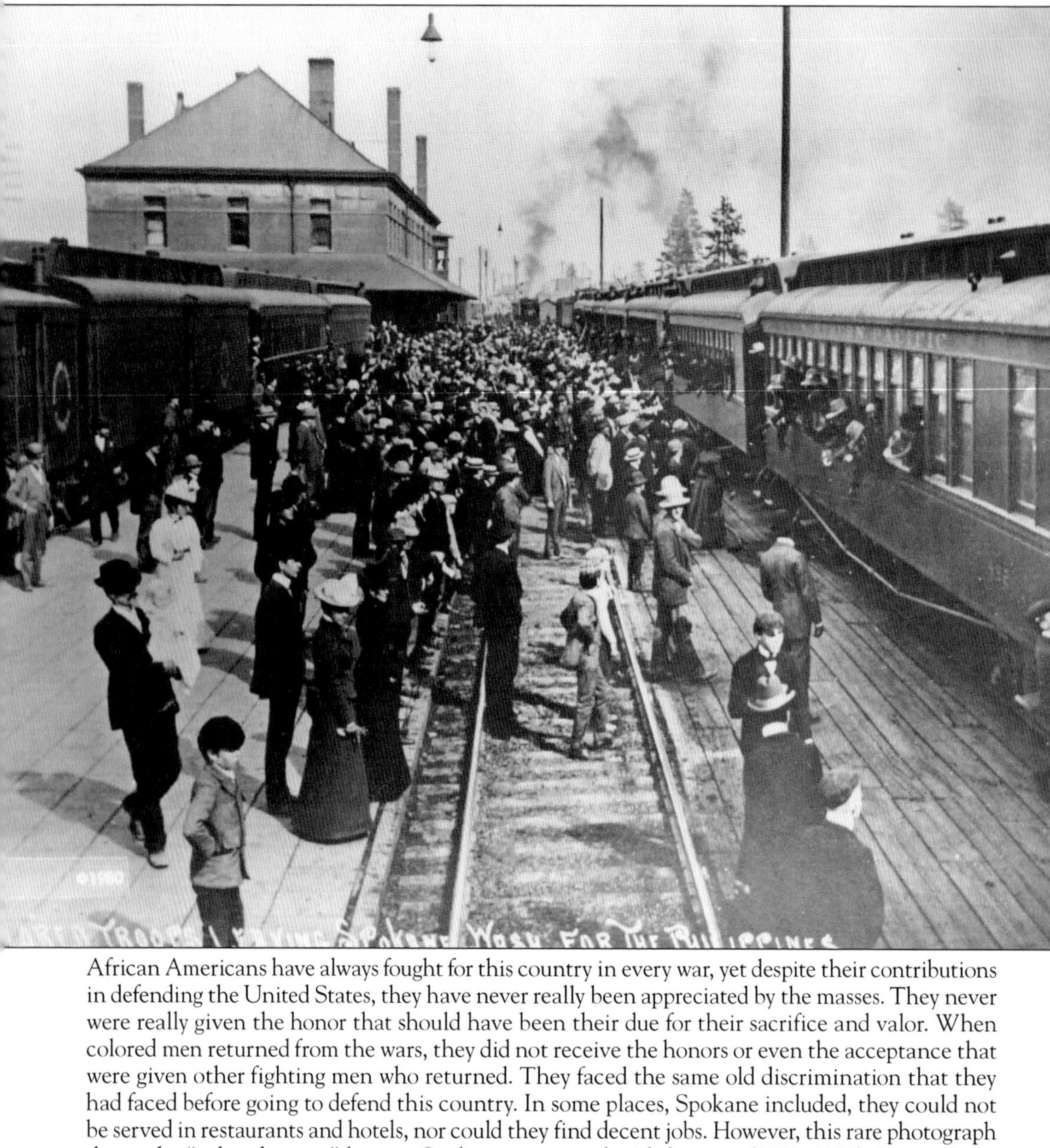

African Americans have always fought for this country in every war, yet despite their contributions in defending the United States, they have never really been appreciated by the masses. They never were really given the honor that should have been their due for their sacrifice and valor. When colored men returned from the wars, they did not receive the honors or even the acceptance that were given other fighting men who returned. They faced the same old discrimination that they had faced before going to defend this country. In some places, Spokane included, they could not be served in restaurants and hotels, nor could they find decent jobs. However, this rare photograph shows the "colored troops" leaving Spokane to go to the Philippines (1898–1899). It must have been quite a spectacle for so many in Spokane to turn out for the occasion. (Courtesy of MAC/ EWHS L87-1.123.)

This c. 1905 photograph is of Sgt. Malbert M. Cooper, a member of the 24th Infantry stationed at Fort George Wright. After his retirement from the military, Sergeant Cooper returned to make his home in Spokane. He remained here the rest of his life. He worked for the White Pine Sash Company.

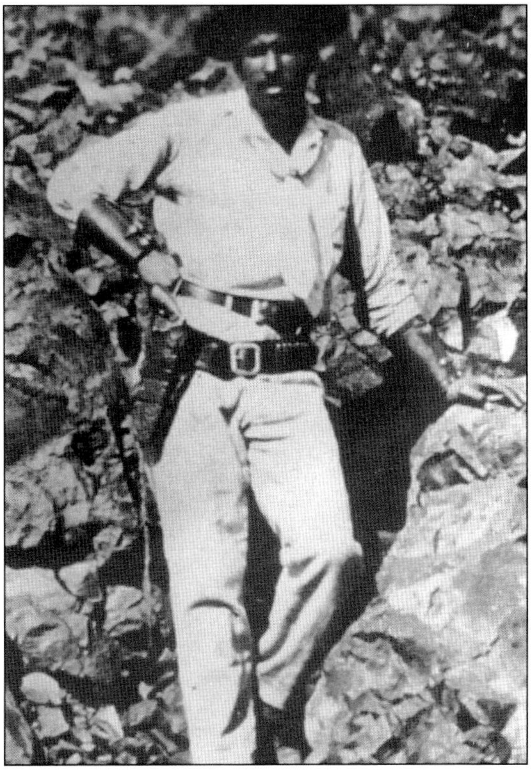

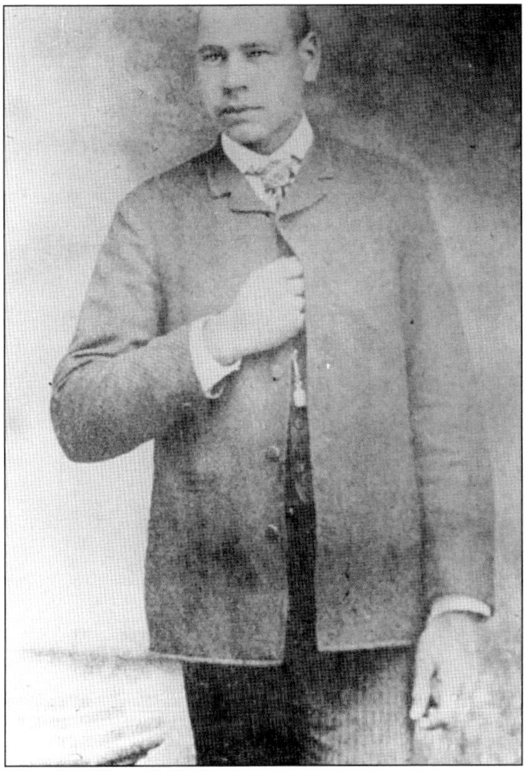

John Presley Boot arrived in Spokane about 1916, around the time he is pictured here. He was a plasterer and built his own home on the city's north side. The children of John P. and Mary Boot are Edna Boot Potter, Wayland W. Boot, and James Cecil Boot. Wayland Boot was a mechanic for Wallace Brothers and ran his own auto mechanic shop behind his home. Some descendants still reside in Spokane.

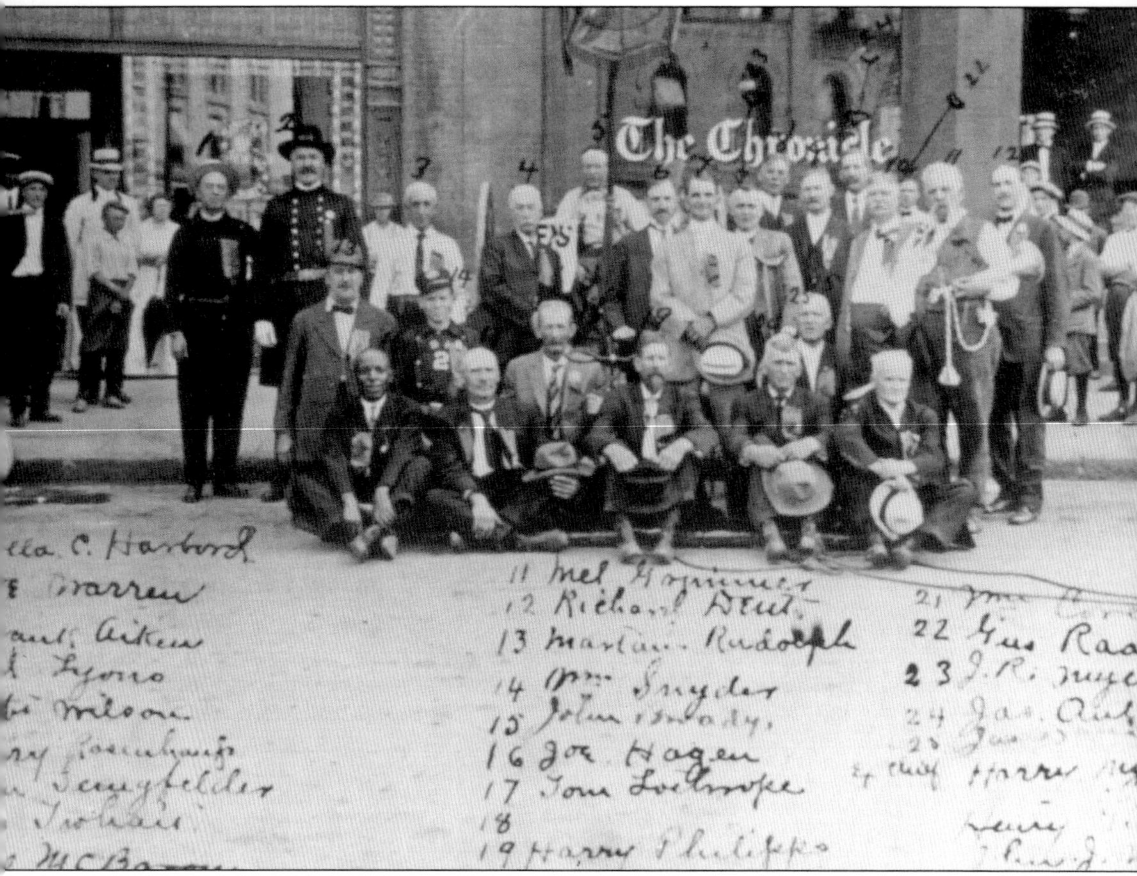

The fire that destroyed the business portion of Spokane Falls in 1889 was a devastating blow to the community. Twenty-five blocks burned and were reduced to ashes. The flames could not be stopped and rapidly spread. The firemen could do little or nothing to stop the inferno. Buildings in the path of the fire were blown up to try to stop the fire from spreading, but it was to no avail. The business portion of the city was literally wiped out. This photograph was taken in 1914, during an anniversary celebration of the Great Fire of 1889 that leveled downtown Spokane Falls. Joseph B. Hagan, who arrived in Spokane Falls in 1888, was a volunteer firefighter (No. 16, first row, far left). Hagan worked as a porter and waiter and eventually became the assistant superintendent of the Spokane and Inland Empire Railroad car service. (Courtesy of Spokane Public Library.)

Three

THE "COLORED MILITARY"

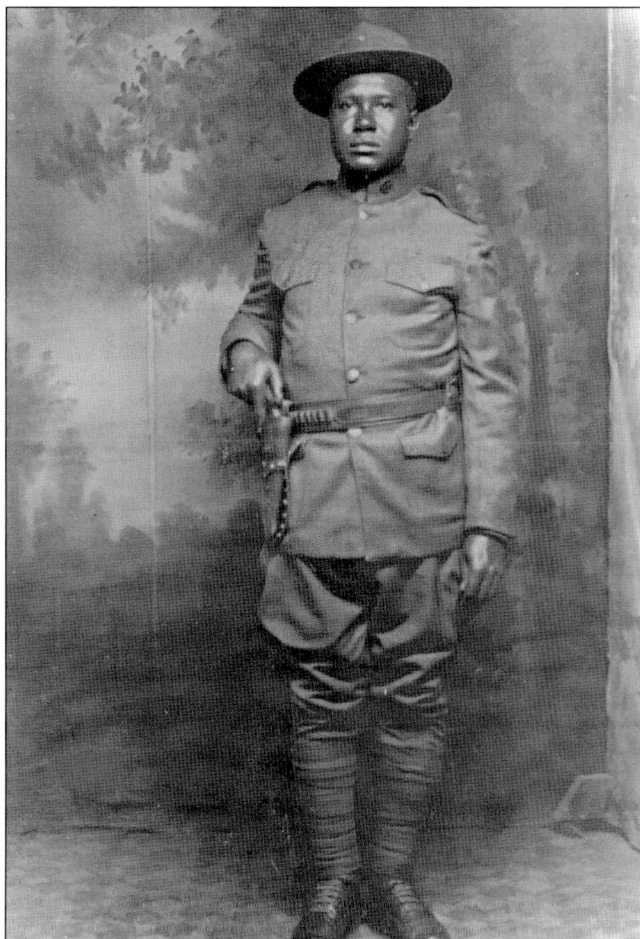

Black servicemen from across the country have been stationed at Fort George Wright, Fairchild Air Force Base, and Geiger Field. Many retired and made their homes in Spokane. This is Ross Mapps, who served in the army in World War I. Mapps was a janitor for Old National Bank and was active in Calvary Baptist Church, where he was a trustee. He had a wife, Gertrude, and a son, Selassie.

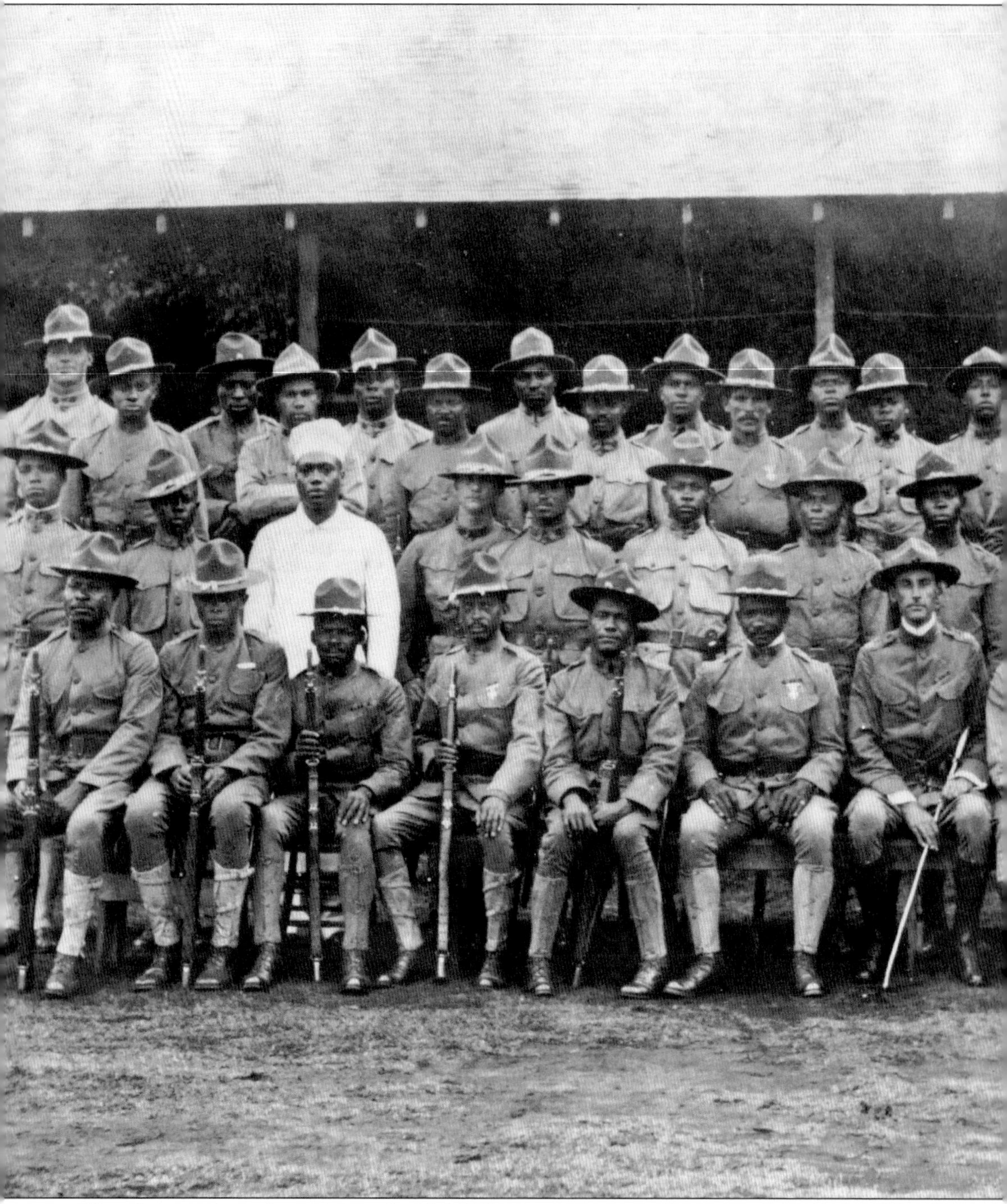

This photograph is of one of the eight 25th Infantry companies at Fort George Wright in Spokane. The photograph most likely was taken when the 25th Infantry returned to Spokane in 1909. Some of these men had fought in the Philippines. They are members of the 2nd and 3rd Battalion of the regiment. These troops brought an advantage to the city of Spokane through their presence

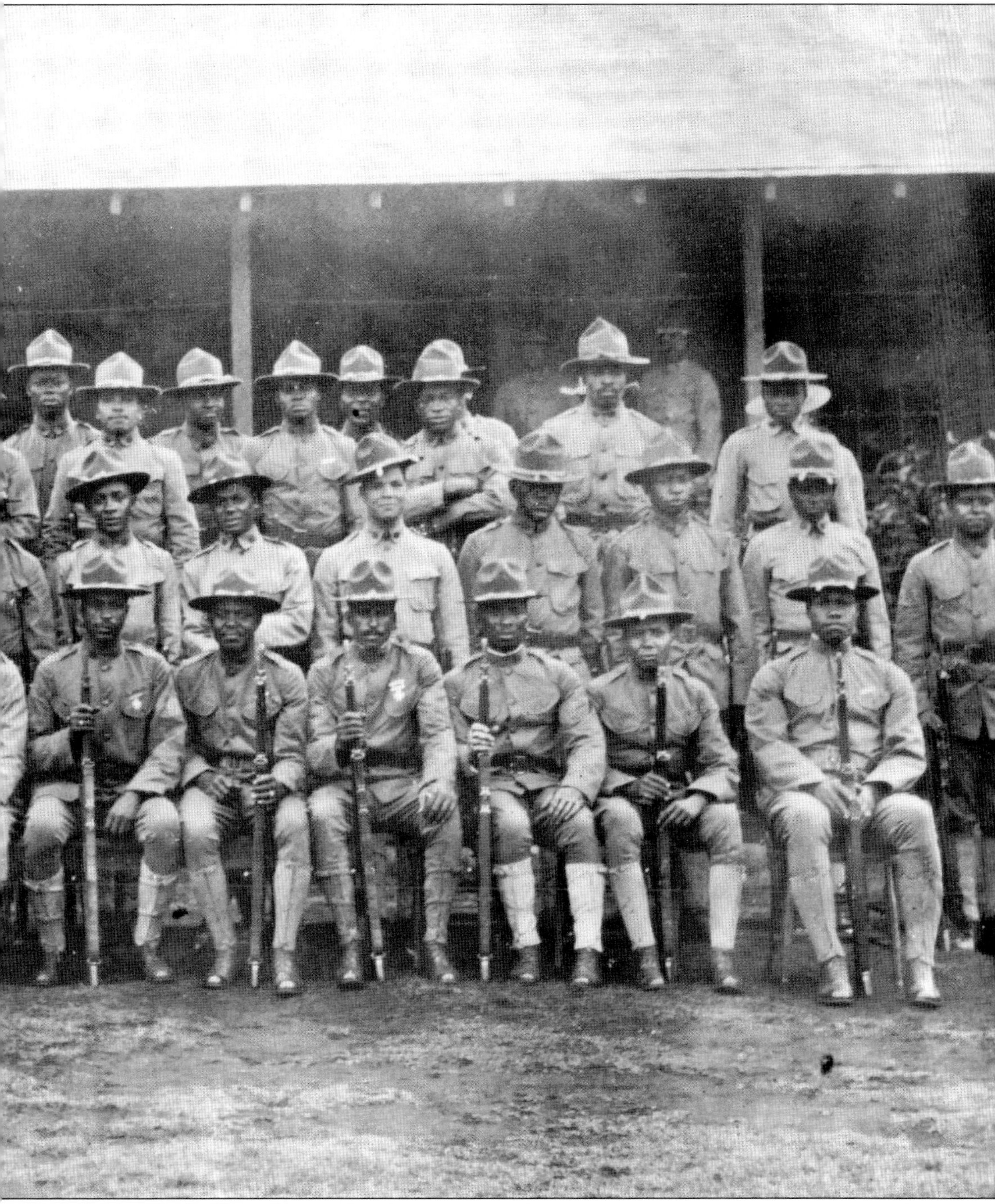

here. The Mounted Orderlies, 25th Infantry, practiced drills in 1911 for the upcoming visit of Col. Theodore Roosevelt to Fort George Wright. Roosevelt visited Spokane and the fort and inspected the black troops stationed there. Some of these men had been at the battles of El Canay and San Juan Hill. (Courtesy of MAC/EWHS L94-24.116.)

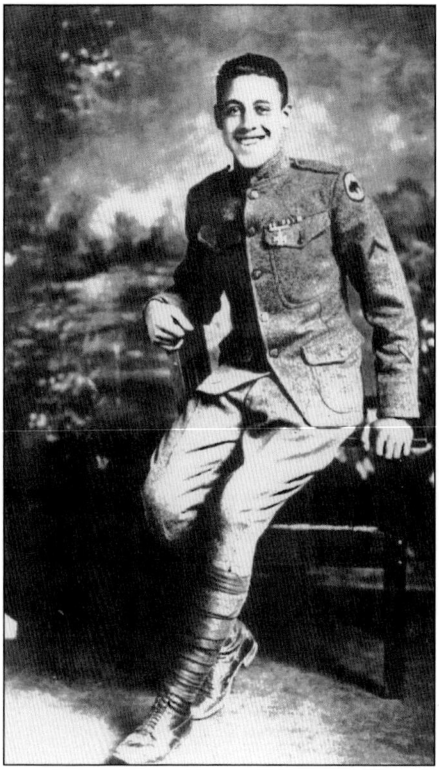

Pfc. Louis Patrick Nichols served in World War I and came to Spokane with his wife, Marie (Shields) Nichols, in 1920. They are the parents of Mildred and Louis Jr., the first African American twins born in Washington state. The couple's other children are Frances (Nichols) Scott and Ruth N. Nichols. Private 1st Class Nichols was born April 15, 1886. He is buried at the Golden Gate Cemetery in San Bruno, California.

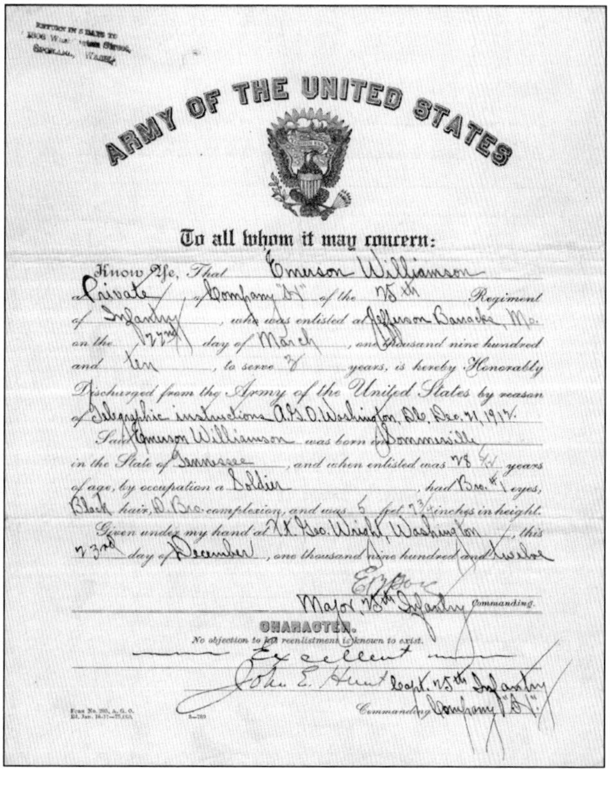

ARMY OF THE UNITED STATES

To all whom it may concern:

Know Ye, That Emerson Williamson a Private, of Company "H" of the 25th Regiment of Infantry, who was enlisted at Jefferson Barracks, Mo. on the 22nd day of March, one thousand nine hundred and ten, to serve 3 years, is hereby Honorably Discharged from the Army of the United States by reason of Telegraphic instructions A.G.O. Washington, D.C. Dec. 21, 1912.

Said Emerson Williamson was born in Sommerville in the State of Tennessee, and when enlisted was 28 4/12 years of age, by occupation a Soldier, had Brown eyes, Black hair, D. Brown complexion, and was 5 feet 7 3/4 inches in height.

Given under my hand at Ft. Geo. Wright, Washington, this 23rd day of December, one thousand nine hundred and twelve

E. M. Boe
Major, 25th Infantry Commanding.

CHARACTER.
No objection to his reenlistment is known to exist.
Excellent
John E. Hunt Capt. 25th Infantry
Commanding Company "H".

Emerson Cole Williamson was honorably discharged from the armed services December 23, 1910. He had served in the Philippines and was discharged at Fort George Wright. He decided not to return to Tennessee, his home state, and continued to live and work in Spokane. He started his own floor refinishing company in Spokane and was known as "The Floor Doctor." This is a copy of his discharge papers.

Capt. Clarence Freeman had many adventures in the army and loved to tell his stories. Freeman returned to Spokane after the war and started his own construction company, along with other enterprises and building projects. With his wife, Frances, he started the first "Job Fair" in Spokane for young job seekers. The Freemans had two sons and one daughter. There is a building bearing his name in downtown Spokane.

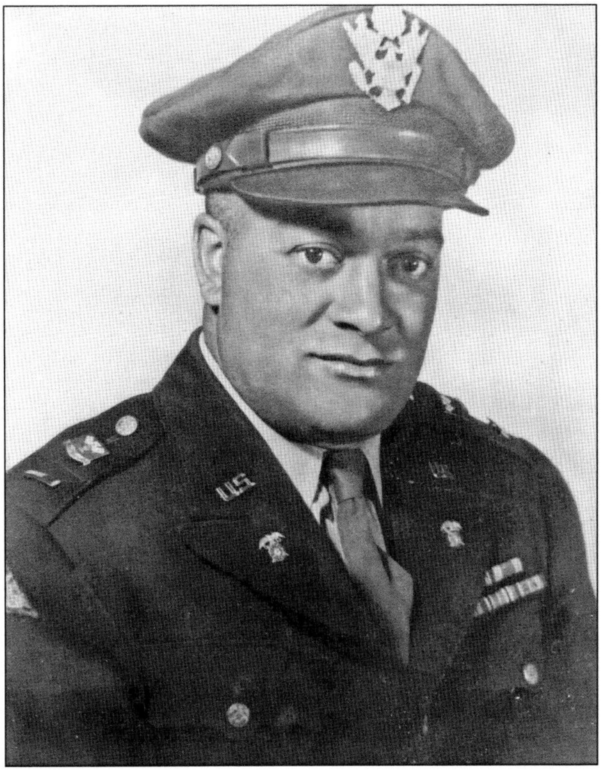

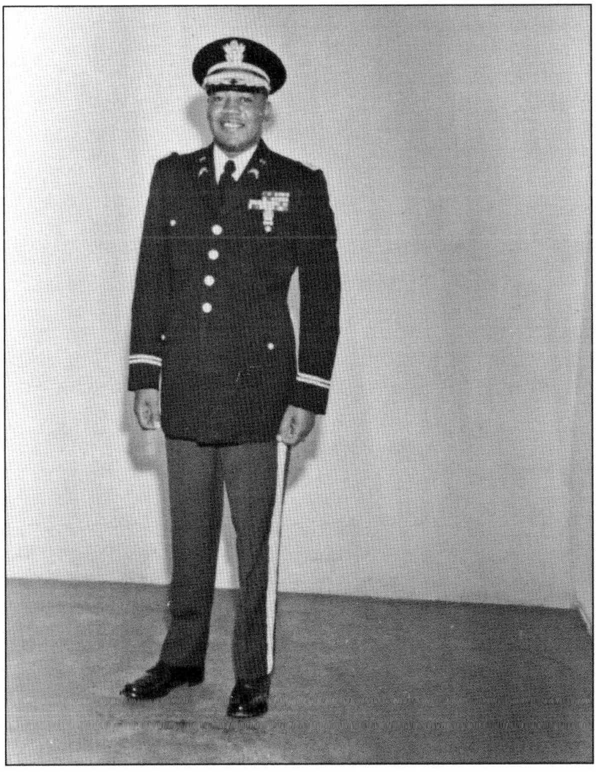

Adrian H. Jones, an army lieutenant colonel and Spokane native, is shown in dress uniform. After retiring, he became head of a program to improve equal employment opportunities in the U.S. Law Enforcement Assistance Administration (LEAA). He has written 15 books and articles on social conflict and collective violence and has lectured on the subject. He is the son of Mary Ann and Hayden Jones from Roslyn, Washington.

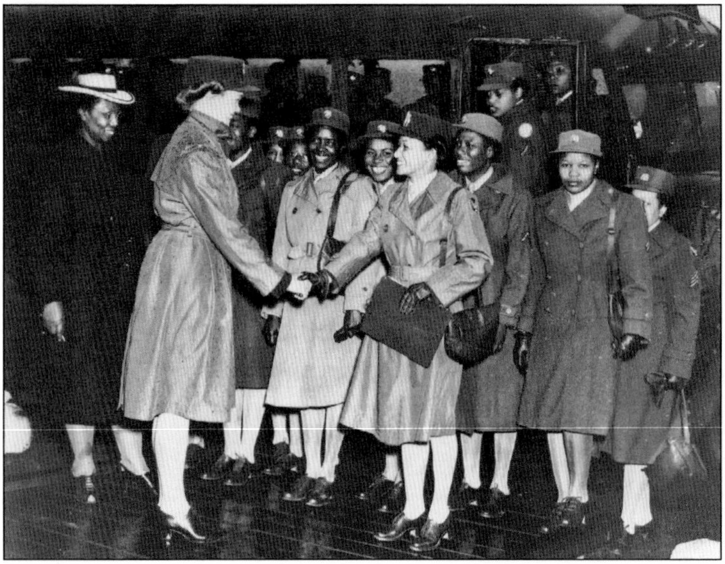

This photograph is of African American women of the Women's Army Corps (WAC) arriving in Spokane. They are greeted by Rosa D. Malone (far left) and a representative from the Women's Service Unit in Spokane. The Women's Army Corps was a significant factor in the morale of the troops in the armed services. They did much to help in World War II. (Courtesy of MAC/EWHS L96-1.2.)

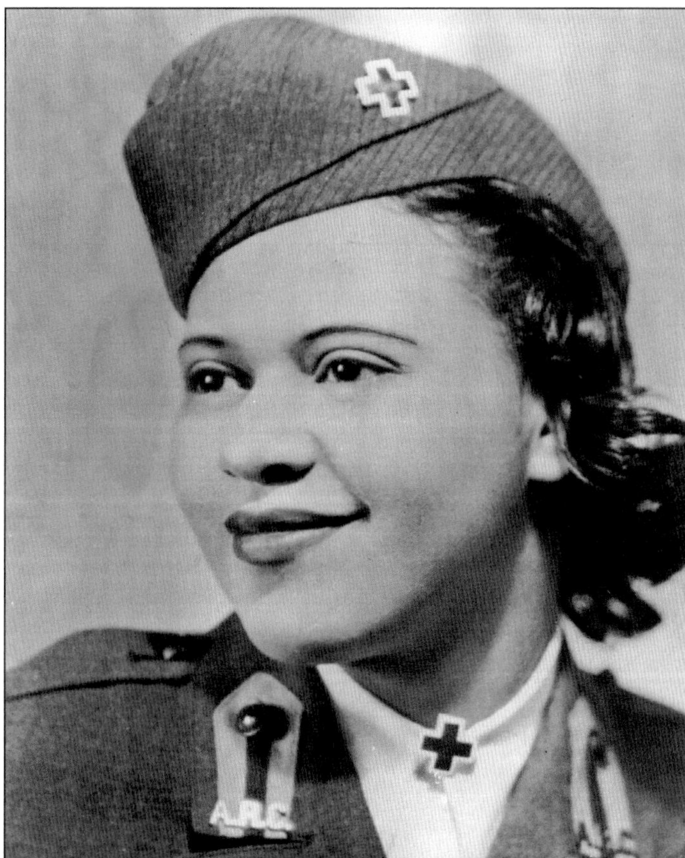

Ruth N. Nichols was born and raised in Spokane. In 1946, she was enrolled at Howard University in Washington, D.C., when she joined an African American unit of the segregated American Red Cross. Nichols was assigned to army special recreation clubs in Korea. The army also was segregated. Ruth also served in the U.S. Women's Army Corps (WAC) during the Korean conflict.

Walter Piper Jr. joined the army during the Vietnam War and became the first from Spokane to be killed in action. His mother, Annie Dotson, was presented the Bronze Star medal. Private 1st Class Piper was cited for heroism in connection with a military operation on February 6, 1966, against a Viet Cong force near the village of Canh Tinh. His courage and devotion to duty were instrumental in defeating the enemy.

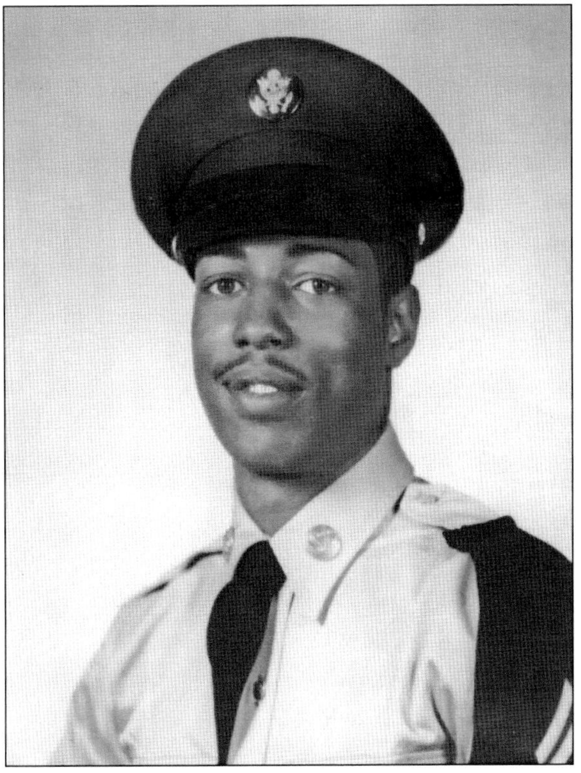

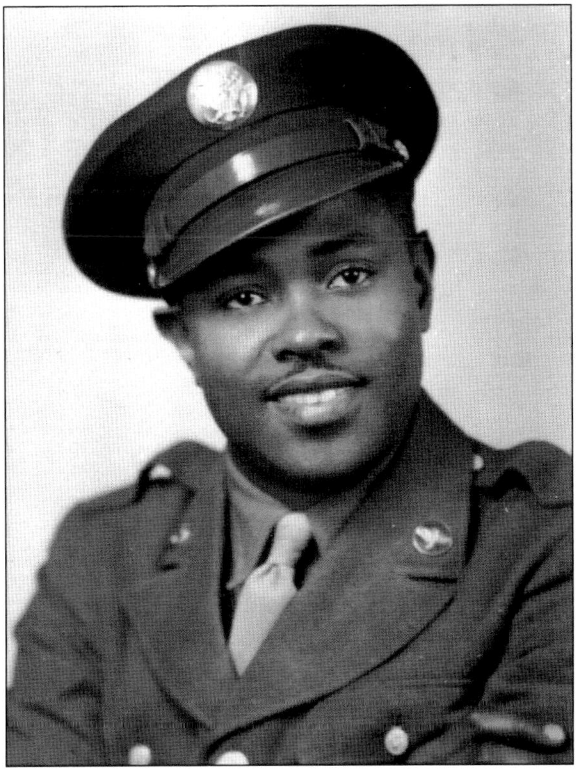

Cpl. Elmo Dalbert, Army Air Corps, served in Colorado Springs, Colorado, and at Wright Patterson Base in Dayton, Ohio, from 1943 to 1946. A longtime Spokane resident with his wife Alta and son Dennis, he was a partner with James Chase in the Chase and Dalbert Body and Fender Shop on Indiana Avenue in Spokane.

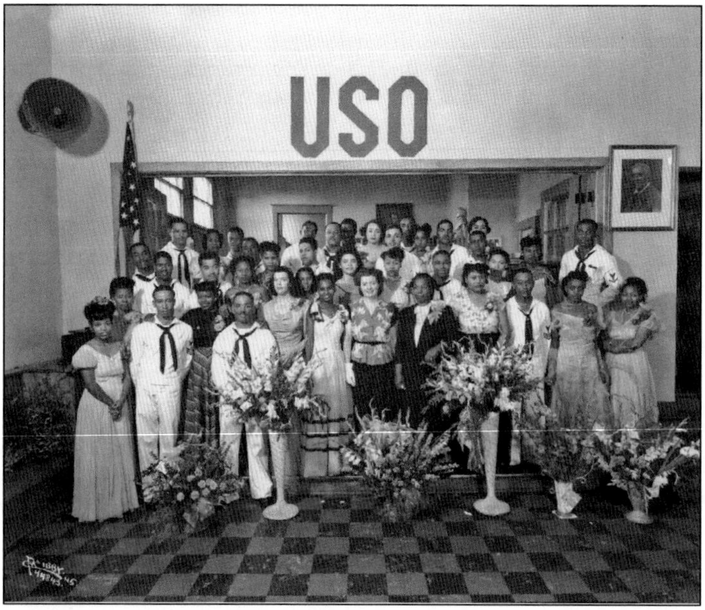

The George Washington Carver USO was established in Spokane at 101 South Division Street during World War II. There was segregation in the military, and the black servicemen and women had no place for entertainment since the white USO was not open to them. This photograph, which includes local residents, was taken at a second anniversary party celebrating the opening of the USO in 1945. (Courtesy of MAC/EWHS L87-1.44843-45.)

PROGRAM

Mistress of Ceremonies - - - Mrs. James Chase

Star-Spangled Banner .... Led by 435th Male Chorus
Invocation .... Most Rev. Bishop White
Vocal Solo .... Mr. Joseph Nelson
Accompanied by Mrs. Nelson of San Diego, California

GREETINGS

Spokane Army Air Field .... Col. David L. Painter
Farragut Naval Station .... Lt. T. J. King
Commanding Officers of Troops .... Capt. Donald A. Bolger
Women's Army Corps .... 1st Lt. Annie L. Brown
Service Men .... 1st Sgt. Hall, 462nd Ava. Sqd.
American Red Cross .... Mrs. Carroll Smith
Churches of Spokane .... Mrs. Charles Holsclaw
Community .... Mrs. Clarence Grubbs
Representative Women's Clubs of Spokane .... Mrs. O. M. Fahey
State Federation of Negro Women's Clubs .... Mrs. Lucile Parker
Tacoma U S O No. 2 .... Mr. Ben Brown
Remarks:
Mr. Harry H. Stoops, Regional Rep. Fed. War Service, Div. of Recreation
Mr. T. O. Hoagland, Field Rep., Div. of Recreation, Comm. War Services
Selections .... 435th Male Chorus
Introduction of Speaker .... Rev. Paul Riley
Guest Speaker .... Miss Margret Mealey
Women's Division, National Catholic Community Services
Parting Words .... Rev. E. B. Reed

OPERATING COMMITTEE

Mr. John T. Little - - - Chairman

Father Paul Riley	Rev. S. J. Holly	Mrs. Clarence Grubbs
Mrs. O. M. Fahey	Mr. Woodard Bass	Rev. E. B. Reed
Mrs. J. F. Farquhar	Mr. Ben Cohn	Capt. Donald Bolger
Mrs. James Chase	Mrs. E. I. Dundee	Mrs. James McHenry
Mr. Nave Lein	Mrs. Lucile Parker	Mrs. Arthur Clausen
	Mrs. James Ford	

•

During 1943-44, 108,000 Service Men and Women from all over the nation have made use of the G. W. Carver Club at

Vesper Services	Negro History Classes
Lectures	Wiener Roasts
Reading, Writing Letters	Picnics, Dances, Barn Parties
Special Interest Groups	Mending
Games	Pool, Ping Pong, Card Parties
Music Appreciation	

Housing for servicemen, servicemen's wives and War workers, etc.

•

During the summer months the garden is used for many of the activities; it has a large Bar B Q pit and many tables and benches which prove very useful.

In closing, we wish to thank all who in any way have contributed to the success of our program. We realize that we are indebted to churches, clubs, and friends who have expressed their faith in us through their interest and support. We trust that as we face the future we will continue to receive your cooperation.

We feel that we are faced with a great opportunity for service.

•

STAFF

Rosa D. Malone - - Director   Mary M. Vallet - - Asst. Director

•

Tea in the Garden

This is the first anniversary program, dated August 13, 1944, for the George Washington Carver USO. The program includes Mrs. James Chase (mistress of ceremonies), Most Reverend Bishop White, Mrs. Charles Holsclaw, Mrs. O. M. Fahey, Rev. E. B. Reed, Rosa D. Malone, Mrs. Clarence Grubbs, and Lucille Parker. The USO was operated by the Women's Division of the National Catholic Community Service. (Courtesy of Ruth N. Nichols.)

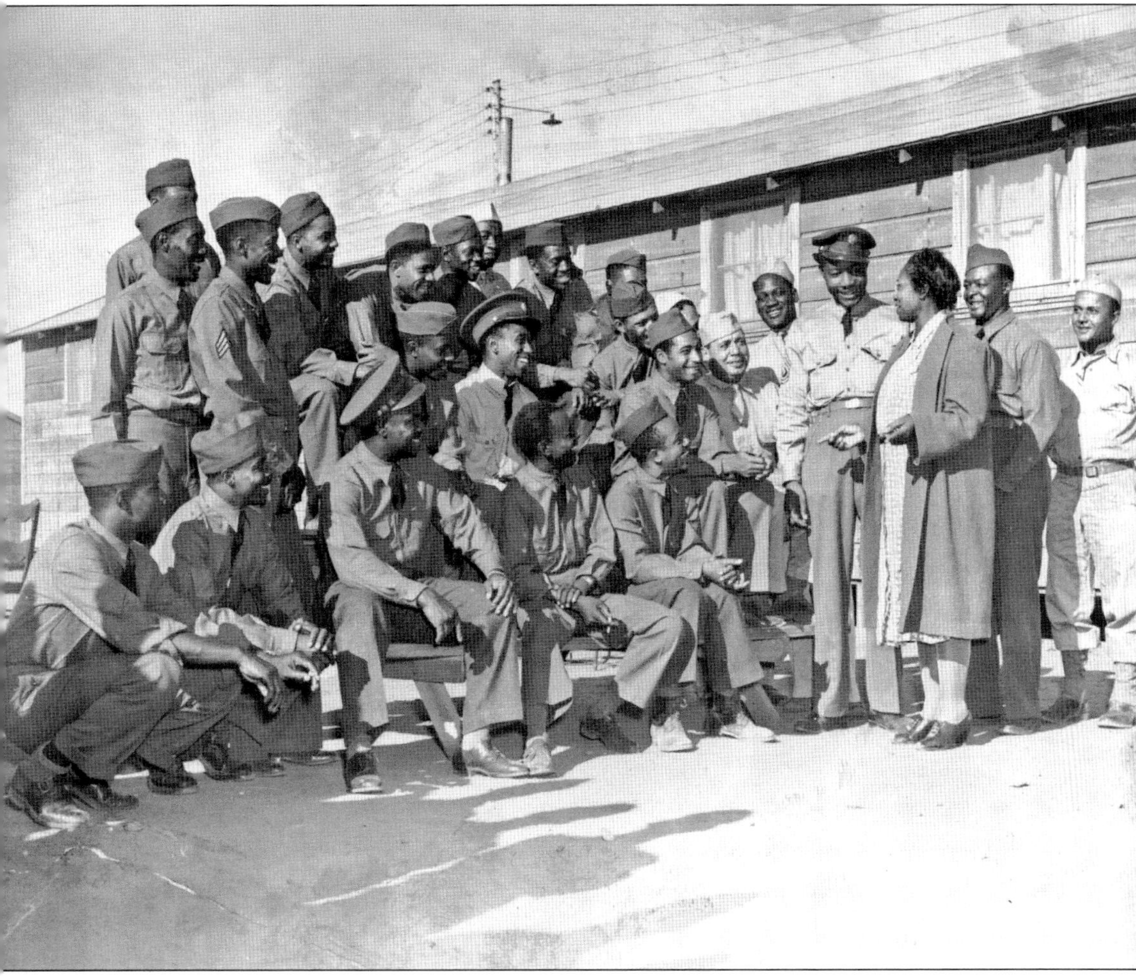

Rosa D. Malone came to Spokane to work as a Work Progress Administration (WPA) supervisor during World War II. She organized the George Washington Carver United Service Organization. Malone, a graduate of Tuskegee Institute in Alabama, was also active in the work of National Catholic Community Services and in civil defense. She was a member of Calvary Baptist Church and the Alabama Chapter of the Order of the Eastern Star. Malone was not only a member of the WPA, she was a valued member of the Spokane community. She became a friend and mentor for many young people and helped to shape their lives. She will always be remembered in the black community as having made a difference. Malone was a personal friend of Nat "King" Cole, Louis Armstrong, Duke Ellington, and prizefighter Joe Louis. She is shown here in a 1945 photograph of the 92nd Aviation Squadron of African American servicemen, taken at Geiger Field, Washington. (Courtesy of MAC/EWHS L96-1.10.)

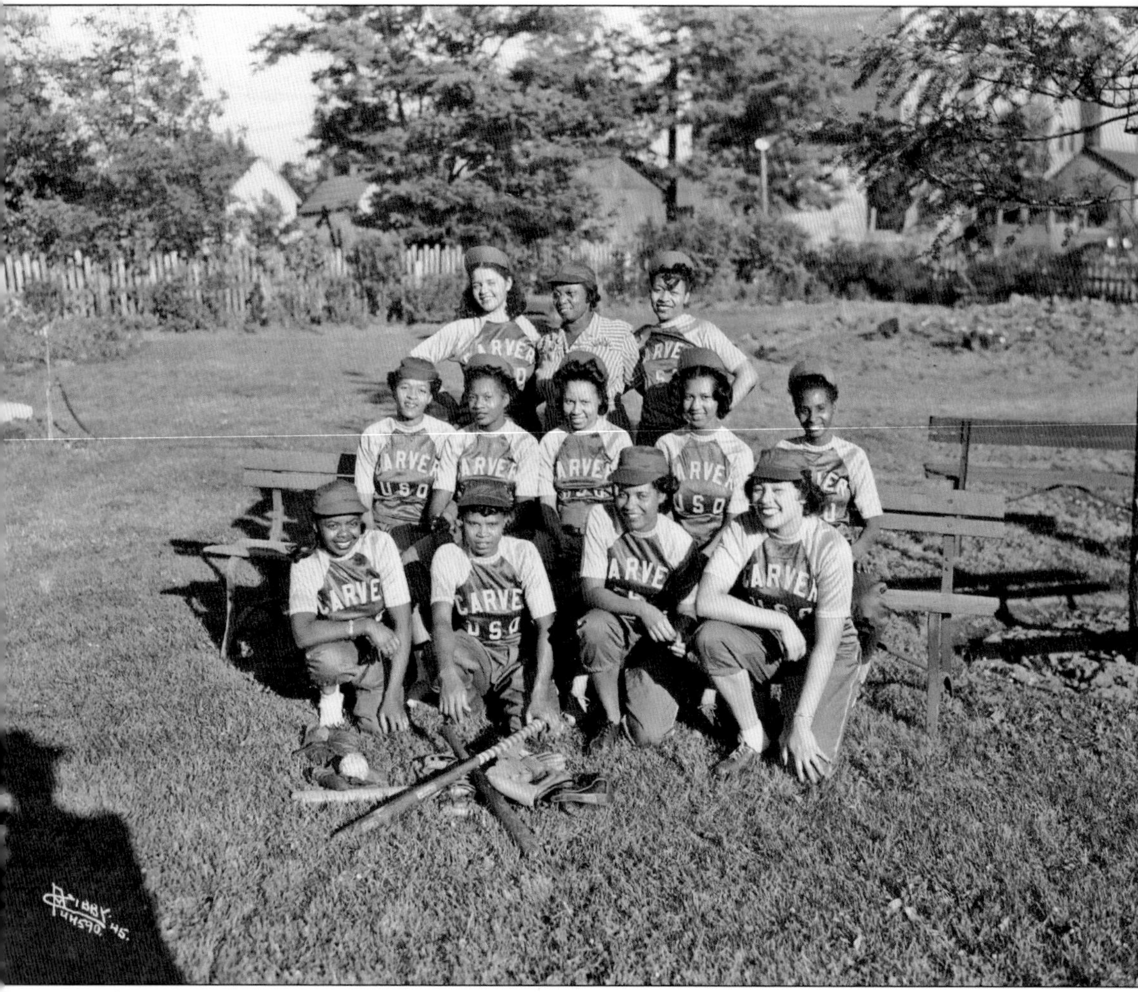

These are 1940s hostesses at the George Washington Carver USO who formed a softball team to entertain both the military and the Spokane community. All of them are not identified, but Rosa D. Malone is in the middle (third row), Jesse Sarto is at far left (second row), and Pauline Lake is in the middle (second row), next to Mary Emma Hill on her left. These young women served as hostesses at the George Washington Carver USO to keep up the morale of servicemen and servicewomen who were away from home. They would serve food, dance, and just visit with the young military. Some of the military were WACs (the Women's Army Corps). The USO was like a home to them. There would be card games, picnics, and barbecues in the large backyard behind the USO. Because of discrimination policies, the black and white military personnel were not allowed then to be part of the same establishment. The USO for white military was in another location. (Courtesy of MAC/EWHS L96-1.12.)

Four

The Black Church

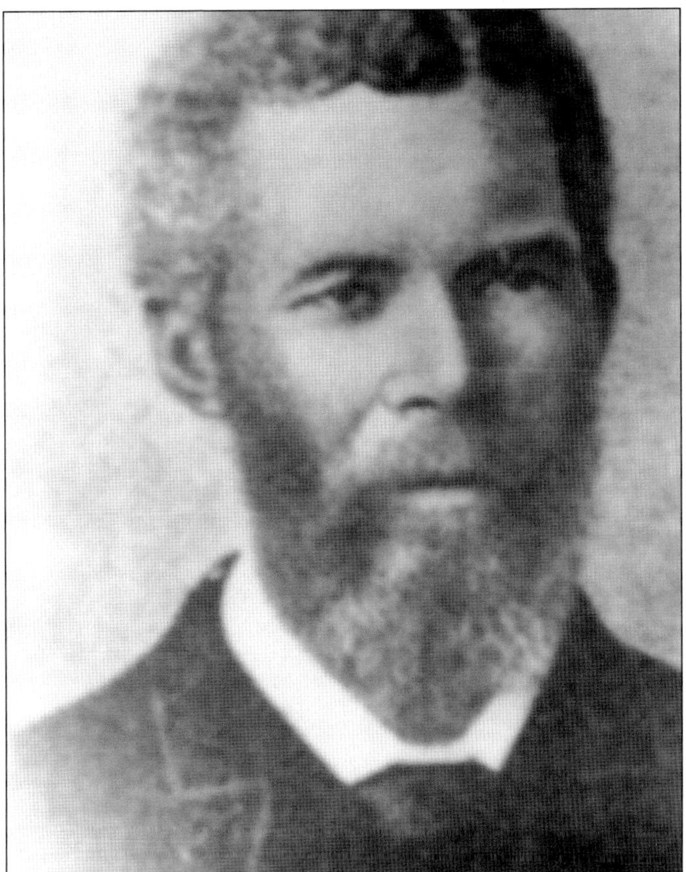

Rev. Peter Barnabas Barrow helped found Calvary Baptist Church, the first historically black church in Spokane, in 1890. He was its pastor from 1895 to 1904. Reverend Barrow founded the Farmer's Alliance in the state of Washington and also organized the Deer Lake Irrigated Orchard Company, a very successful black-owned apple orchard project. Reverend Barrow was killed in a streetcar accident in Tacoma, Washington, while attending a church convention.

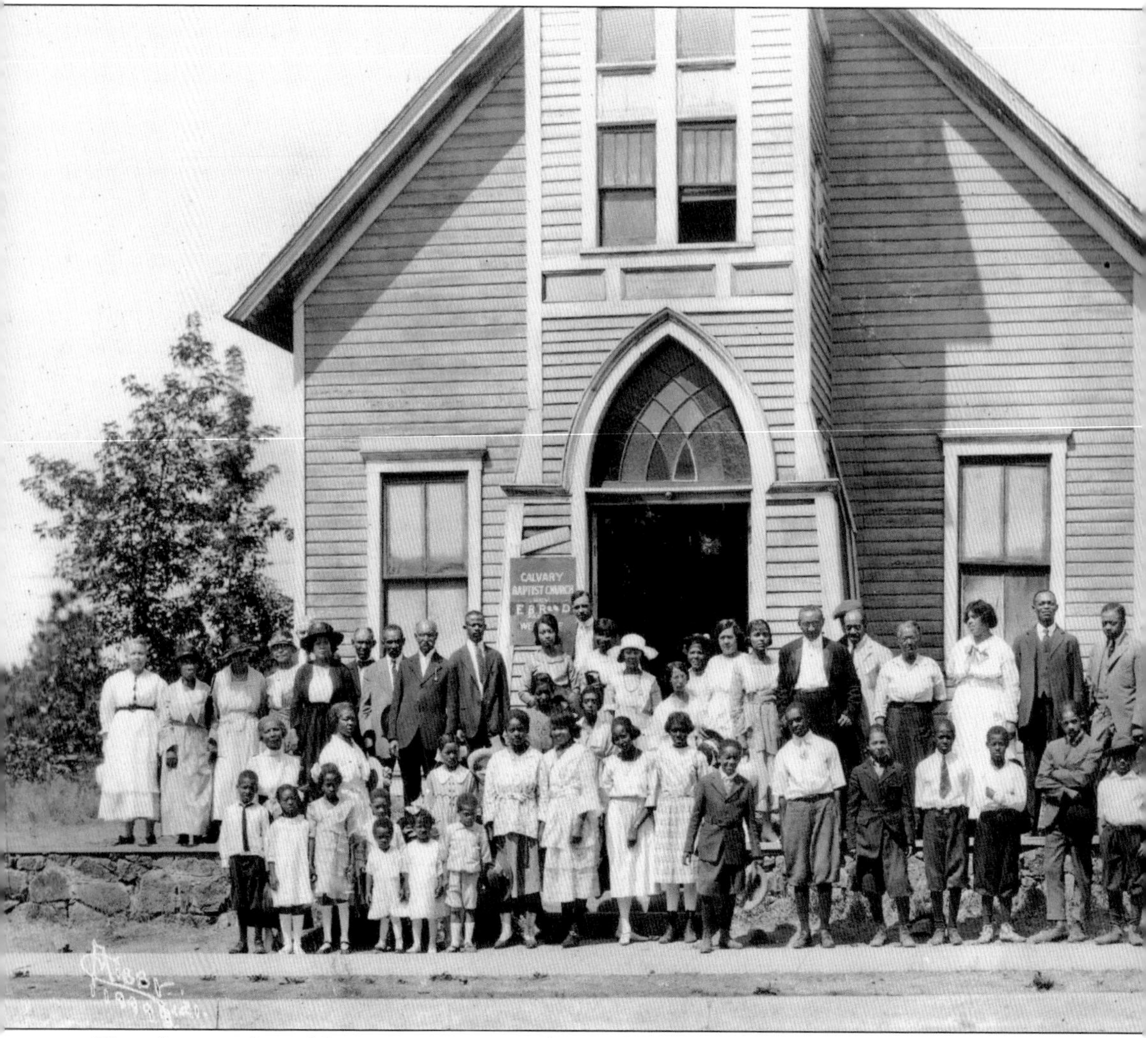

This photograph is of the congregation standing in front of Calvary Baptist Church in 1919. Rev. Emmett Reed, the pastor, is standing next to his wife, Pam Reed. Irene and Wallace Hagin Sr. are right in front of the church sign. Thelma (Reed) Weiseger and Wallace Hagin Jr. are two of the children in the first row. This small group of parishioners of Calvary Baptist Church later moved to the building now located at Third Avenue and Cowley Street in Spokane. This is the first home of Calvary, but they persevered and built a large brick building plus a parsonage. Through the dedication of Reverend Reed and other ministers, Calvary is a much respected and revered part of the Spokane community. Many souls have been saved, and many prayers and songs have emanated from this building.

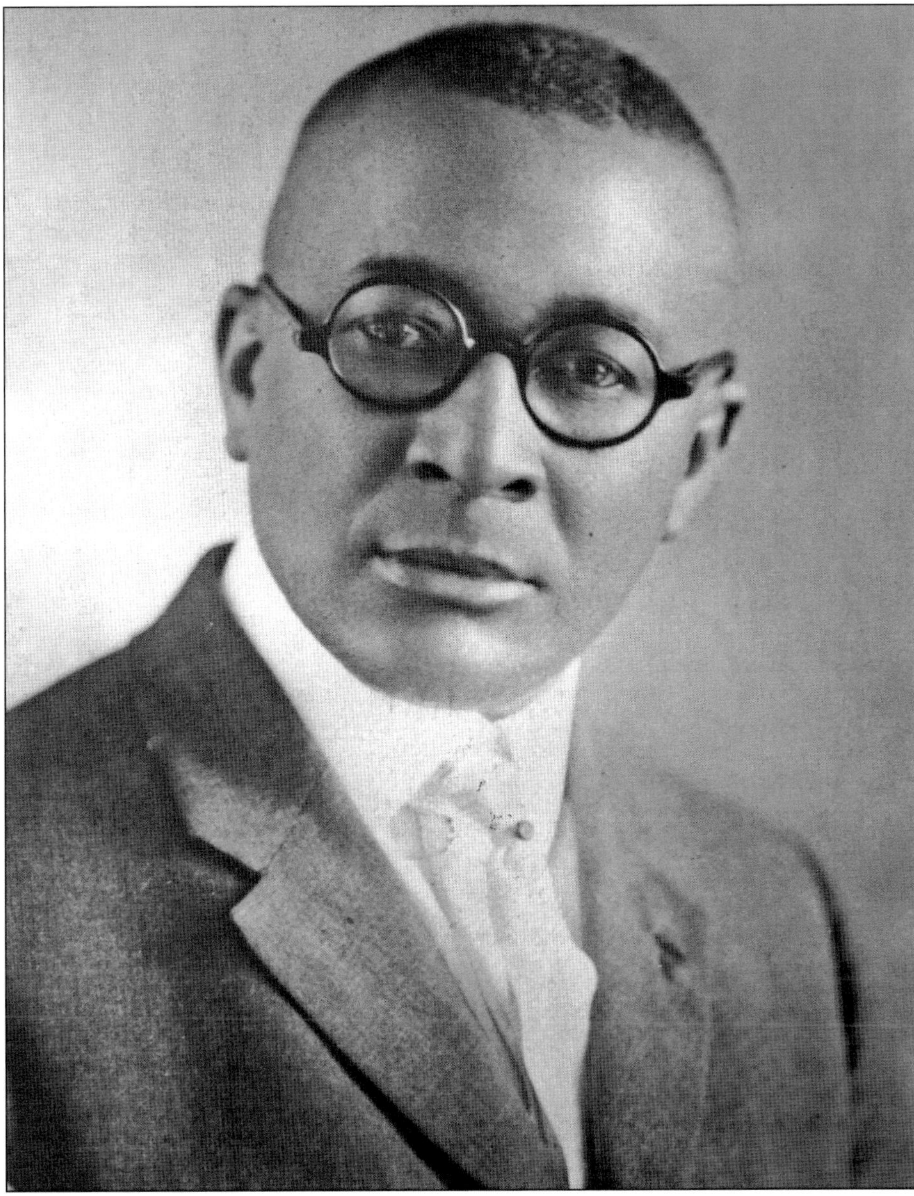

Rev. Emmett B. Reed pastored Calvary for 41 years, from 1919 until his death in 1961. Ordained in San Jose, California, in 1905, he was moderator of the Washington Baptist Association (Negro) for 31 years and was a director of the National Baptist Convention. Reverend Reed was a dedicated minister and "hands-on" pastor. When anyone was in trouble with the law or any other indiscretion, he was right there to give his service, no matter what the situation. He was very much respected, and he tried to break down the barriers of discrimination. Reverend Reed was the first black minister to start interdenominational services in the community. Many Sunday evenings, the church choir would sing at other churches, and they in turn would sing at Calvary. Many speakers came to Calvary, and there was a feeling of harmony in the gatherings. When Reverend Reed passed away, there was a great void in the whole community. Reverend Reed had three children: Thelma (Reed) Weiseger, Emetta Jones, and Emmett B. Reed Jr. Reverend Reed is buried at Pines Cemetery in the Spokane Valley.

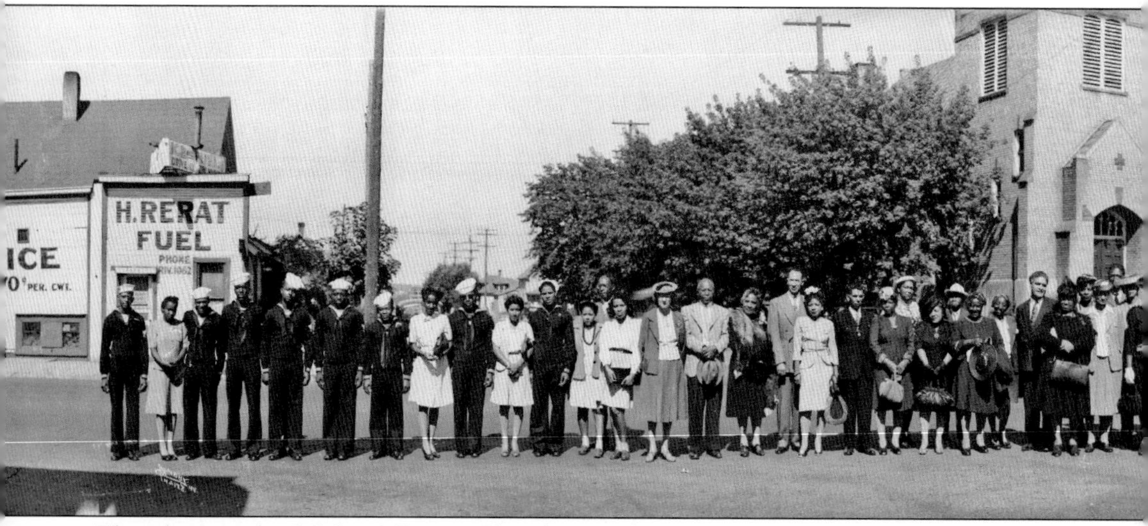

This photograph of Calvary Baptist Church was taken in 1944. The full congregation is lined up in front of the church and down the block. As can be seen in the photograph, there are a few military men. They represent all of the military, men and women, who were stationed in and around the city. Rev. Emmett B. Reed was the pastor. Notables in the photograph include Ross and Gertrude Mapps and their son Selassie, Mr. and Mrs. Grubbs, Abner and Hester Hill and

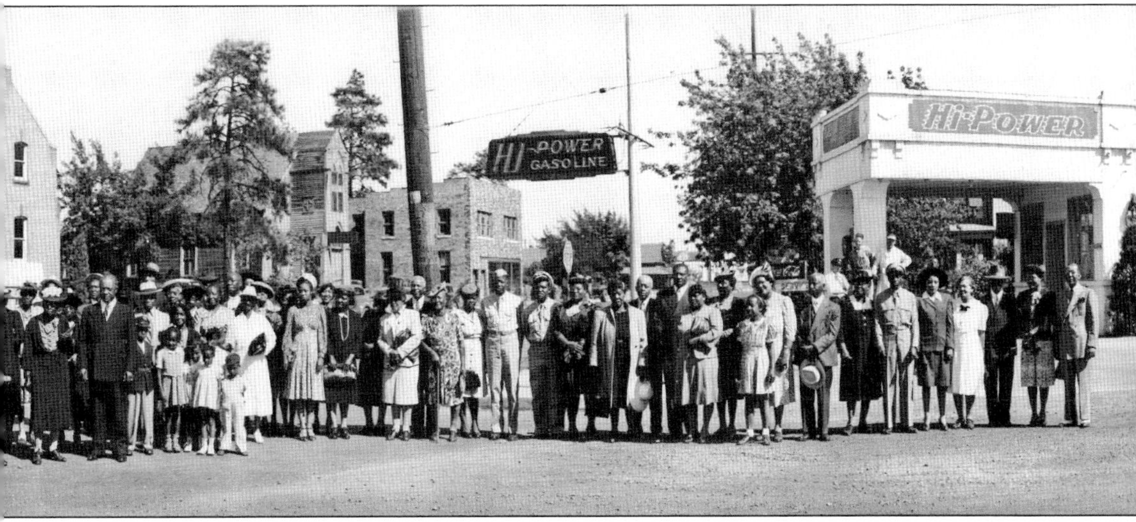

their family, Mr. and Mrs. Sylvester Lake and their daughters Sylvia and Mona, Mr. and Mrs. Carole Curtley, Mr. and Mrs. Ben Lewis, and Mr. and Mrs. Wellington. This photograph was taken on a Sunday morning after church. (Courtesy of Thelma (Reed) Weiseger, daughter of Rev. Emmett B. Reed.)

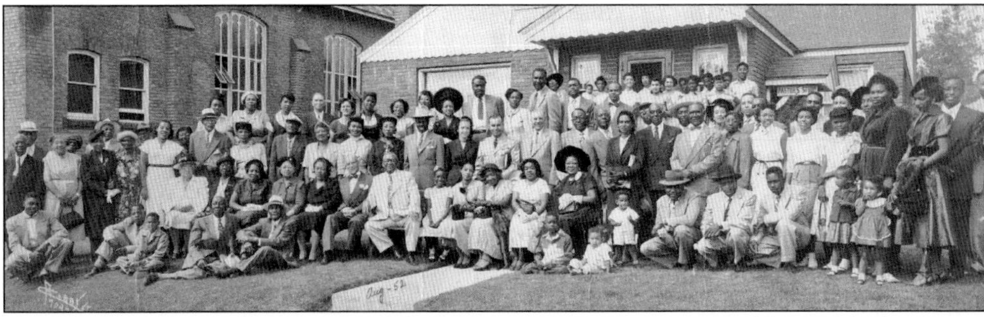

This photograph was taken in front of the parsonage at Calvary. Some of the people shown were from Bethel AME Church. Bethel finished services before Calvary; therefore, its members came to Calvary to meet friends and socialize. Some members of Bethel are Lillian Strong and her daughter Charlotte. Reverend Reed is in front wearing a white suit. This photograph was taken in August 1952. (Courtesy of MAC/EWHS, L97-56.433.)

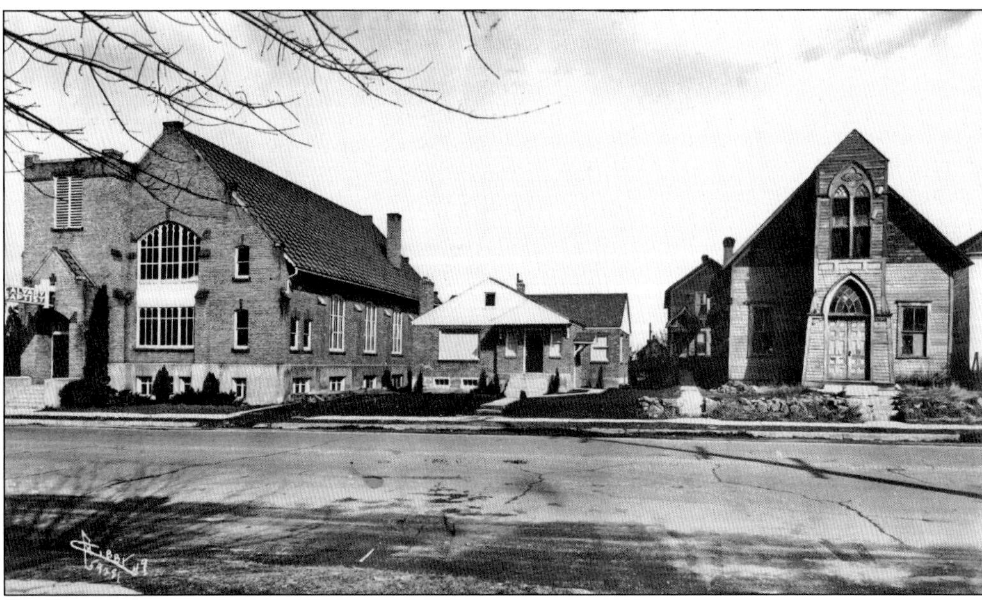

This photograph of Calvary Baptist Church shows the new church building and parsonage, along with the old church in the background. Although the old and new were never actually seen together in a photograph, this composite was done for a newspaper article that was printed in the *Spokesman Review and Chronicle*. The new church was constructed in 1927, and the parsonage was built in 1945.

Bethel African Methodist Episcopal Church, shown in 1910, was the second black church organized in Spokane. This photograph shows the church congregation in front of the new building. The wreckage of the old building is also shown. The church was located at Fifth Avenue and Pine Street. When the church relocated, the beautiful stained-glass windows were taken to the new church building.

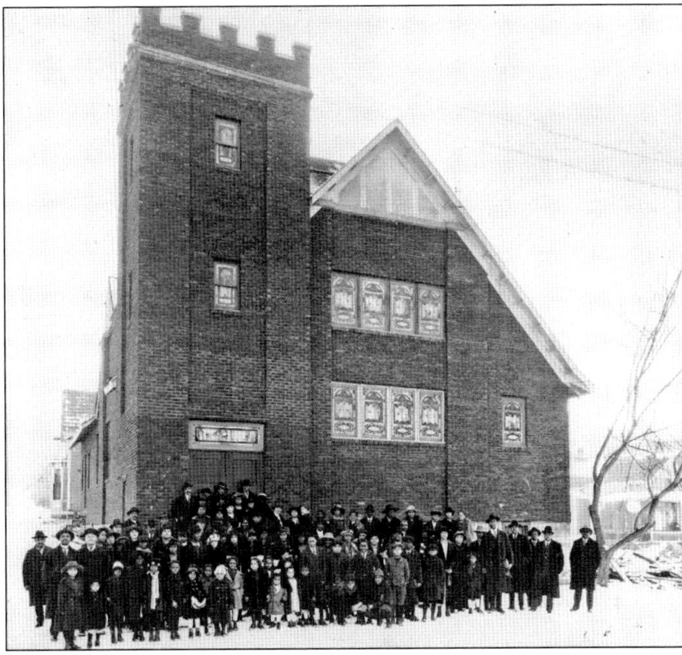

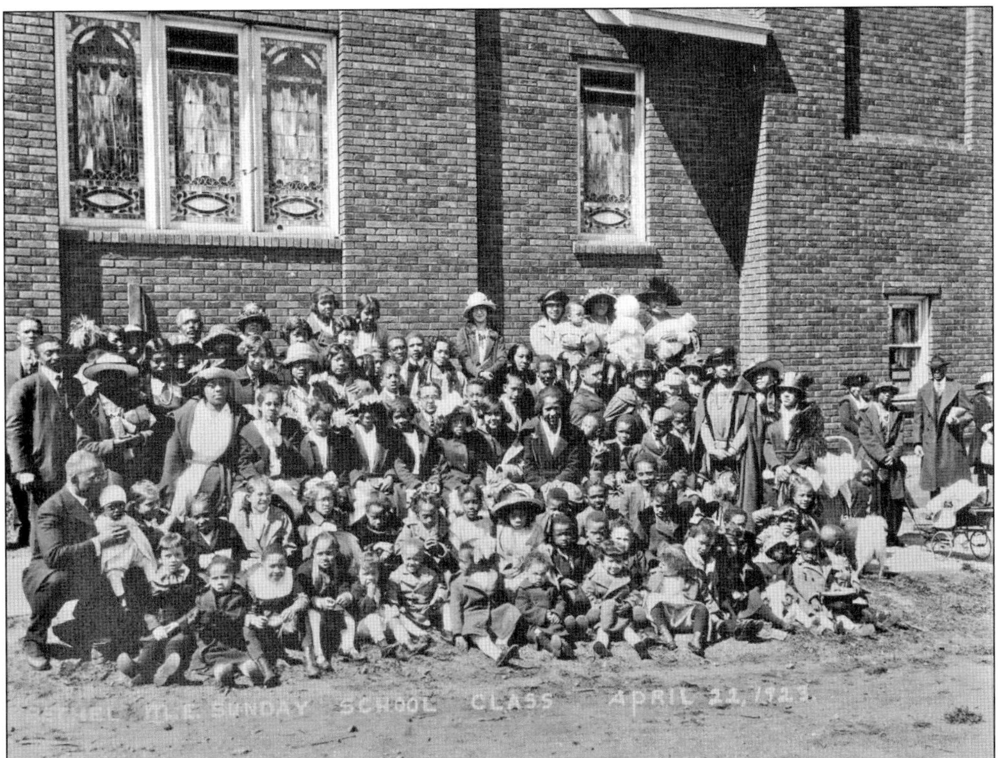

This photograph of the Bethel AME Sunday school was taken April 22, 1923. Sunday school has always been important in the black community. The religious instruction that a child is given is very important to the rest of his or her life. The black church has always given much attention to its children, primarily to prepare them for citizenship and leadership. Children were, and are, our future.

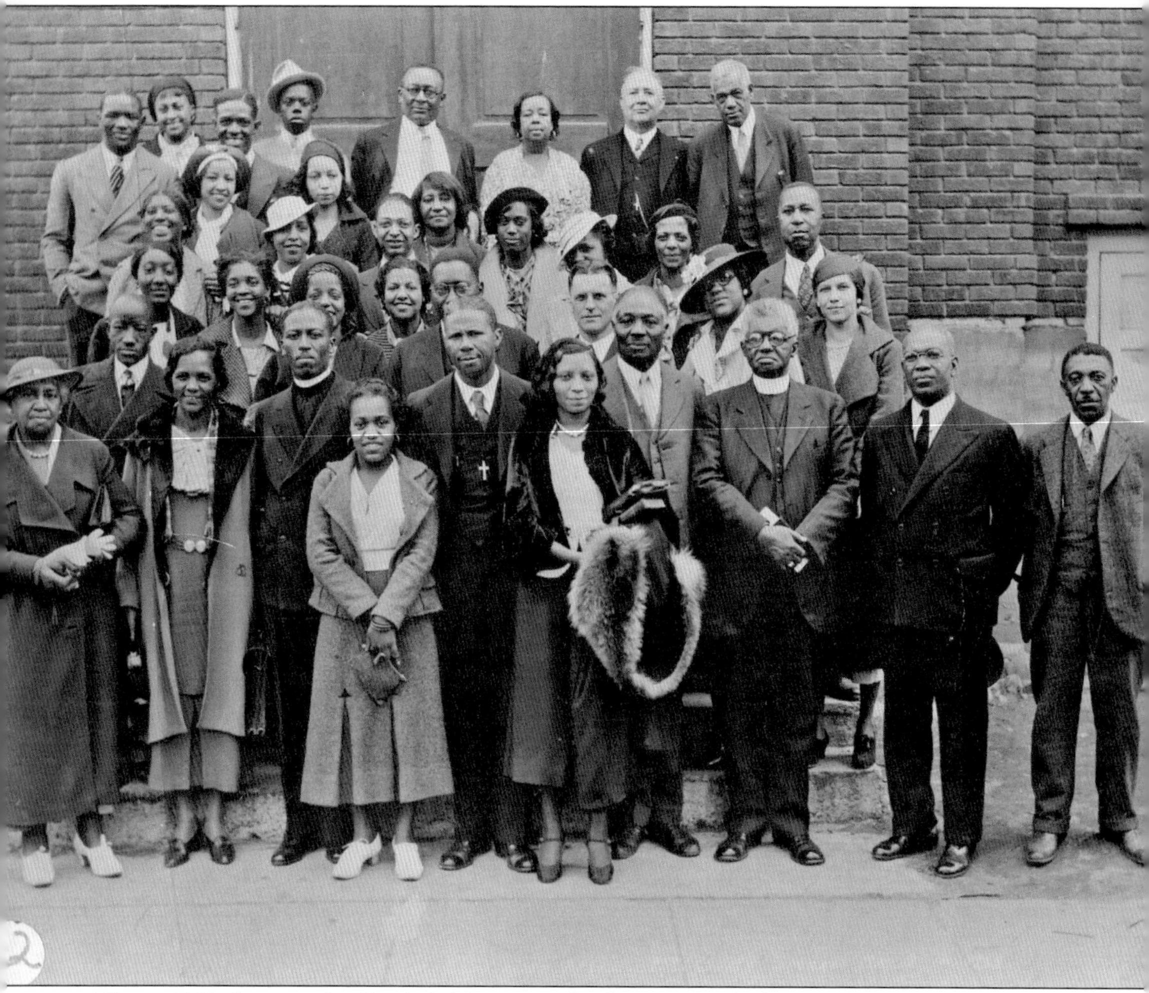

This c. 1920 photograph of Bethel African Methodist Episcopal Church was taken in 1931 on the steps in front of the church building at Fifth Avenue and Pine Street in Spokane. Rev. Emmett B. Reed, pastor of Calvary Baptist Church, may have been the speaker at Bethel. He is pictured at the top of the steps, in the middle, in front of the door. Others pictured are Lillian Stokes, wife of F. A. Stokes, and Frances Freeman. Bethel AME Church, initially named St. Paul's Methodist Church, was the first African American Methodist church in the Spokane community. It had a large congregation and a fine Sunday school program and choir. The church had a lovely building with many stained-glass windows. Members of the church purchased the windows and had their names commemorated there. When the church was later moved to the new location, those windows were moved to the new church.

Rev. George W. White, seen in his Sunday best in this 1890 photograph, was the first pastor of St. Paul's Church (later known as Bethel African Methodist Episcopal Church). Many fine pastors led the faithful at Bethel. Many things were accomplished by the congregation. After years at Fifth Avenue and Pine Street, another church building was constructed by Clarence Freeman, a contractor and longtime member of the church.

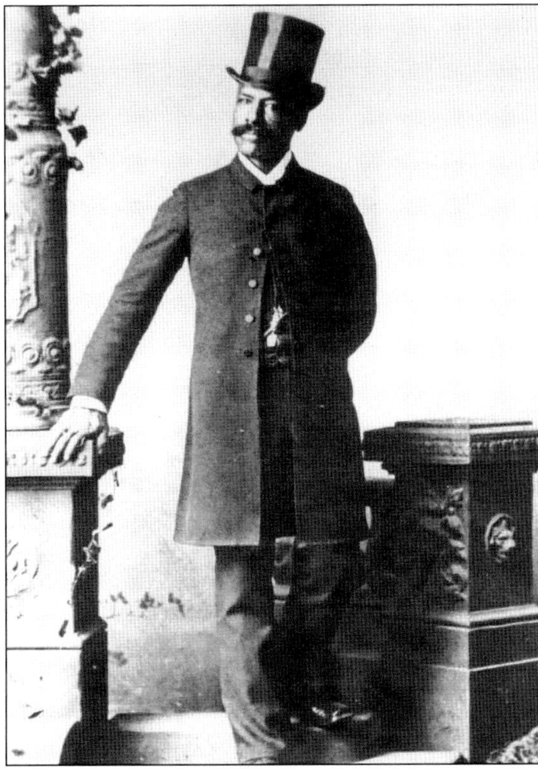

This photograph was taken Mother's Day 1936 at Bethel African Methodist Episcopal Church. The congregation would have a special service honoring mothers. Many times, the mother with the youngest children or the most elderly mother would be awarded a prize. Mother's Day was always a special day in the black church. There was always a large attendance at the Mother's Day observance. (Courtesy of MAC/EWHS, L87-1.8887-36.)

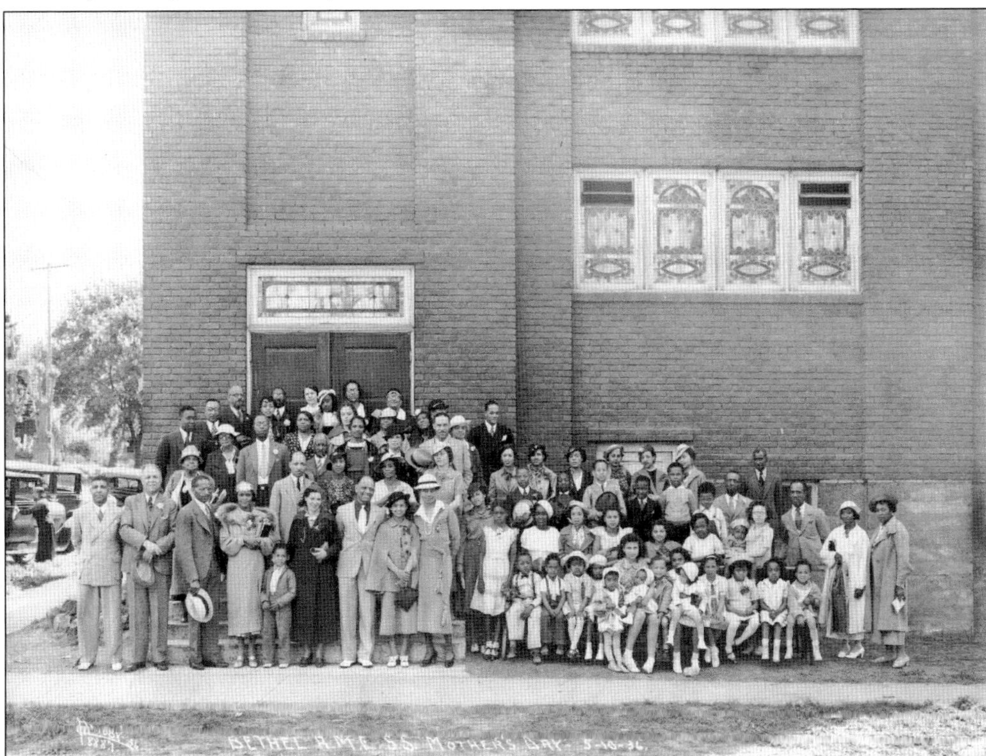

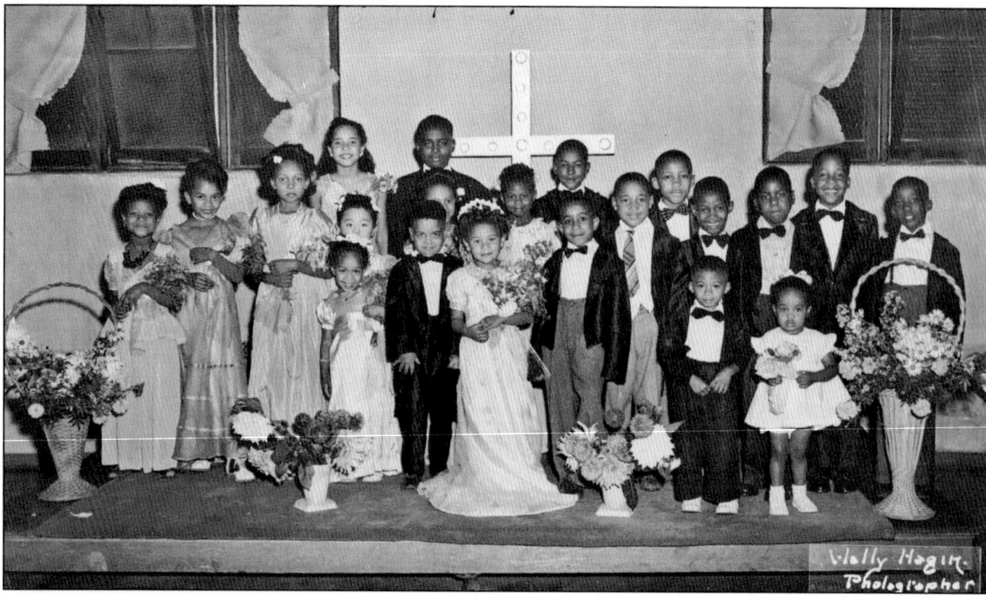

The church was the lifeblood of the African American community, not only for religious instruction but also for fun. This photograph, taken September 26, 1947, at Calvary Baptist Church, depicts a Tom Thumb wedding. All of the participants are children. The event was sponsored by the Neon Club. The groom is Clarence Freeman Jr., and the bride is Wallene Hagin. It was always fun to watch. (Courtesy of MAC/EWHS, L97-56.165.)

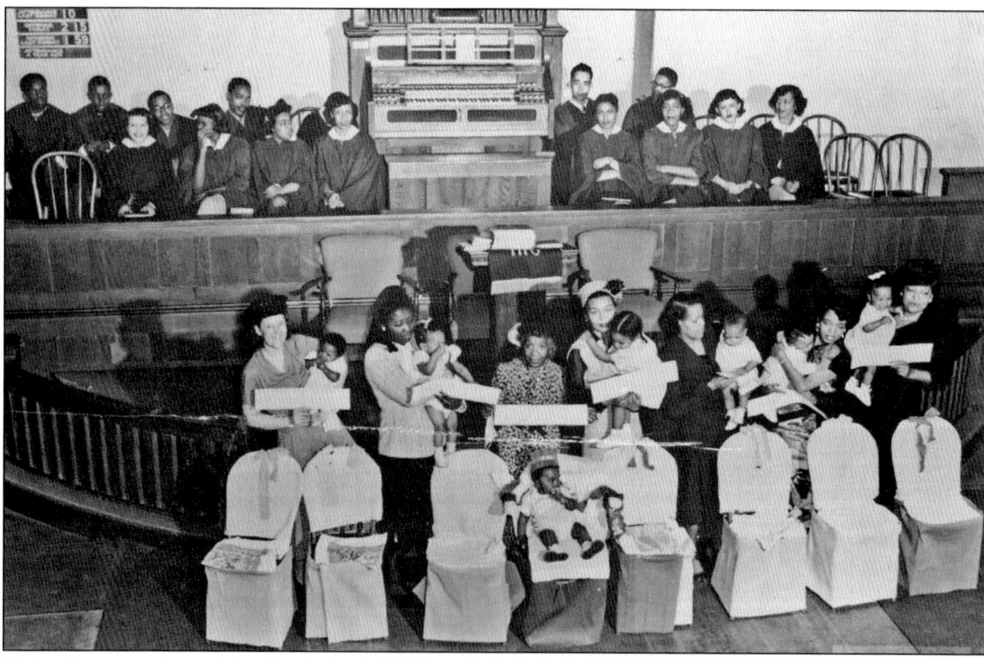

This photograph is of the Bethel AME Church baby contest in 1948. From left to right are (front row) sponsors Stella Carr, Amy Carter, Lillian Strong, unidentified, Bailey Pierce, and Frances Freeman; (second row) choir members Evelyn Burnette, Alice Mims, Charlotte Strong, Jerrelene (Hill) Williamson, Russlyne Hagin, Lillian (Hill) Carter, Lois Bernestien, and Mary (Hill) McFarlin; (third row) three unidentified, Sam Williamson, Leroy Wilson, and Warren Smith.

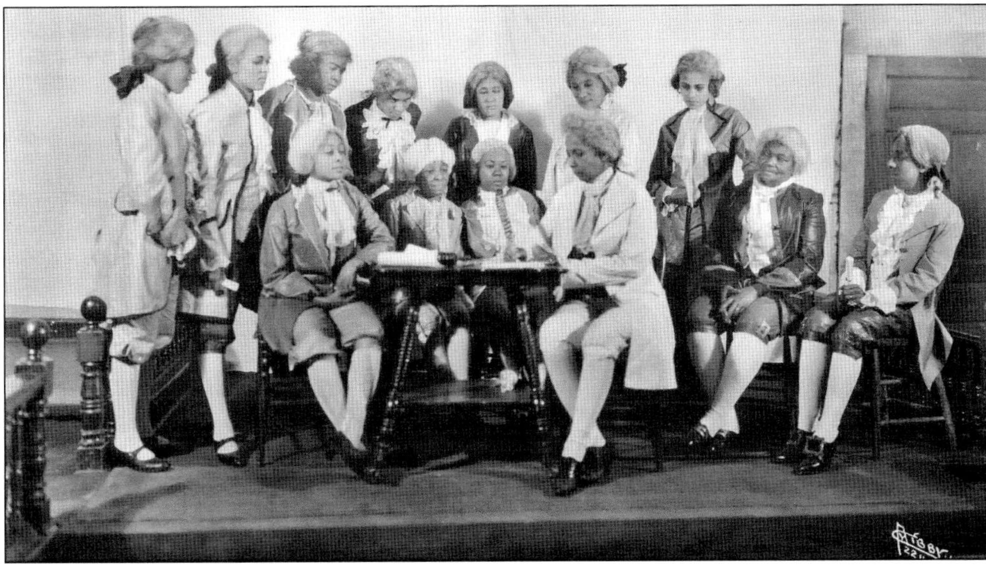

This is the reenactment of the signing of the Declaration of Independence by the Women of Calvary in 1922. Irene Hagin is seated on the far left. Another fun event was the "Devil's Funeral," just like a regular funeral, coffin and all. When people looked in the coffin, they saw their own reflection in a mirror. Devil's food cake and ice cream were served. (Courtesy of MAC/EWHS, L97-56.315.)

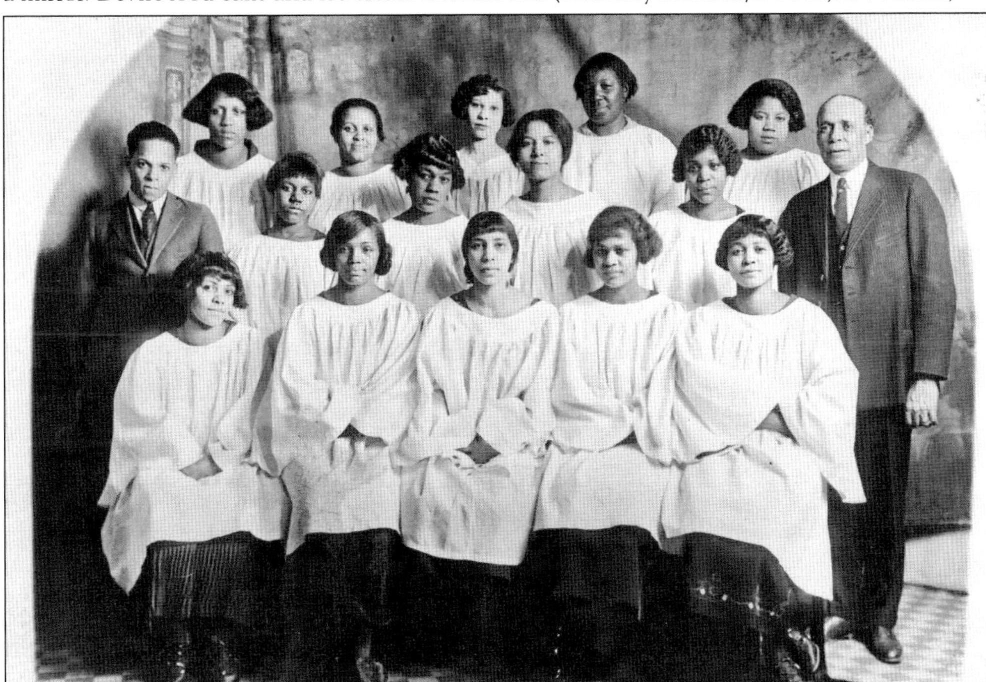

This photograph of the Bethel African Methodist Episcopal Church choir is from around 1930. Elbert Breckenridge (left) is the grandson of Lucy and Henry Breckenridge, who came to Spokane from Roslyn, Washington. The minister is on the right. Among the members of the choir are the Lipscomb sisters, who had a singing group and were well known for their beautiful voices. They performed in many venues around Spokane.

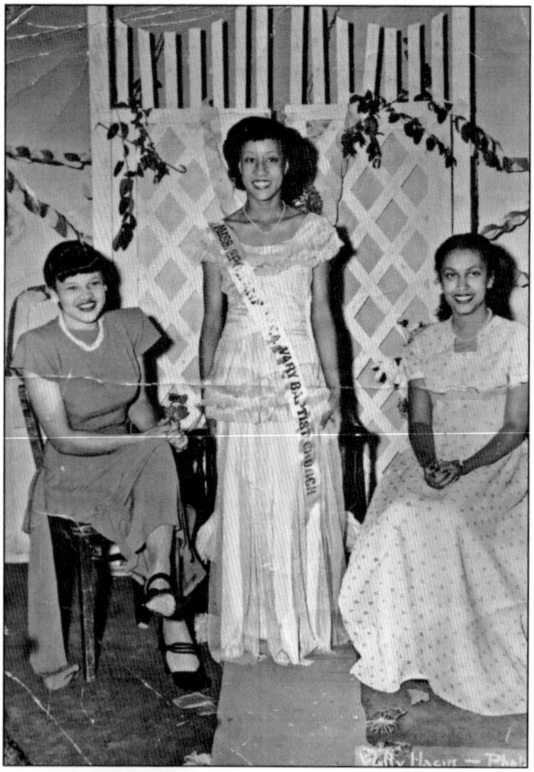

This is the contest for Miss Spokane of Calvary Baptist Church in 1949. The winner, in the middle, is Jerrelene (Hill) Williamson. On the right is Russlyne Hagin, and on the left is Lois Bernestien. The contest was a fund-raiser for Calvary. The person who sold the most tickets was the winner. Another fund-raiser during Reverend Reed's pastorate was Calvary's famous fried chicken dinners, which many Spokane residents would attend.

This is a photograph of Bethel African Methodist Episcopal Church showing the new stucco and wood structure under construction. The address at this time was on Newark Avenue and Laura Street. The address has since been changed to 645 Richard Allen Court. The pastor of Bethel, at this writing, is Rev. Lonnie Mitchell, and his wife is Elisha. The new church was built by Freeman-Goebel Contractors.

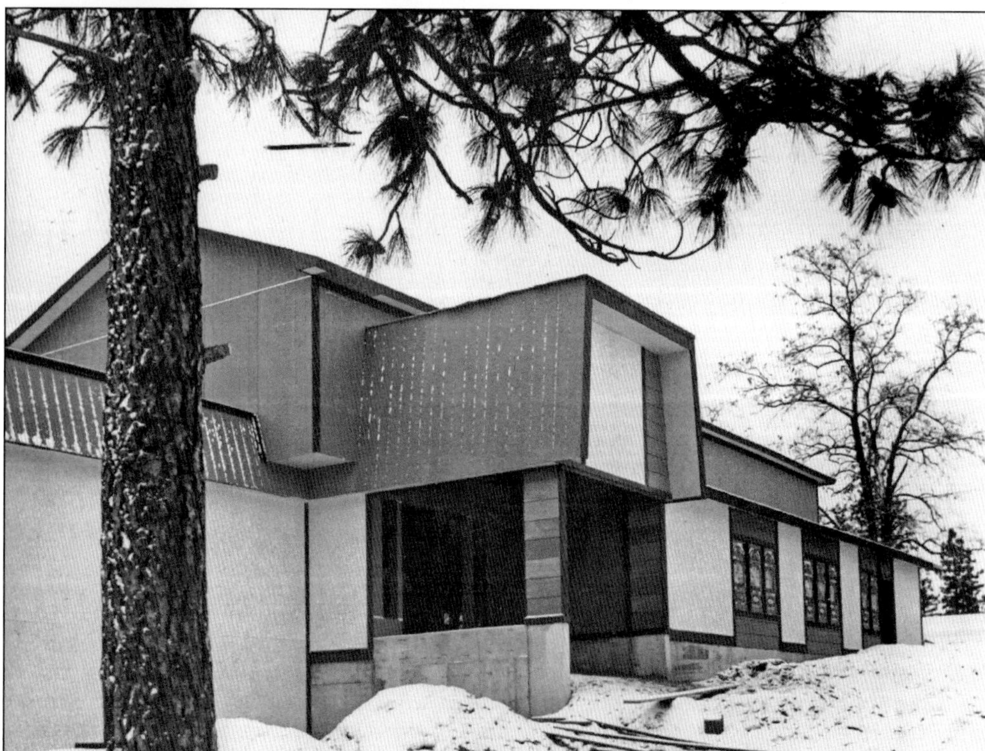

This is the 100th anniversary of Calvary Baptist Church in 1990. The celebration theme was "Daring to Be Different." Calvary, established in 1890, has been an integral part of the African American community and of the overall Spokane community. The church has stood on the corner of Third Avenue and Cowley Street for many years. Calvary's motto is "The Friendly Church." At this writing, Calvary is 119 years old.

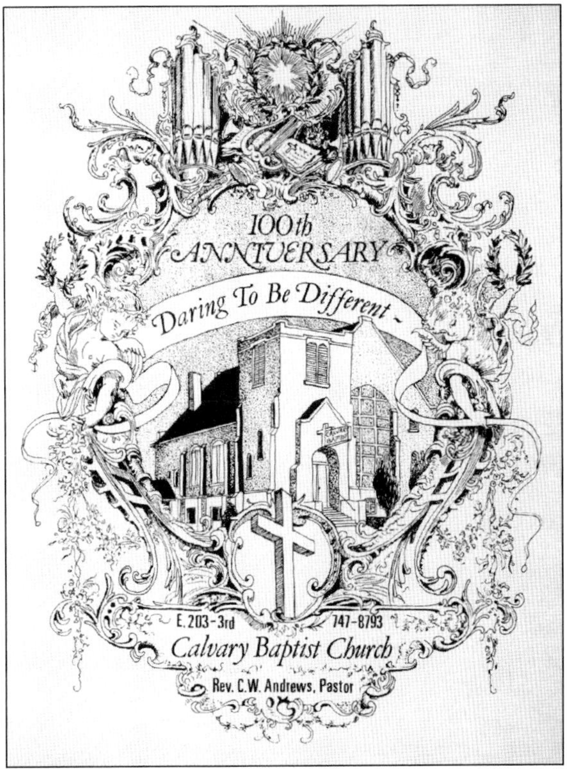

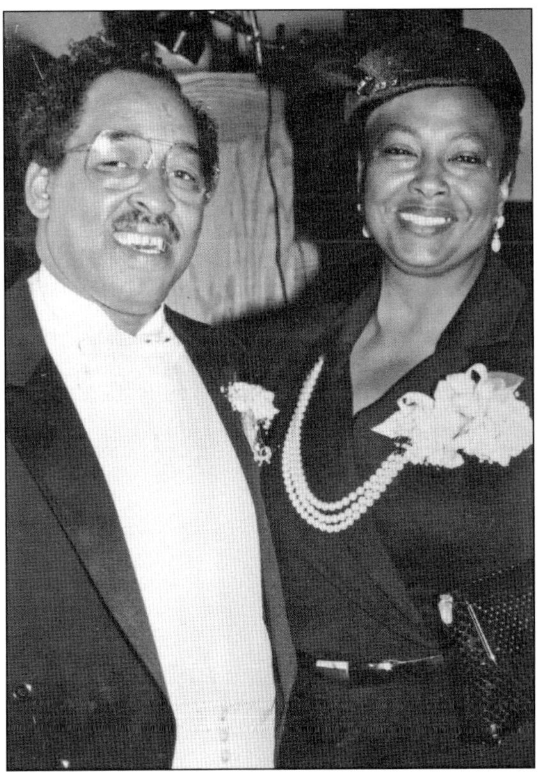

This photograph is of Rev. C. W. Andrews and his wife, Doris. They came to Calvary with their children, Chester Jr., Darryl, Kenneth, Dana, and Lyn. Reverend Andrews was installed as pastor in May 1975. At this writing, he is the present pastor. Through his pastorate, religious instruction still is being performed at the church.

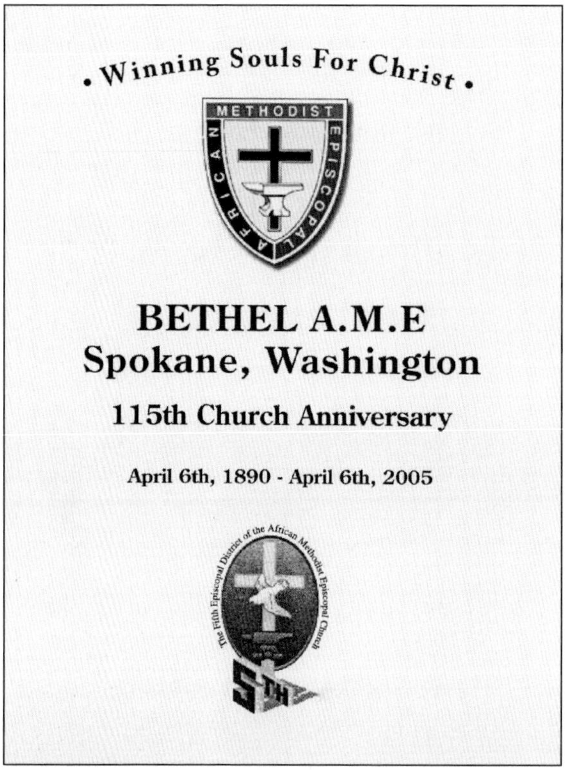

This photograph shows the program for the 115th anniversary of the Bethel African Methodist Episcopal Church. Bethel AME was organized on April 6, 1890, by the Reverend A. C. Augustus, presiding elder, in the home of Mrs. D. F. C. Washington. Among those present were Mr. and Mrs. L. W. Williams, Ed Whitlock, J. B. Harkins, J. P. Crew, E. H. Holmes, and Mrs. C. J. Flowers.

Shown here are members of the Calvary Baptist Church Senior Choir, along with the pastor of Calvary, Rev. C. W. Andrews (second row, center). This choir not only sang at the church but was featured in other venues throughout the city and the state. The choir sang on television Christmas programs and also made a recording. Chester Andrews Jr. (first row) was the pianist.

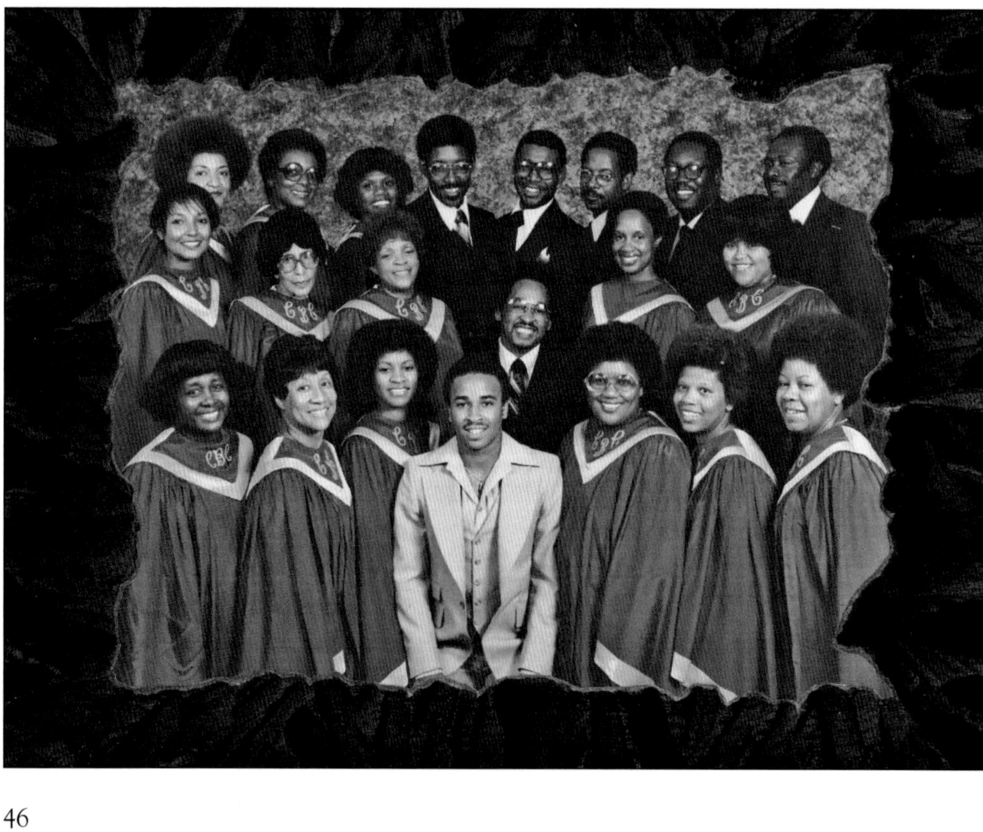

Five

DISCRIMINATION AND RACISM

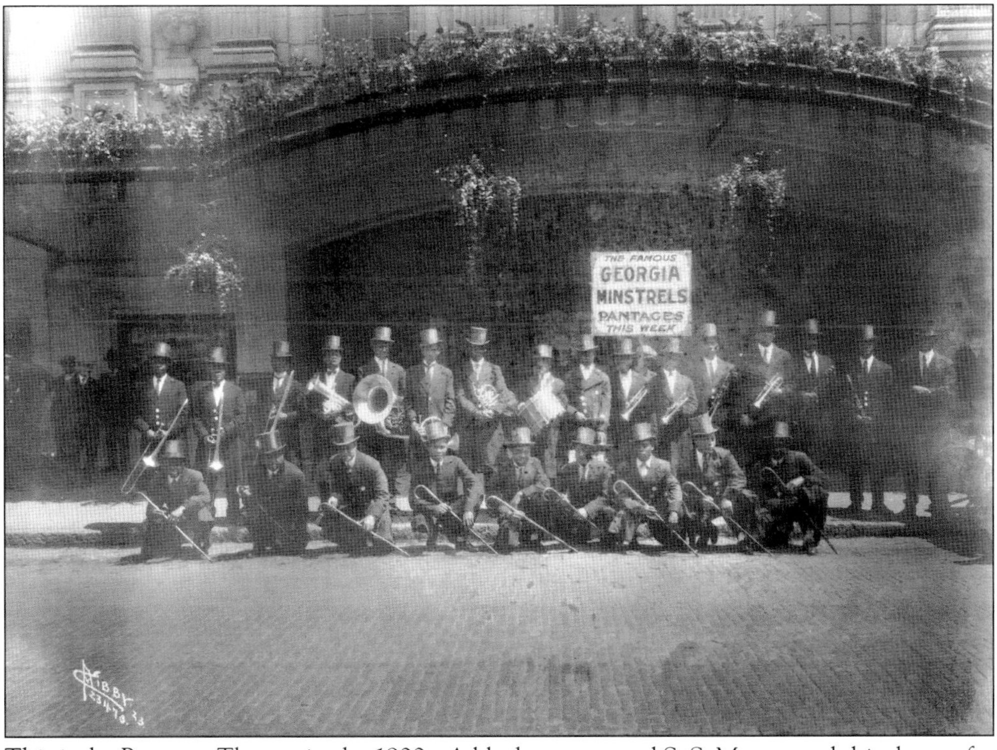

This is the Pantages Theatre in the 1900s. A black man named S. S. Moore sued this theater for trying to make him sit in the balcony. He won the case and was awarded $200. Jurors remarked, "A man ought to be able to sit where he wants to sit," according to Jim Kershner in *Columbia Magazine*. Because of this action, blacks later were able to sit anywhere in Spokane theaters.

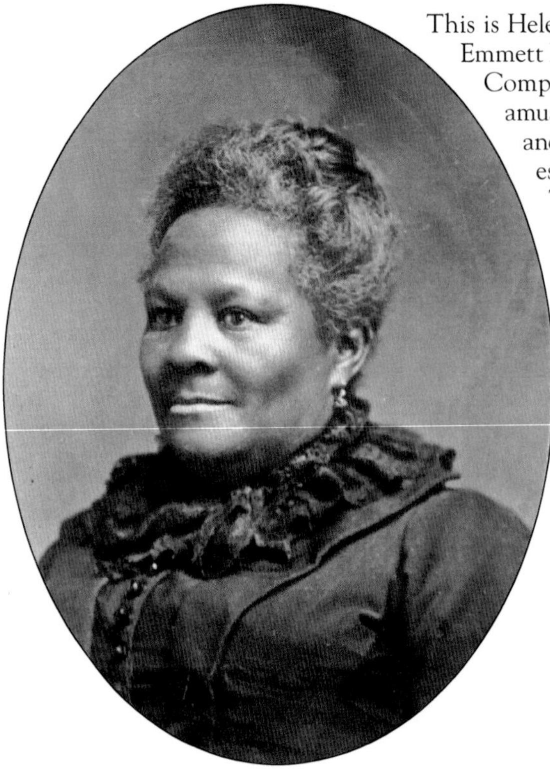

This is Helen Holmes, mother of Emmett Holmes Sr. Emmett Holmes sued the Washington Water Power Company, the owner of Natatorium Park, an amusement park on the city's west side. Emmett and his family were refused service in an eating establishment in the park. He lost the case. The judge's ruling was, "They had the right to refuse service," as reported by Joseph Franklin in *All Through the Night*.

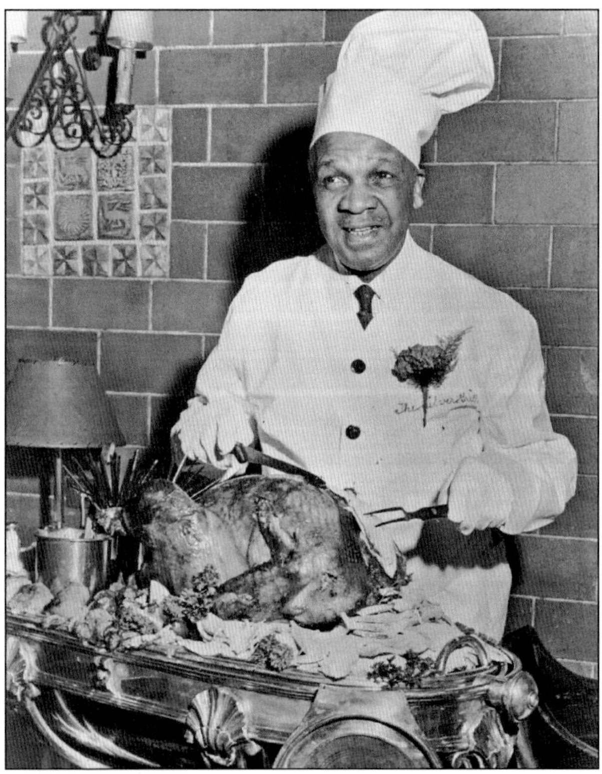

Clarence Taylor was a dining room steward at the Spokane (Ridpath) Hotel for 50 years until retirement in 1952. Some businesses had "Whites Only" signs that Rev. Emmett Reed and F. A. Stokes would try to get removed. Praise is due Harold I. "Shine" McKenna's Fern Ice Cream Parlor for welcoming blacks in the 1940s. African Americans have been called "colored," "brown," "Negro," "black," and the "N" word, which this author refuses to perpetuate.

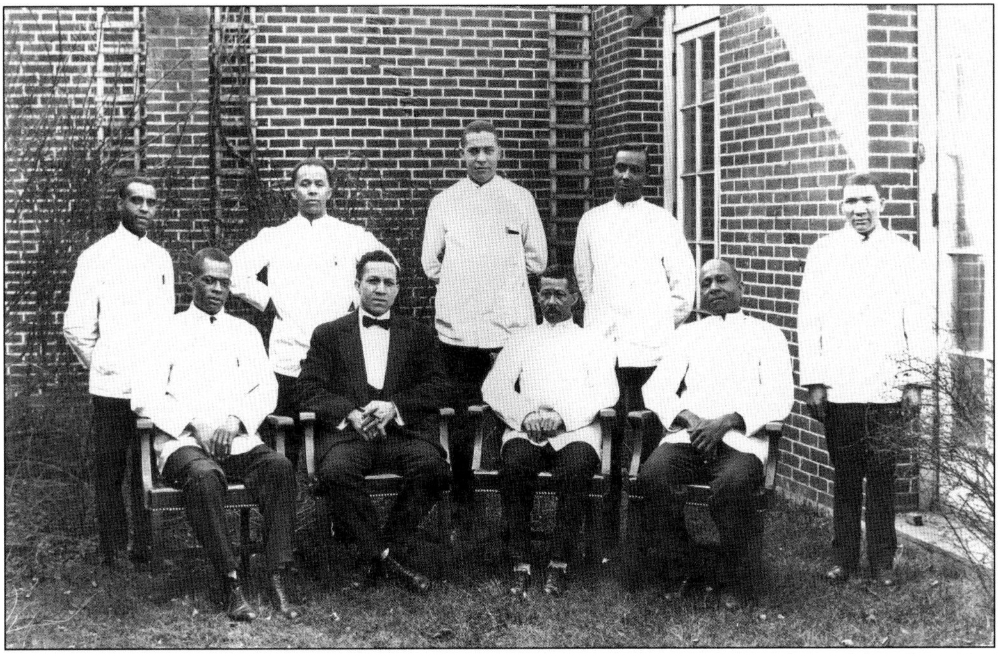

This photograph was taken at the Spokane Club in 1920. These waiters are dressed for a busy day at work. The man in the black suit is probably the head waiter or leader. Many black men and women in Spokane worked at this then-private club for whites only, for at least a time. (Courtesy of MAC/EWHS L87-1.17546-20.)

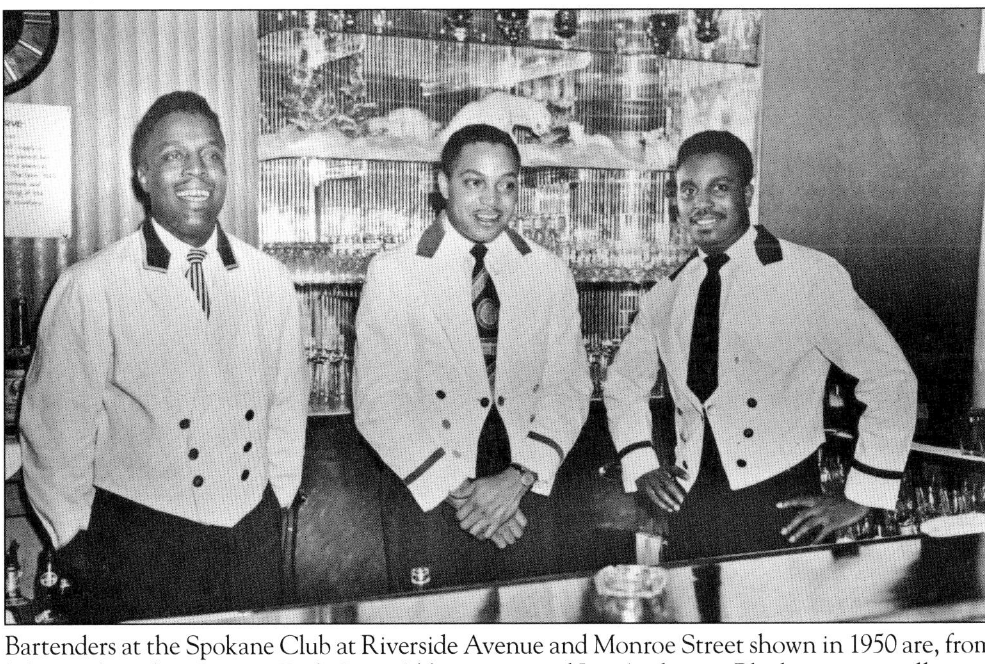

Bartenders at the Spokane Club at Riverside Avenue and Monroe Street shown in 1950 are, from left to right, John "Sonny" Teel, Gene Abbyington, and Jun Anderson. Black men generally were limited to work as janitors, hotel bellhops, and construction workers. Women were domestics, cared for white children, or were hotel maids. Many did laundry for white women in their homes. Later, black women worked in the backs of dress stores, preparing clothes.

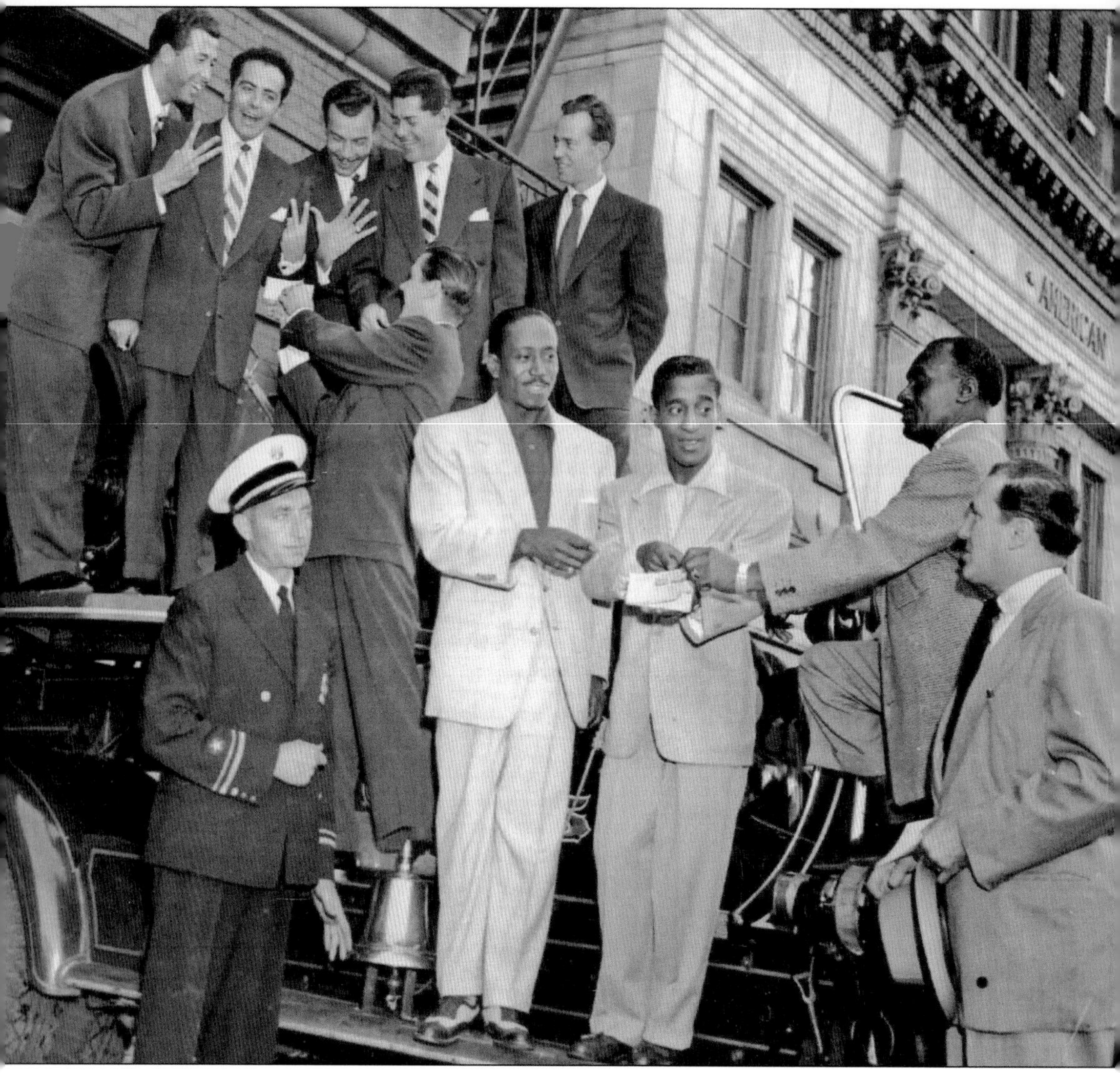

Sammy Davis Jr. was refused service at the exclusive Davenport Hotel and wrote about it in his book, *Yes, I Can*. He, his father, and his uncle came to Spokane to perform a show at the Orpheum Theatre. This 1950s photograph of Davis was taken at the fire station next to the American Legion Building in Spokane. Louis Armstrong also was refused lodging at the Davenport Hotel and was leaving from the airport when concert promoters convinced him to return for his show. In the 1940s, the Harlem Globetrotters had to eat and sleep at a boardinghouse across from Bethel AME Church because they were not able to find other lodging. Blacks also could not work at the Davenport Hotel. Spokane was not unique in clamoring to see black entertainers but being unwilling to accept them as equals. Across the country, they were barred from many hotels, clubs, and restaurants except when performing, and even then they were forced to use the back door. (Courtesy of Joy and John Obde.)

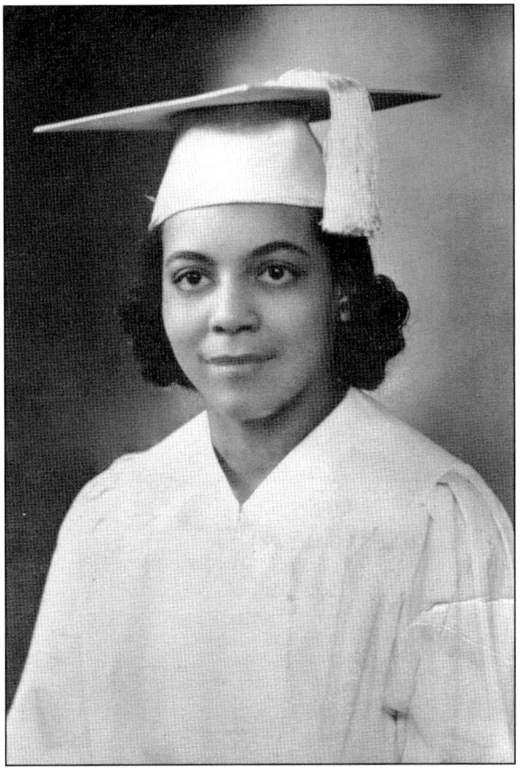

A little-known story of discrimination at the Davenport Hotel happened in 1937, when singer Marian Anderson stayed there. Some Marycliff High School girls went to interview her, and a black girl in the group was told to use the freight elevator. The other girls said, "We'll all go on the freight elevator." This young black girl, Frances (Nichols) Scott, later became the first black female attorney in Spokane.

Discrimination against blacks was prevalent in Spokane restaurants. Blacks could not go everywhere, but they had "their own:" Virgil's Chicken Dinner Shack (shown here in 1940), owner Virgil Sexton; the Willow Inn, owner Walter Derrick; the Ebony Cafe, owner Frank Hopkins; the Porters' and Waiters' Club, owner Algier Ball; the Golden Bird, owner Tommy Rutledge; Sam's Pit, owner Sam Willis; and more.

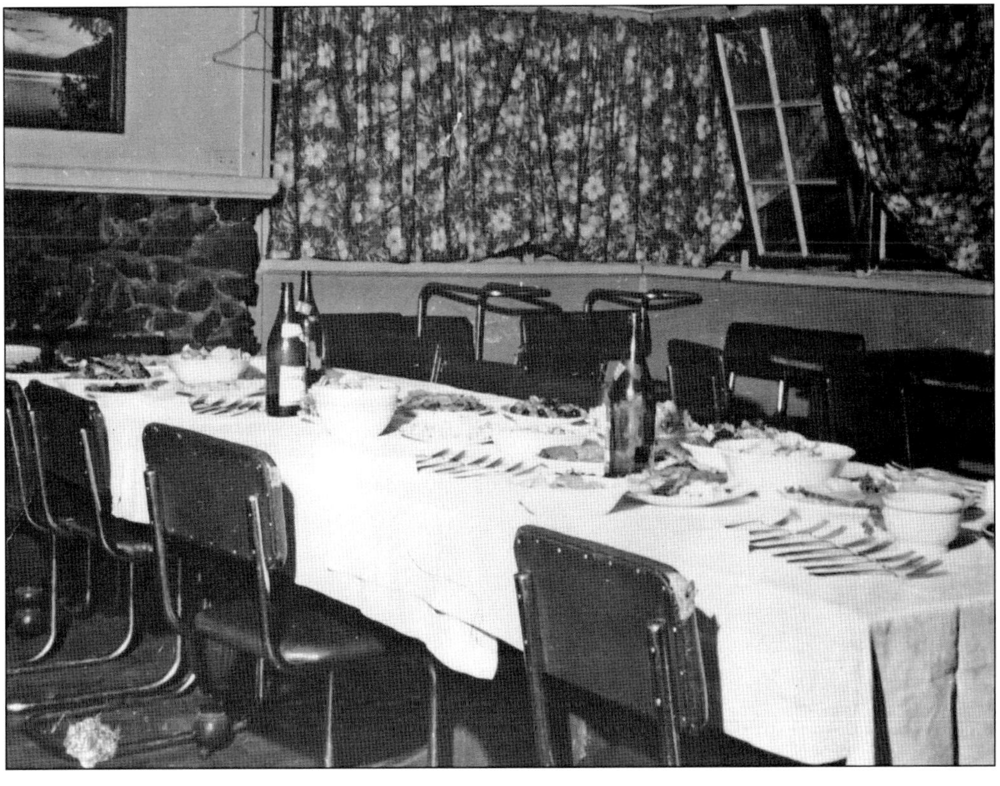

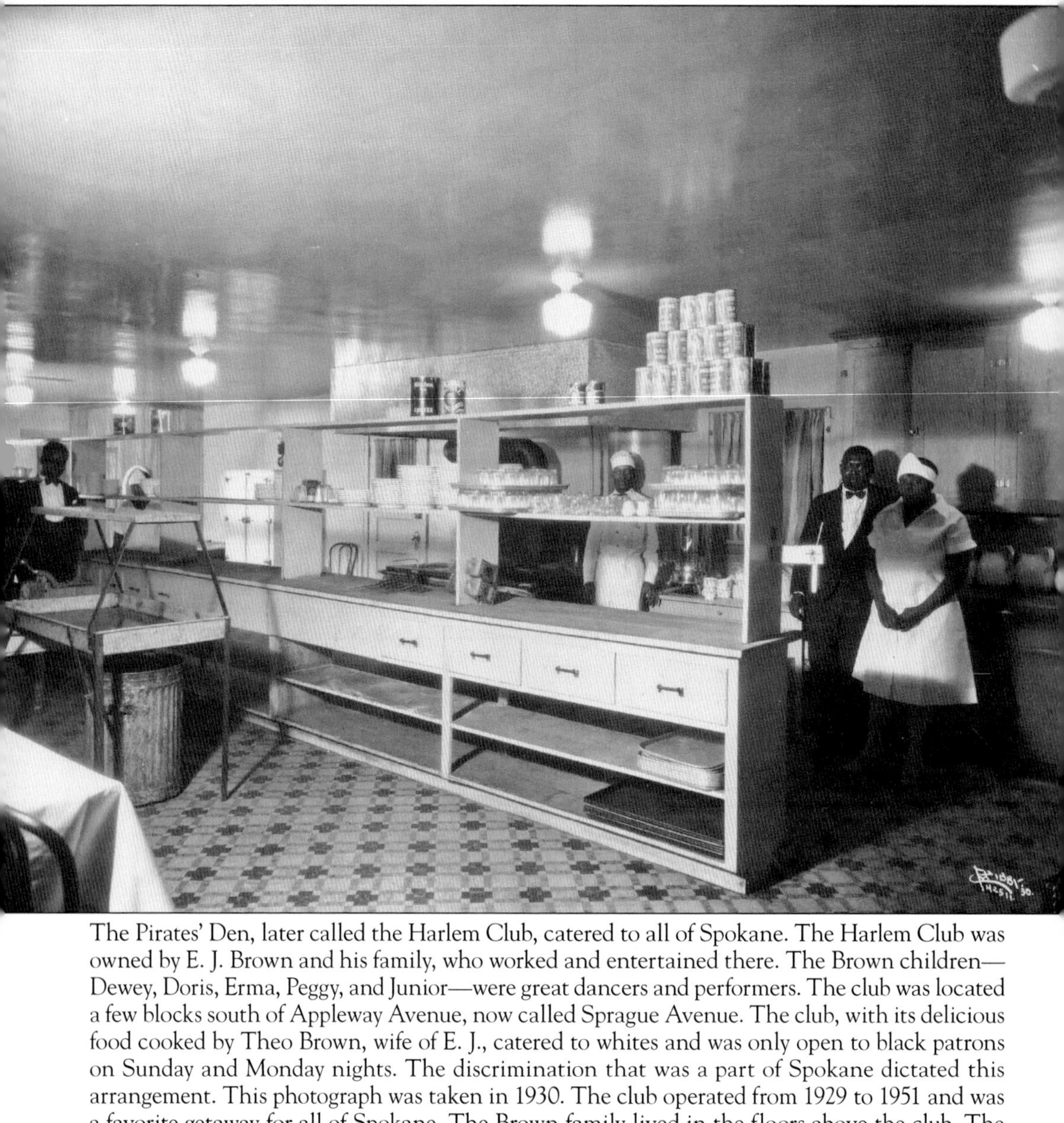

The Pirates' Den, later called the Harlem Club, catered to all of Spokane. The Harlem Club was owned by E. J. Brown and his family, who worked and entertained there. The Brown children—Dewey, Doris, Erma, Peggy, and Junior—were great dancers and performers. The club was located a few blocks south of Appleway Avenue, now called Sprague Avenue. The club, with its delicious food cooked by Theo Brown, wife of E. J., catered to whites and was only open to black patrons on Sunday and Monday nights. The discrimination that was a part of Spokane dictated this arrangement. This photograph was taken in 1930. The club operated from 1929 to 1951 and was a favorite getaway for all of Spokane. The Brown family lived in the floors above the club. The club burned down in 1951 from some faulty electric wiring. It was a great loss to the Spokane community. E. J. Brown built a home for his family at 5901 East Eighth Avenue, which was not too far from where the club was located. (Courtesy of MAC/EWHS L87-1.42511-30.)

This is a copy of the menu at Happy's Restaurant. It was located at 208 Shadle Center on the northwest side of Spokane and was owned by Rev. Percy "Happy" Watkins and his family. It was called Happy's Soul Food Restaurant and Barbeque. Reverend Watkins and his wife, Etta, have four sons, Percy Jr., John, James, and Paul. At this writing, he is pastor of New Hope Baptist Church.

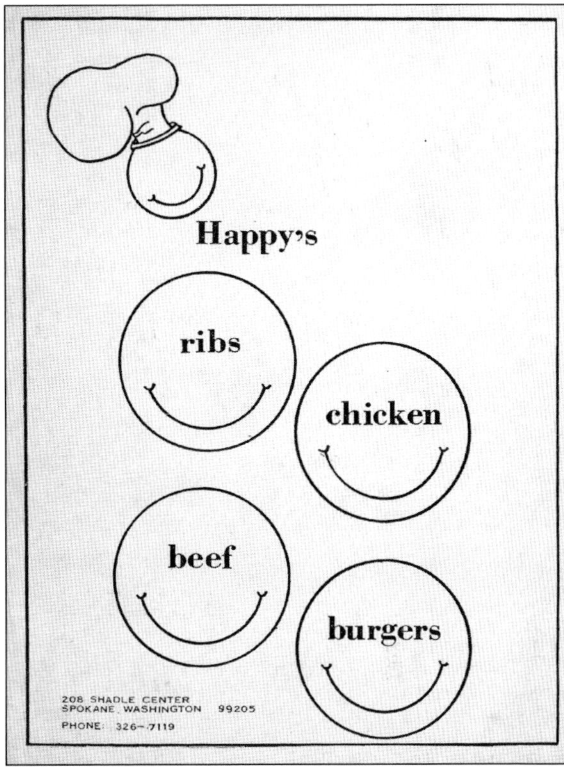

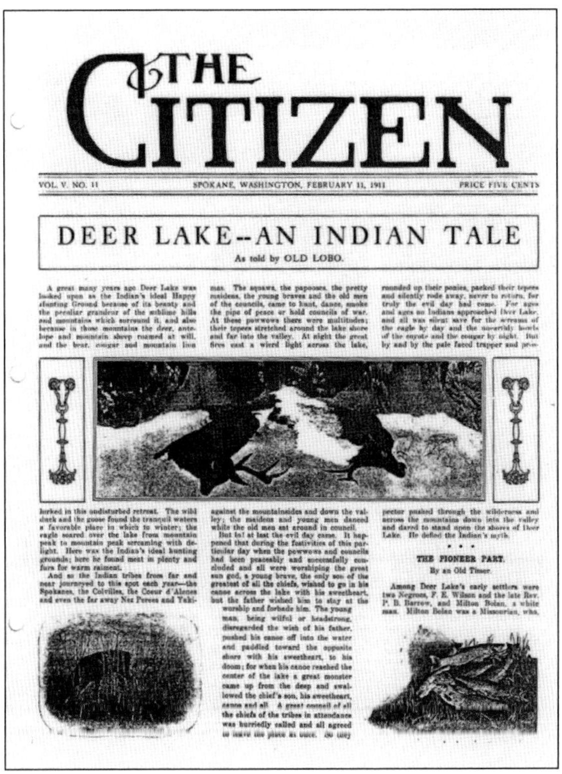

THE CITIZEN

VOL. V. NO. 11 SPOKANE, WASHINGTON, FEBRUARY 11, 1911 PRICE FIVE CENTS

DEER LAKE--AN INDIAN TALE

As told by OLD LOBO.

A great many years ago Deer Lake was looked upon as the Indian's ideal Happy Hunting Ground because of its beauty and the peculiar grandeur of the sublime hills and mountains which surround it, and also because in those mountains the deer, antelope and mountain sheep roamed at will, and the bear, cougar and mountain lion lurked in this undisturbed retreat. The wild duck and the goose found the tranquil waters a favorable place in which to winter; the eagle soared over the lake from mountain peak to mountain peak screaming with delight. Here was the Indian's ideal hunting grounds; here he found meat in plenty and furs for warm raiment.

And so the Indian tribes from far and near journeyed to this spot each year—the Spokanes, the Colvilles, the Coeur d'Alenes and even the far away Nez Perces and Yakimas. The squaws, the papooses, the pretty maidens, the young braves and the old men of the councils, came to hunt, dance, smoke the pipe of peace or hold councils of war. At these powwows there were multitudes; their tepees stretched around the lake shore and far into the valley. At night the great fires cast a wierd light across the lake, against the mountainsides and down the valley; the maidens and young men danced while the old men sat around in council.

But lo! at last the evil day came. It happened that during the festivities of this particular day when the powwows and councils had been peaceably and successfully concluded and all were worshiping the great sun god, a young brave, the only son of the greatest of all the chiefs, wished to go in his canoe across the lake with his sweetheart, but the father wished him to stay at the worship and forbade him. The young man, being wilful or headstrong, disregarded the wish of his father, pushed his canoe off into the water and paddled toward the opposite shore with his sweetheart, to his doom; for when his canoe reached the center of the lake a great monster came up from the deep and swallowed the chief's son, his sweetheart, canoe and all. A great council of all the chiefs of the tribes in attendance was hurriedly called and all agreed to leave the place at once. So they rounded up their ponies, packed their tepees and silently rode away, never to return, for truly the evil day had come. For ages and ages no Indians approached Deer Lake, and all was silent save for the screams of the eagle by day and the unearthly howls of the coyote and the cougar by night. But by and by the pale faced trapper and prospector pushed through the wilderness and across the mountains down into the valley and dared to stand upon the shores of Deer Lake. He defied the Indian's myth.

* * *

THE PIONEER PART.

By an Old Timer.

Among Deer Lake's early settlers were two Negroes, F. E. Wilson and the late Rev. P. B. Barrow, and Milton Bolan, a white man. Milton Bolan was a Missourian, who,

The black community had its own newspapers through the years: the *Citizen*, published by Charles Barrow; the *Star*, published by I. C. Johnson and his wife; the *Forum*; the *Voice of the West*; the *Western Star*; and the *Black Shoppers Guide*. Later there was the *African American Voice*, published by Robert Lloyd and his wife, Diane. This is the front of the *Citizen* newspaper, February 11, 1911.

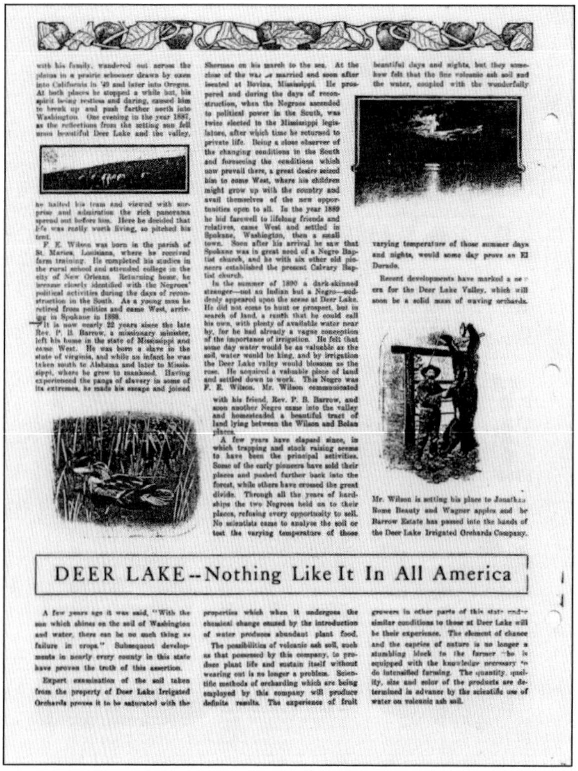

with his family, wandered out across the plains in a prairie schooner drawn by oxen into California in '49 and later into Oregon. At both places he stopped a while but, his spirit being restless and daring, caused him to break up and push farther north into Washington. One evening in the year 1887, as the reflections from the setting sun fell upon beautiful Deer Lake and the valley, he halted his team and viewed with surprise and admiration the rich panorama spread out before him. Here he decided that life was really worth living, so pitched his tent.

F. E. Wilson was born in the parish of St. Maries, Louisiana, where he received farm training. He completed his studies in the rural school and attended college in the city of New Orleans. Returning home, he became closely identified with the Negroes' political activities during the days of reconstruction in the South. As a young man he retired from politics and came West, arriving in Spokane in 1888.

It is now nearly 22 years since the late Rev. P. B. Barrow, a missionary minister, left his home in the state of Mississippi and came West. He was born a slave in the state of virginia, and while an infant he was taken south to Alabama and later to Mississippi, where he grew to manhood. Having experienced the pangs of slavery in some of its extremes, he made his escape and joined Sherman on his march to the sea. At the close of the war he married and soon after located at Bovina, Mississippi. He prospered and during the days of reconstruction, when the Negroes ascended to political power in the South, was twice elected to the Mississippi legislature, after which time he returned to private life. Being a close observer of the changing conditions in the South and foreseeing the conditions which now prevail there, a great desire seized him to come West, where his children might grow up with the country and avail themselves of the new opportunities open to all. In the year 1889 he bid farewell to lifelong friends and relatives, came West and settled in Spokane, Washington, then a small town. Soon after his arrival he saw that Spokane was in great need of a Negro Baptist church, and he with six other old pioneers established the present Calvary Baptist church.

In the summer of 1890 a dark-skinned stranger—not an Indian but a Negro—suddenly appeared upon the scene at Deer Lake. He did not come to hunt or prospect, but in search of land, a ranch that he could call his own, with plenty of available water near by, for he had already a vague conception of the importance of irrigation. He felt that some day water would be as valuable as the soil, water would be king, and by irrigation the Deer Lake valley would blossom as the rose. He acquired a valuable piece of land and settled down to work. This Negro was F. E. Wilson. Mr. Wilson communicated with his friend, Rev. P. B. Barrow, and soon another Negro came into the valley and homesteaded a beautiful tract of land lying between the Wilson and Bolan places.

A few years have elapsed since, in which trapping and stock raising seems to have been the principal activities. Some of the early pioneers have sold their places and pushed further back into the forest, while others have crossed the great divide. Through all the years of hardships the two Negroes held on to their places, refusing every opportunity to sell. No scientists came to analyse the soil or test the varying temperature of those beautiful days and nights, but they somehow felt that the fine volcanic ash soil and the water, coupled with the wonderfully varying temperature of those summer days and nights, would some day prove an El Dorado.

Recent developments have marked a new era for the Deer Lake Valley, which will soon be a solid mass of waving orchards.

Mr. Wilson is setting his place to Jonathan Rome Beauty and Wagner apples and the Barrow Estate has passed into the hands of the Deer Lake Irrigated Orchards Company.

DEER LAKE--Nothing Like It In All America

A few years ago it was said, "With the sun which shines on the soil of Washington and water, there can be no such thing as failure in crops." Subsequent developments in nearly every county in this state have proven the truth of this assertion.

Expert examination of the soil taken from the property of Deer Lake Irrigated Orchards proves it to be saturated with the properties which when it undergoes the chemical change caused by the introduction of water produces abundant plant food.

The possibilities of volcanic ash soil, such as that possessed by this company, to produce plant life and sustain itself without wearing out is no longer a problem. Scientific methods of orcharding which are being employed by this company will produce definite results. The experience of fruit growers in other parts of this state under similar conditions to those at Deer Lake will be their experience. The element of chance and the caprice of nature is no longer a stumbling block to the farmer who is equipped with the knowledge necessary to do intensified farming. The quantity, quality, size and color of the products are determined in advance by the scientific use of water on volcanic ash soil.

An inside page of the *Citizen* newspaper tells the story of F. E. Wilson, who first came to Deer Lake, Washington, in 1890 in search of land. He was described as a "dark skinned stranger, not an Indian, but a negro." Wilson communicated with his friend P. B. Barrow, and they formed the Deer Lake Irrigated Orchard Company. This information is from the *Citizen* newspaper, dated February 11, 1911.

This is a copy of the *Spokane Star* newspaper dated April 12. From articles in the paper itself, it seems to be from about 1945 or 1946. Bernice Adams is on the cover. She was a well-known entertainer around Spokane. The paper was published by I. C. Johnson and his wife. They owned a publishing shop on Third Avenue for many years. This copy was Vol. 1, No. 1.

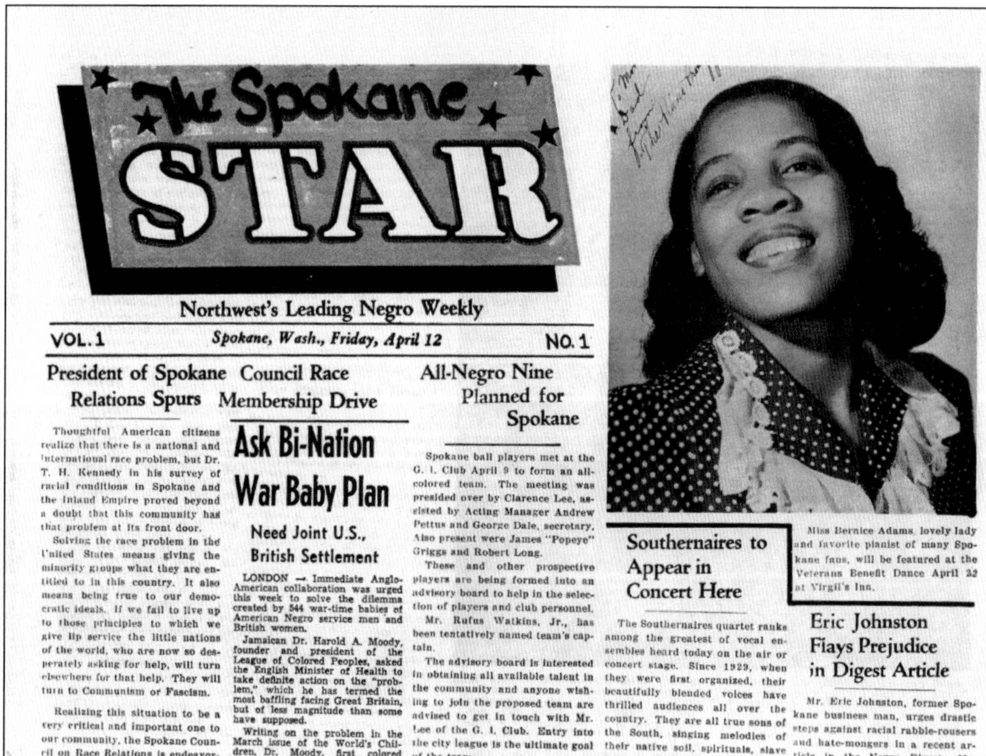

The Spokane STAR

Northwest's Leading Negro Weekly

VOL. 1 — Spokane, Wash., Friday, April 12 — NO. 1

President of Spokane Council Race Relations Spurs Membership Drive

Thoughtful American citizens realize that there is a national and international race problem, but Dr. T. H. Kennedy in his survey of racial conditions in Spokane and the Inland Empire proved beyond a doubt that this community has that problem at its front door.

Solving the race problem in the United States means giving the minority groups what they are entitled to in this country. It also means being true to our democratic ideals. If we fail to live up to those principles to which we give lip service the little nations of the world, who are now so desperately asking for help, will turn elsewhere for that help. They will turn to Communism or Fascism.

Realizing this situation to be a very critical and important one to our community, the Spokane Council on Race Relations is endeavor-

Ask Bi-Nation War Baby Plan

Need Joint U.S., British Settlement

LONDON — Immediate Anglo-American collaboration was urged this week to solve the dilemma created by 544 war-time babies of American Negro service men and British women.

Jamaican Dr. Harold A. Moody, founder and president of the League of Colored Peoples, asked the English Minister of Health to take definite action on the "problem," which he has termed the most baffling facing Great Britain, but of less magnitude than some have supposed.

Writing on the problem in the March issue of the World's Children, Dr. Moody, first colored chairman of a British Missionary

All-Negro Nine Planned for Spokane

Spokane ball players met at the G. I. Club April 9 to form an all-colored team. The meeting was presided over by Clarence Lee, assisted by Acting Manager Andrew Pettus and George Dale, secretary. Also present were James "Popeye" Griggs and Robert Long.

These and other prospective players are being formed into an advisory board to help in the selection of players and club personnel.

Mr. Rufus Watkins, Jr., has been tentatively named team's captain.

The advisory board is interested in obtaining all available talent in the community and anyone wishing to join the proposed team are advised to get in touch with Mr. Lee of the G. I. Club. Entry into the city league is the ultimate goal of the team.

Miss Bernice Adams, lovely lady and favorite pianist of many Spokane fans, will be featured at the Veterans Benefit Dance April 22 at Virgil's Inn.

Southernaires to Appear in Concert Here

The Southernaires quartet ranks among the greatest of vocal ensembles heard today on the air or concert stage. Since 1929, when they were first organized, their beautifully blended voices have thrilled audiences all over the country. They are all true sons of the South, singing melodies of their native soil, spirituals, slave songs, and Negro popular songs.

Eric Johnston Flays Prejudice in Digest Article

Mr. Eric Johnston, former Spokane business man, urges drastic steps against racial rabble-rousers and hate-mongers in a recent article in the Negro Digest. Mr.

The *Black Shoppers' Guide* was a paper of ideas, issues, and comments. This first copy, a Glover Publication dated 1969, cost 25¢ and was Vol. 1, No 1. The newspaper noted, "The *Black Shoppers Guide* was established because some citizens are disturbed by the complacency and indifference of many residents in Spokane." The editor was Paul Pradia, the women's editor was Carol Richey, and the youth editor was Jennifer (Williamson) Roseman.

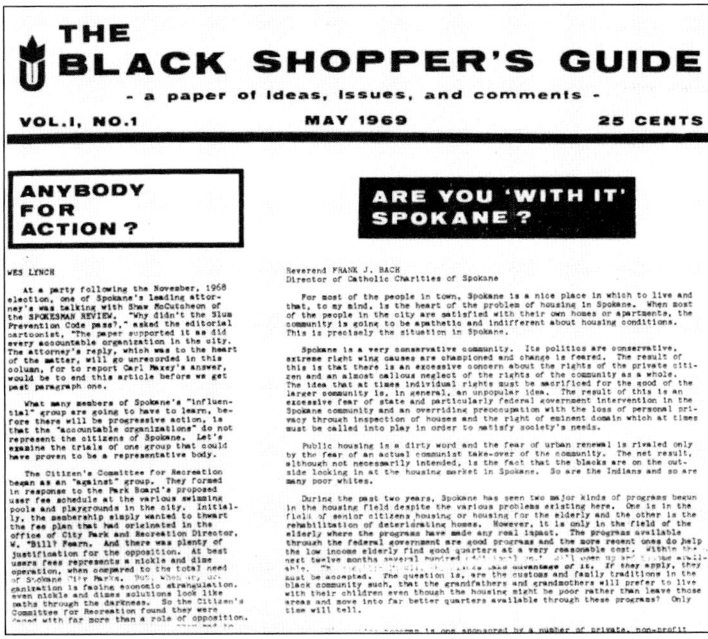

THE BLACK SHOPPER'S GUIDE

- a paper of ideas, issues, and comments -

VOL.I, NO.1 MAY 1969 25 CENTS

ANYBODY FOR ACTION?

WES LYNCH

At a party following the November, 1968 election, one of Spokane's leading attorney's was talking with Shaw McCutcheon of the SPOKESMAN REVIEW. "Why didn't the Slum Prevention Code pass?," asked the editorial cartoonist, "The paper supported it as did every accountable organization in the city. The attorney's reply, which was to the heart of the matter, will go unrecorded in this column, for to report Carl Maxey's answer, would be to end this article before we get past paragraph one.

What many members of Spokane's "influential" group are going to have to learn, before there will be progressive action, is that the "accountable organizations" do not represent the citizens of Spokane. Let's examine the trials of one group that could have proven to be a representative body.

The Citizen's Committee for Recreation began as an "against" group. They formed in response to the Park Board's proposed user fee schedule at the various swimming pools and playgrounds in the city. Initially, the membership simply wanted to thwart the fee plan that had originated in the office of City Park and Recreation Director, W. "Bill? Fearn. And there was plenty of justification for the opposition. At best users fees represents a nickle and dime operation, when compared to the total need of Spokane City Parks. But, when an organization is facing economic strangulation, even nickle and dimes solutions look like paths through the darkness. So the Citizen's Committee for Recreation found they were faced with far more than a role of opposition.

ARE YOU 'WITH IT' SPOKANE?

Reverend FRANK J. BACH
Director of Catholic Charities of Spokane

For most of the people in town, Spokane is a nice place in which to live and that, to my mind, is the heart of the problem of housing in Spokane. When most of the people in the city are satisfied with their own homes or apartments, the community is going to be apathetic and indifferent about housing conditions. This is precisely the situation in Spokane.

Spokane is a very conservative community. Its politics are conservative, extreme right wing causes are championed and change is feared. The result of this is that there is an excessive concern about the rights of the private citizen and an almost callous neglect of the rights of the community as a whole. The idea that at times individual rights must be sacrificed for the good of the larger community is, in general, an unpopular idea. The result of this is an excessive fear of state and particularly federal government intervention in the Spokane community and an overriding preoccupation with the loss of personal privacy through inspection of houses and the right of eminent domain which at times must be called into play in order to satisfy society's needs.

Public housing is a dirty word and the fear of urban renewal is rivaled only by the fear of an actual communist take-over of the community. The net result, although not necessarily intended, is the fact that the blacks are on the outside looking in at the housing market in Spokane. So are the Indians and so are many poor whites.

During the past two years, Spokane has seen two major kinds of programs begun in the housing field despite the various problems existing here. One is in the field of senior citizens housing or housing for the elderly and the other is the rehabilitation of deteriorating homes. However, it is only in the field of the elderly where the programs have made any real impact. The programs available through the federal government are good programs and the more recent ones do help the low income elderly find good quarters at a very reasonable cost. Within the next twelve months several hundred [illegible] will open up and [illegible] available. [illegible] advantage of it. If they apply, they must be accepted. The question is, are the customs and family traditions in the black community such, that the grandfathers and grandmothers will prefer to live with their children even though the housing might be poor rather than leave those areas and move into far better quarters available through these programs? Only time will tell.

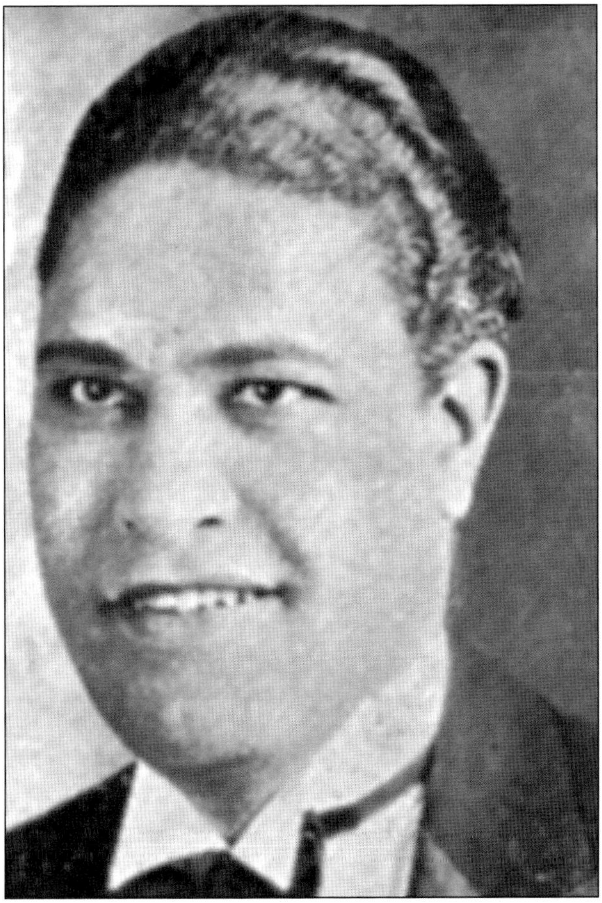

A black man could not get his hair cut in a white barbershop. Carole Curtley opened a shop located at 31 West Riverside Avenue and later moved to Division Street. His motto was "Appearance is yours for the asking." Other barbers were Long, "Bubba" Griggs, Ella, and many more. Not all of the barbers had shops, but they kept the black man "lookin' good." This photograph was taken around 1940.

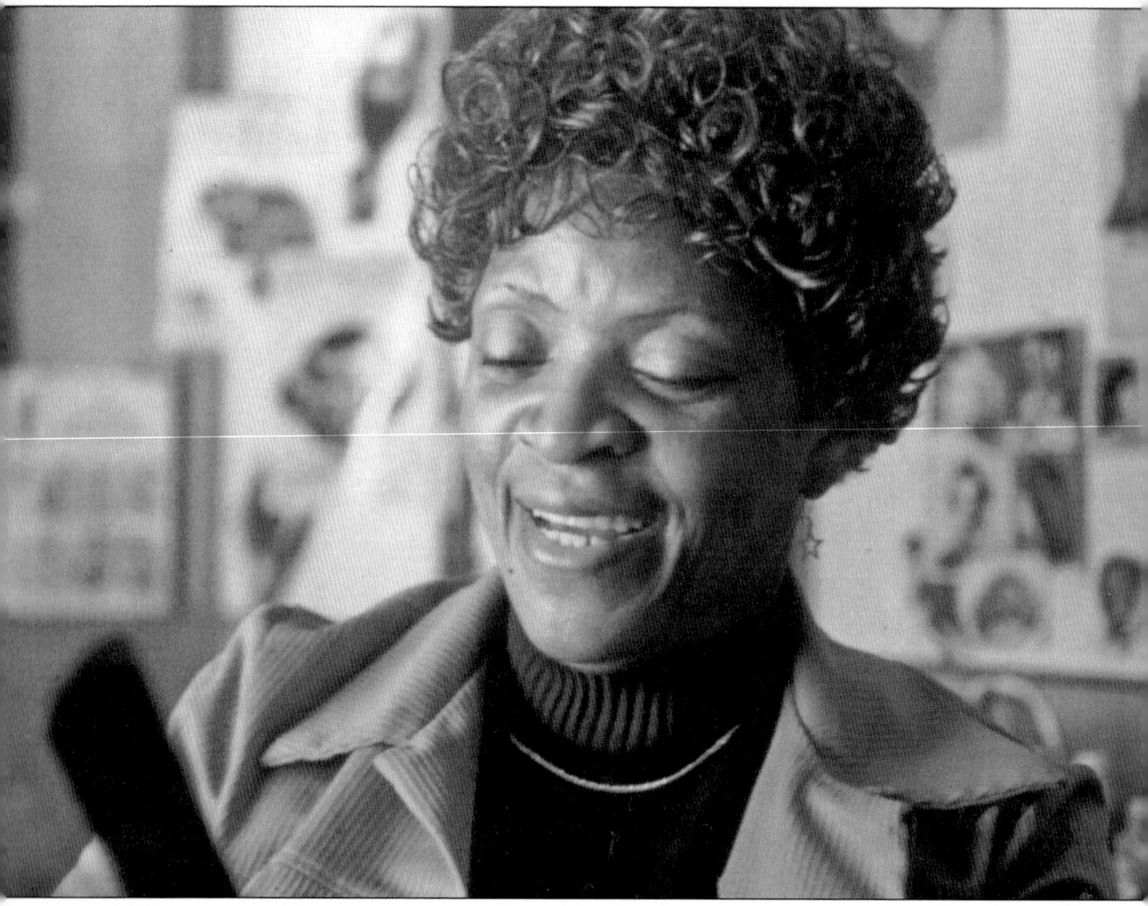

Black women could not go to white salons to have their hair done. Sarah Q. Gardner started a hair salon in her home. Many of Spokane's black women went to her home to get their hair done. Her expertise in caring for hair was well known, and she had many homemade remedies for loss of hair and other kinds of hair problems. Also, one could catch up on the latest gossip at her shop. She eventually opened a shop on East Sprague Avenue and then another shop at East Sprague and Stone Street. She was always busy. This photograph was taken at her shop on Sprague and Stone. The Gardners—Sarah, Levi, and their two children—were longtime Spokane residents. Sarah Gardner at one time even ran for the Spokane City Council. She was a beloved member of the Spokane community. To this day it is painful to think of it, but she was murdered in her shop September 17, 1987. Her killer was never officially identified. The photograph is from around 1979.

Six

SOCIAL CLUBS AND ORGANIZATIONS

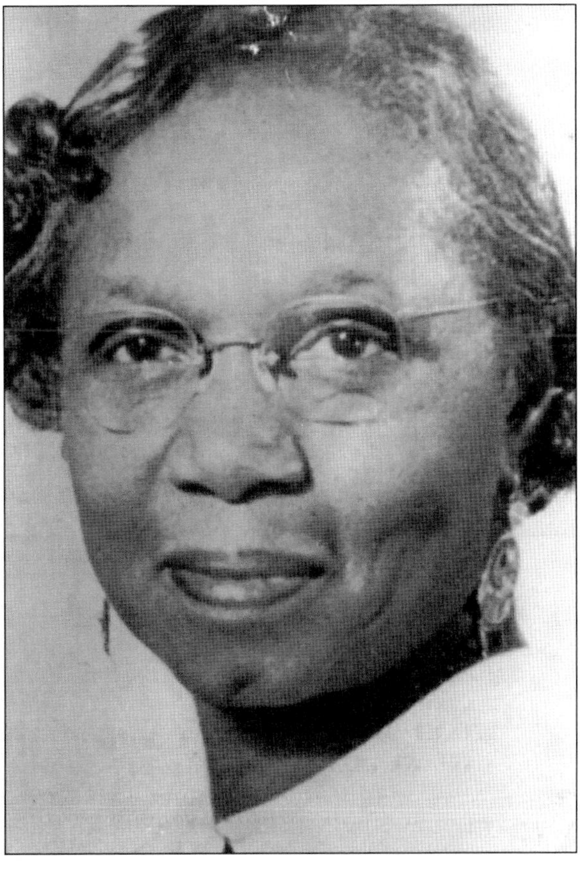

Rosa D. Malone came to Spokane as an administrator in the Works Project Administration. She helped found the Booker T. Washington Community Center, a place for blacks to congregate and spend leisure time. It was a great asset to blacks. Malone was a graduate of Tuskegee Institute in Alabama. She also helped establish a USO for black military in this city. The photograph is dated May 30, 1939.

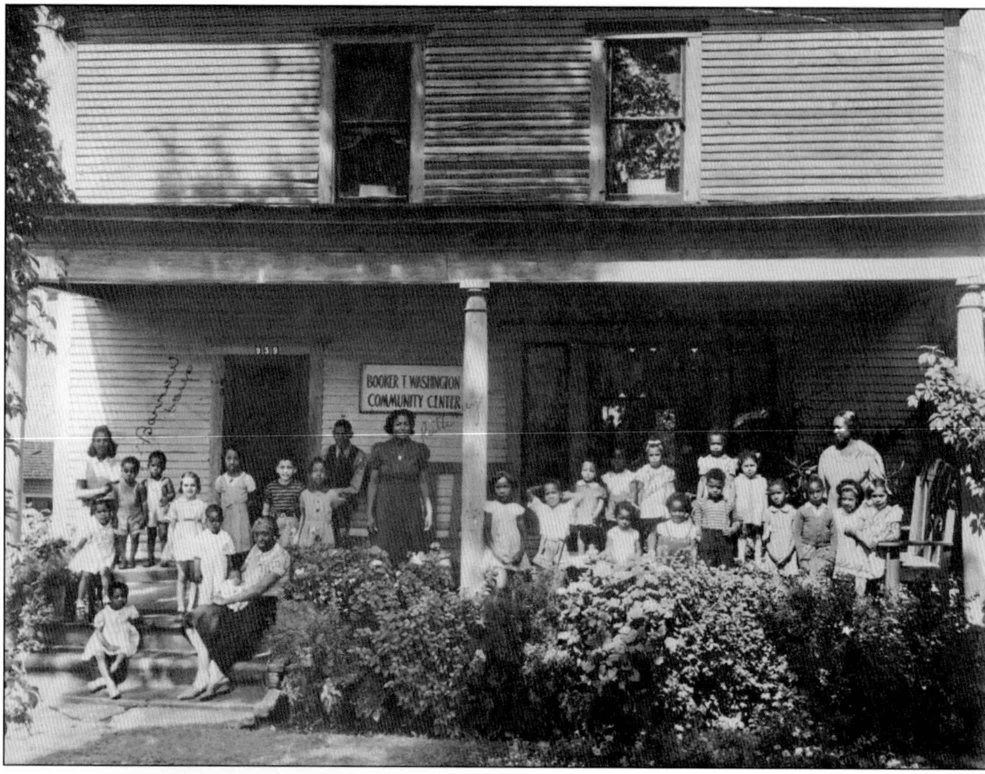

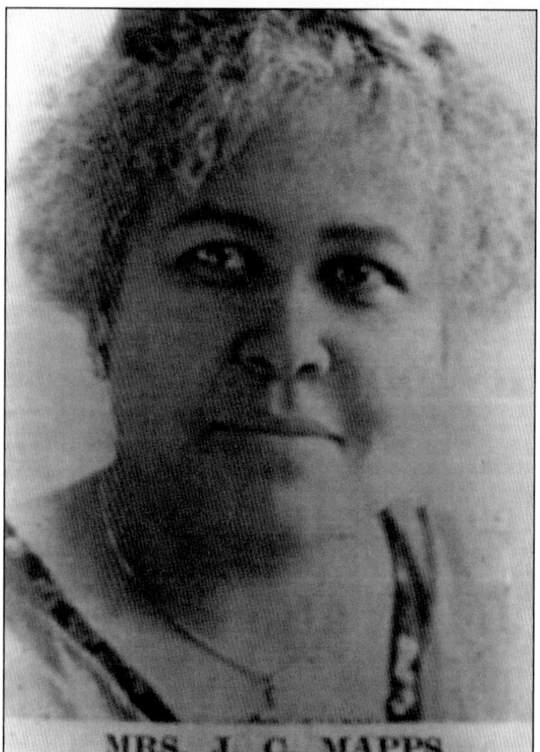

The Booker T. Washington Community Center served as a day care center. Rosa D. Malone (far right) and other adult attendants are shown here with the children. Jerrelene Williamson is one of the children in front of the door. Her sisters are also in this photograph. Malone died in Spokane of an illness after an automobile accident in which she was a passenger.

Arriving in Spokane in 1907, Helen Mapps became a leader in women's activities. She was one of the founders of the Wednesday Art Club and a founder and president of the Colored Women's Federation of Washington. During World War I, she was given a citation for the countless hours she devoted to Red Cross volunteer work. This photograph is from about 1920.

The Wednesday Art Club members during the 1960s were, from left to right, (first row) Lila Robinette, Frances Nichols Scott, Nora Daw (wife of Rev. Matthew Daw, pastor of Calvary Baptist Church), Bennie Coltrane, and Lillian McHenry; (second row) Marie Nichols Maley, Pauline Lake, Corrine Workcuff, Eleanor Chase, Mabel Coates, and Annie Freeman. The Wednesday Art Club was a community-oriented club.

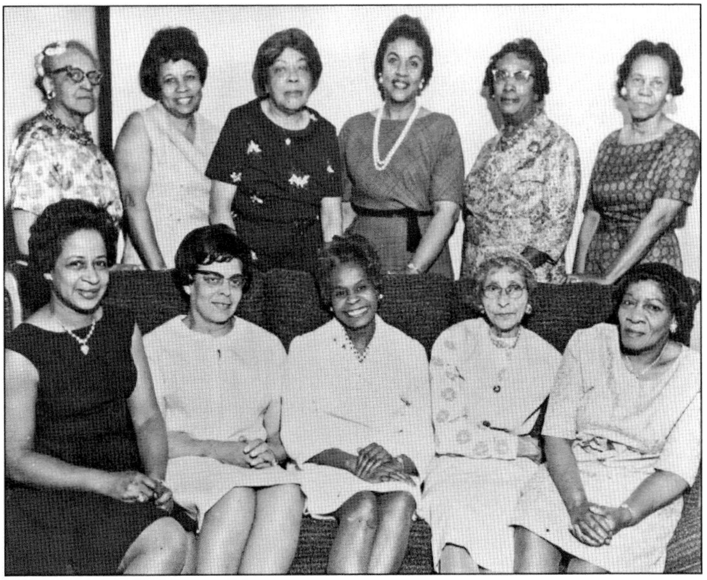

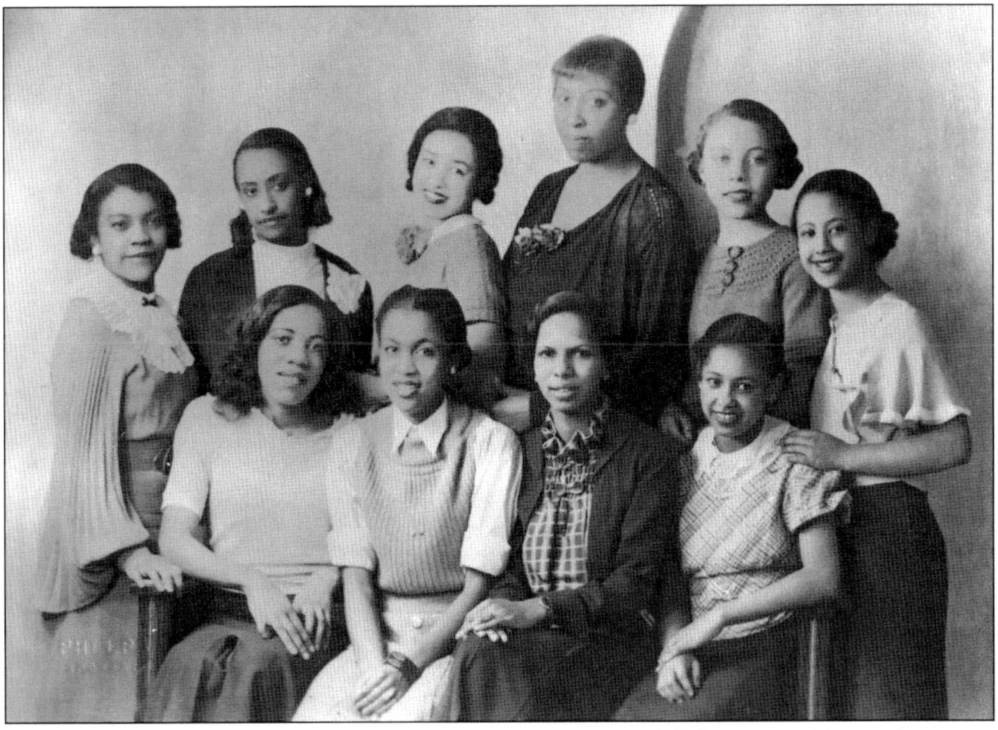

The Phillis Wheatley Club, shown here around 1940, was a club for young African American women. Pictured from left to right are (first row) Bernice (Weiseger) Adams, Eleanor (Barrow) Chase, Helen (Coltrane) Reed, and Ruth Richardson; (second row) Alta (Finley) Dalbert, Marjorie (Boyd) Wellington, Madeline Smith, Alvernon Evans (advisor), Zerelda Gordon, and Isabelle Richardson. This club was named after the famous poet Phillis Wheatley.

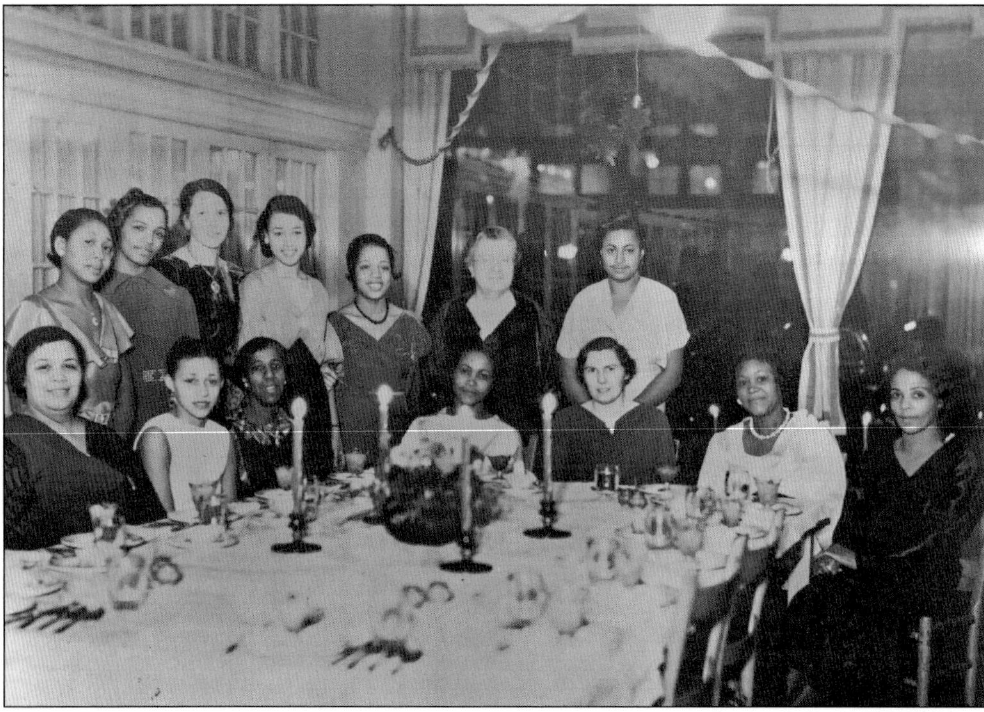

The Ashanti Club was a social club named for the West African people of Ghana. It held many events to socialize and keep the young people entertained. Some women in the photograph are (standing) Lillian Stokes (third from left) and Frances Freeman (fifth from left), who provided this photograph; (seated) Olive Barrow (third from left), the mother of Eleanor (Barrow) Chase. The photograph was taken in December 1935.

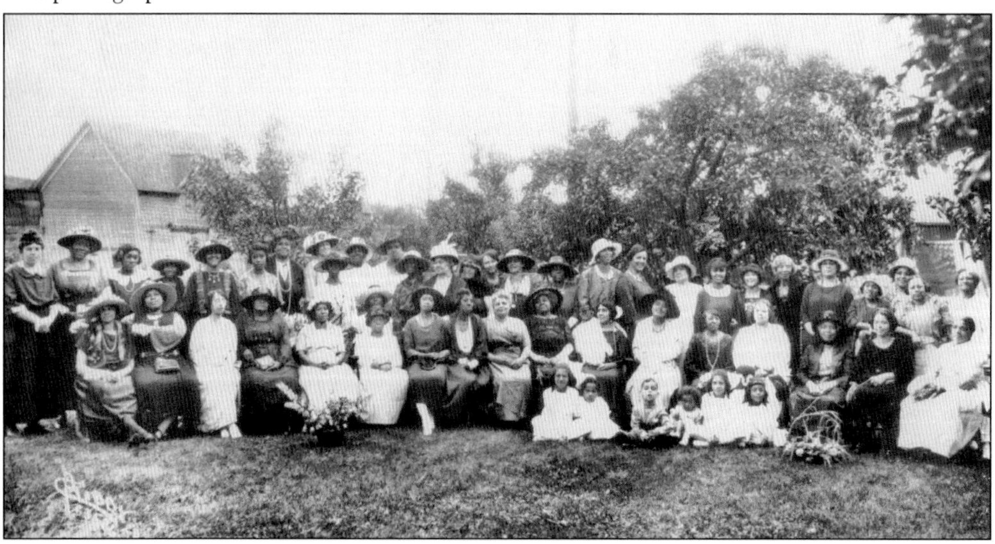

The Pierian Club was a literary club for black women who wished to elevate themselves by reading and studying the arts. The word *pierian* means "relating to learning or poetry." These women were of the philosophy that by studying and learning, one could elevate the black community in stature. This photograph was taken around 1923, at a gathering for the black community sponsored by the club.

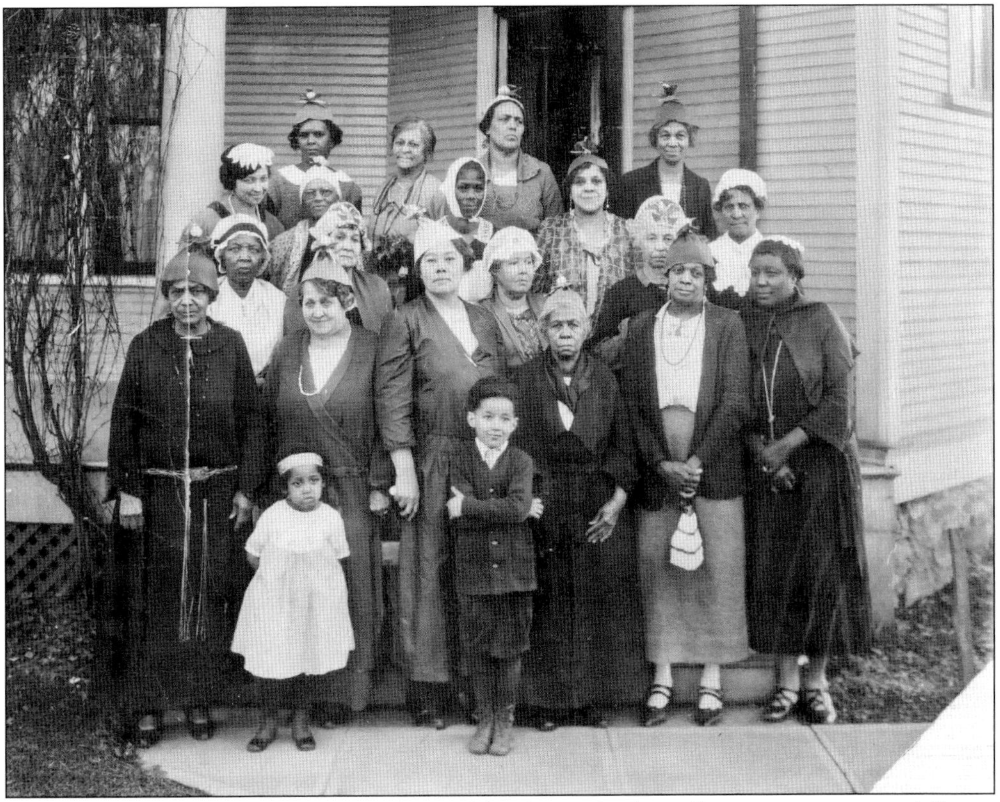

This unique photograph is of the Grandmas' Club taken in Spokane. Everyone is wearing a different and unusual hat that they made. The little girl and boy are probably someone's grandchildren. This photograph was collected during the Centennial Tribute to Northwest Black Pioneers in 1989. It probably was taken in the 1920s.

The Crest Club was a social club for African American women that was affiliated with the YWCA in Spokane. Members of the club photographed around 1940 are, from left to right, Bailey Pierce, Susan Reed, Pauline Lake, Thelma Reed, Willabelle Tucker, Mrs. Terry (the advisor), Frances Scott, Francita Burnette, Francell Hagin, Frances Freeman, and Marion Cristman.

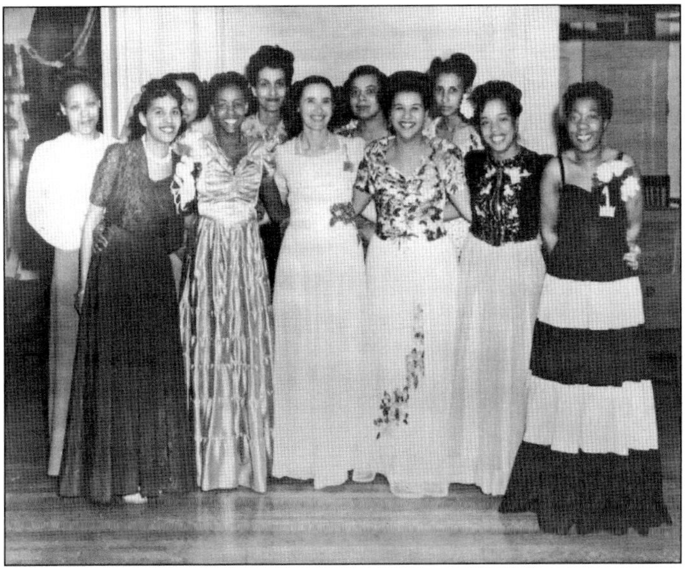

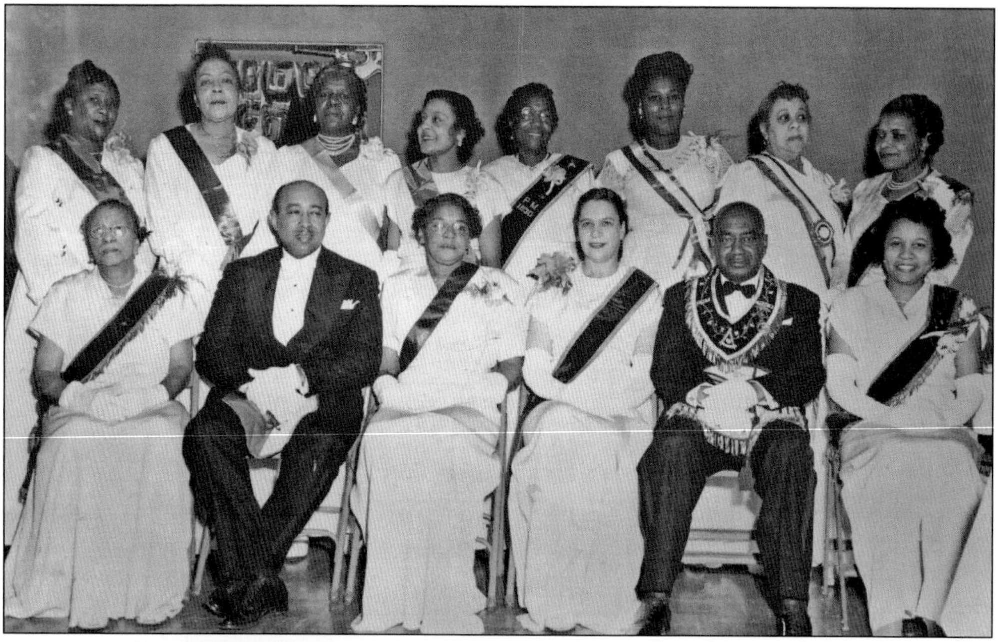

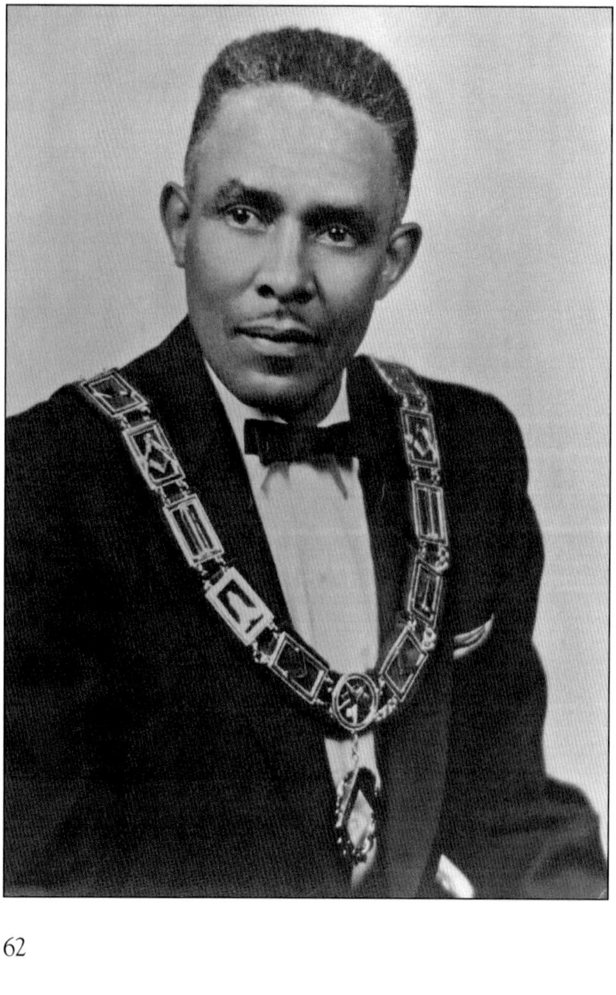

This photograph is of Chapter 3, Order of the Eastern Star, Spokane, Washington. Shown are (first row) Sister Sims, Past Matron (P.M.); W. Vernon Scott, Past Master (P.M.); Sister Mathis, P.M.; Sister Stokes, P.M.; Brother E.J. Brown, P.M.; and Sister Pauline Lake, P.M.; (second row) unidentified; Sister C. Workcuff; Sister Stubbs; Sister G. Breckenridge; Sister F. Brazil, P.M.; Sister Loree Thompson; Sister Daisy Campbell; and Sister T. Brown, P.M.

Prince Hall Grand Masonic Lodge welcomed Sylvester J. Lake (33rd degree, Inland Empire Lodge No. 3, F&AM) as its Most Worshipful Grand Master. His wife, Pauline Lake (P.M., Spokane Chapter 3, Order of the Eastern Star), became the order's Grand Queen in 1950 and Grand Worthy Matron of the Prince Hall Grand Chapter in 1964. She was the first African American woman bailiff in Spokane courts.

This is a *c.* 1970 photograph of the Wednesday Art Club. From left to right are (seated) Pauline Lake, Willabelle Tucker, Frances Nichols Scott, and Seletta Campbell; (standing) unidentified, Marie Nichols Maley, Josephine Barrow, Shirley Oliver, unidentified, and Mabel Coates. These women were not only members of the Wednesday Art Club, they were also good friends.

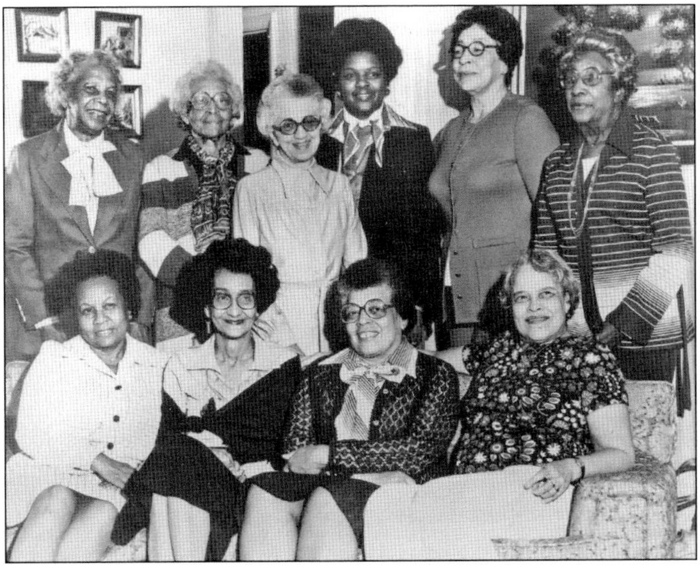

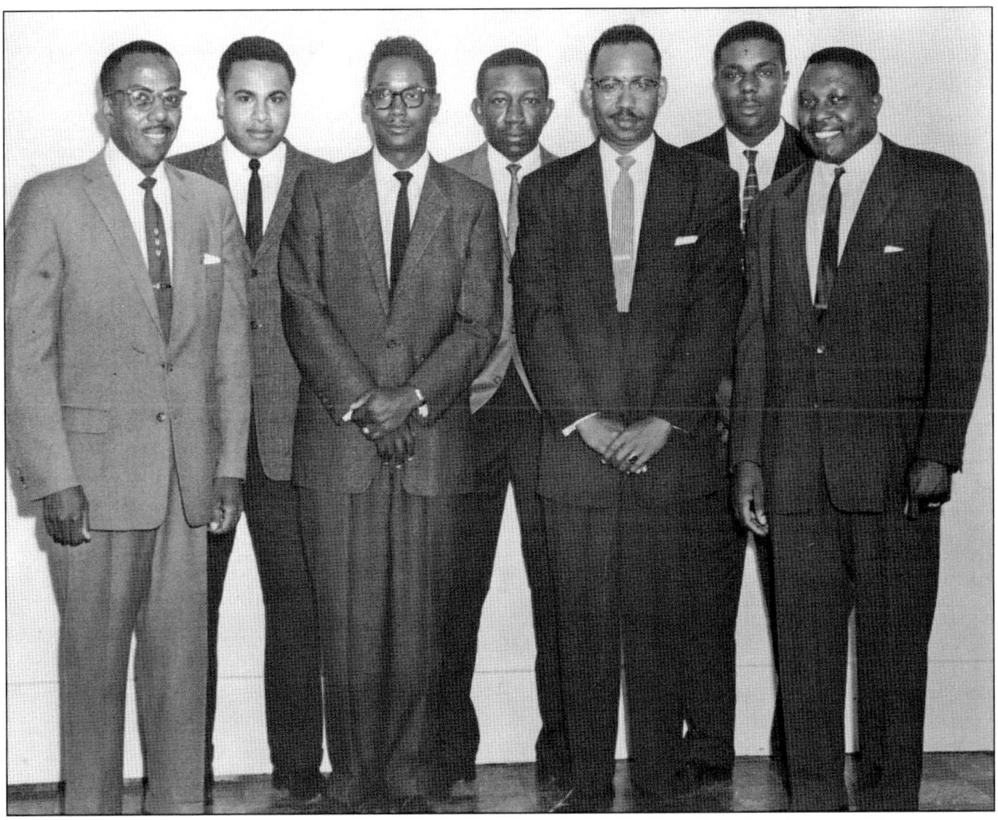

This *c.* 1950 photograph is of the Men's Philanthropic and Social Club. The photograph represents all the men's clubs that were a part of the black community in Spokane. Pictured here from left to right are Kirk Barrow, Oliver Gibson, two unidentified, Henry Hawkins, Carl Jones, and unidentified. This club planned entertainment and social functions for the black community.

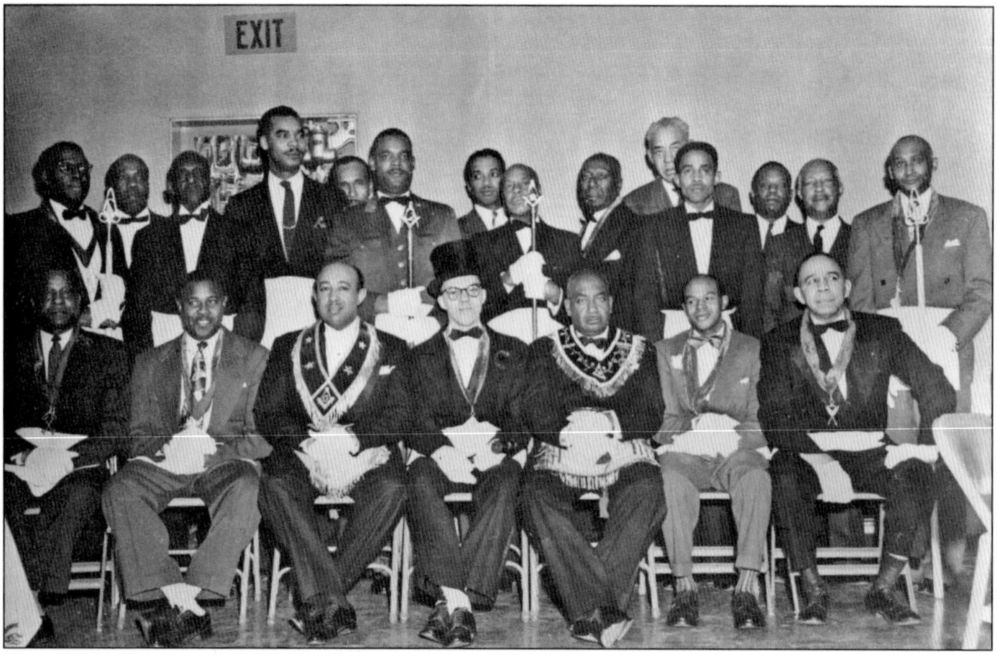

This is Inland Empire Lodge No. 3 Free and Accepted Masons of Spokane, Washington, Prince Hall Affiliation (P.H.A.). Shown from left to right (but only known by last name) are (first row) Workcuff, Dalbert, Scott, Dunn, Worshipful Master Brown, McHenry Jr., and Baldwin; (second row) Coates, Moorehead, Stubbs, Chase, Mathis, unidentified, Tucker, Brazil, Grubbs, Thompson, Lake, Breckenridge, Clay, and McHenry Sr. The photograph was taken in 1954.

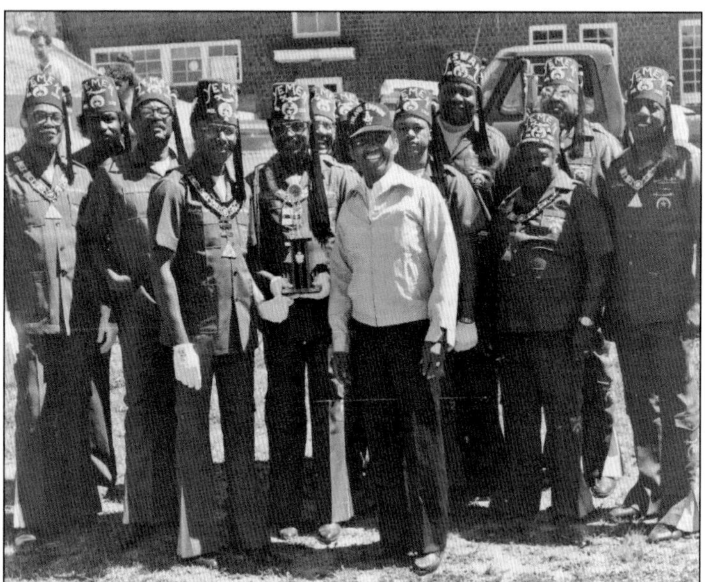

The first lodge of Negro Masons in Washington was started as a club in May 1889 at Roslyn, Washington. It was organized by district deputy grand master J. E. Shepperson and received its charter in 1897. This photograph was taken in the 1990s in Roslyn, over 100 years later. Most Worshipful Grand Master Billy V. Morris (in ball cap) is shown with Yemen Temple No. 152 (the Prince Hall Shriners) drill team. They won the competition.

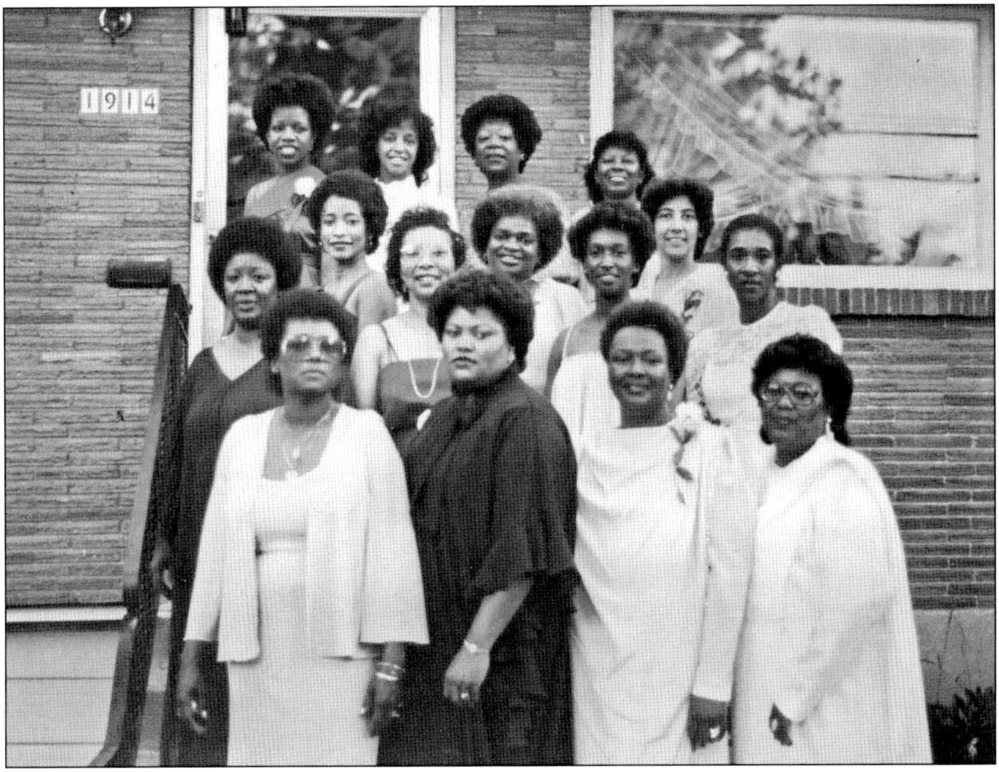

The Spokane chapter of The Links Inc. was founded by Shirley Oliver, Christine Mead, and Sylvia (Lake) Finley. The Links Inc. strives to improve the quality of life and the pursuit of excellence through local, national, and international service. Shown above from left to right are (first row) Berder Jones, Adrian Williams, Doris Andrews, and Teresa Hunter; (second row) Dorothy Webster, Thelma Claiborne, Fannie Bush, and Mildred Ritchie; (third row) Vickie Welch, Mary Langford, and Janice Lovelace; (fourth row) Inez Chubb, Terri Rowland, V. Anne Smith, and Emelda Brown. The photograph was taken in 1978. At this writing, Dorothy Webster is director of administrative services for the City of Spokane and V. Anne Smith is president of the Spokane NAACP. Sylvia (Lake) Finley, the daughter of Sylvester and Pauline Lake, also is shown in a 1961 photograph (right) when she was homecoming princess at Central Washington University.

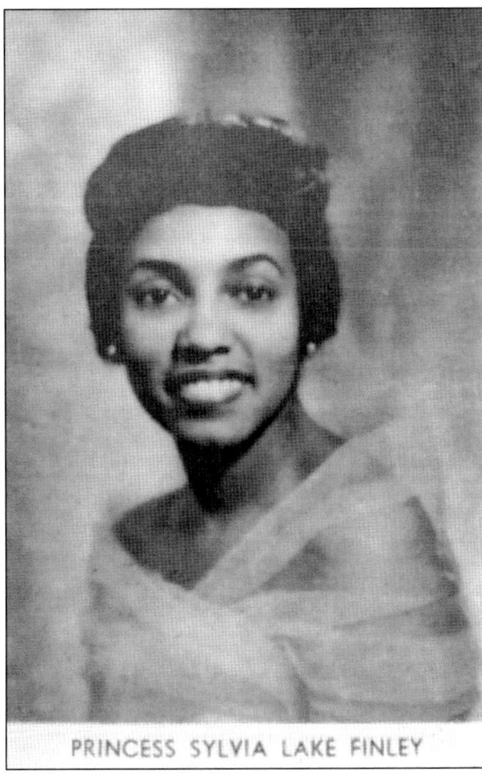

PRINCESS SYLVIA LAKE FINLEY

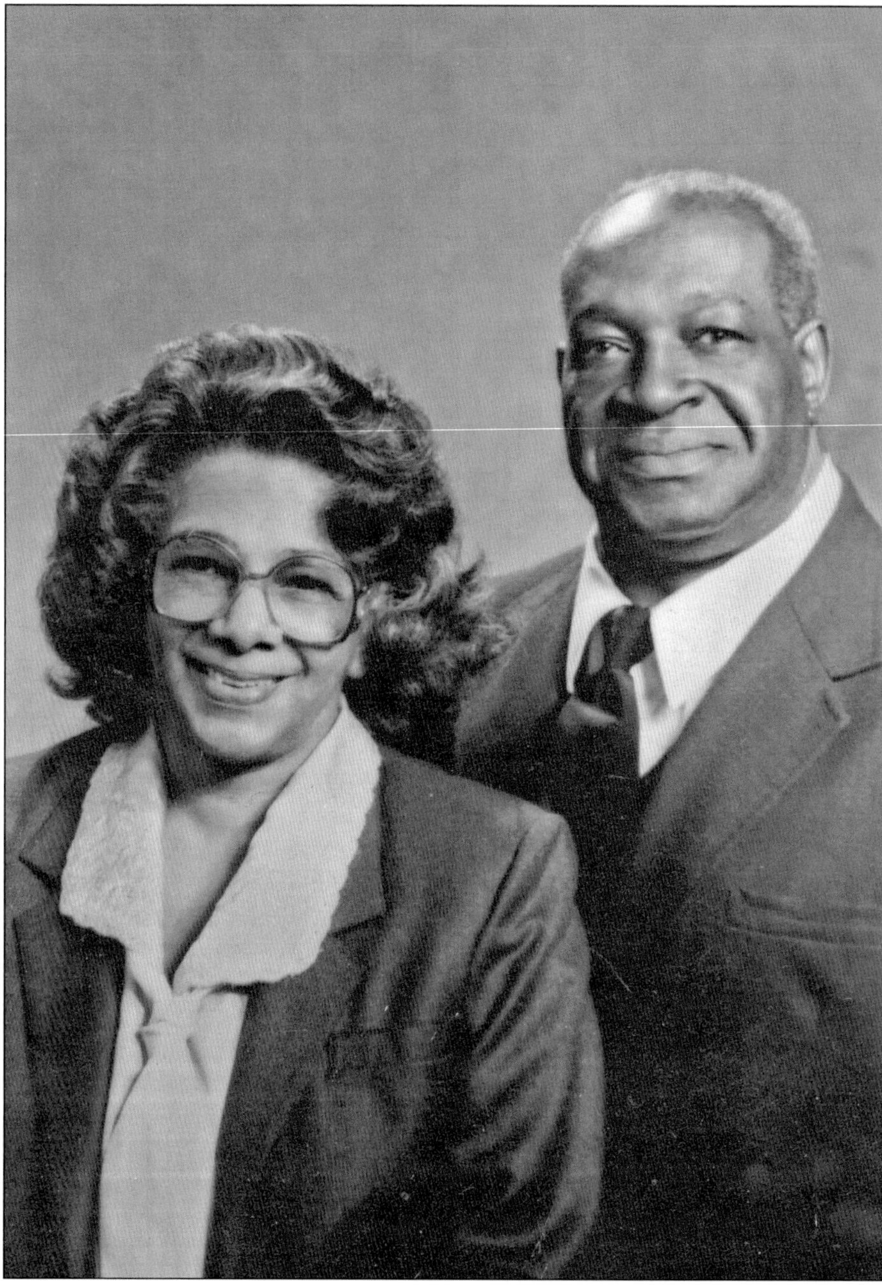

The Spokane chapter of the NAACP was founded in 1923. Its first president was Rev. E. B. Reed. Pictured here are Rev. James Sims and Lydia Sims. Among the other presidents to serve were F. A. Stokes, one of the organizers of the NAACP, in 1919, and James Chase. During World War II, Lydia and Rev. James Sims moved to Spokane from Newark, New Jersey. He was an Army Air Force soldier stationed at Geiger Airfield. Reverend Sims was elected president of the NAACP in 1956. Lydia Sims was the first African American female president of the NAACP in the Spokane chapter. The Simses are the parents of twin sons, Ronald and Donald Sims, and James McCormick. Ron Sims has been very active in politics in Washington state. After Rev. James Sims passed away in the 1990s, Lydia Sims retired to Edmonds, Washington.

Seven

Black-Owned Businesses

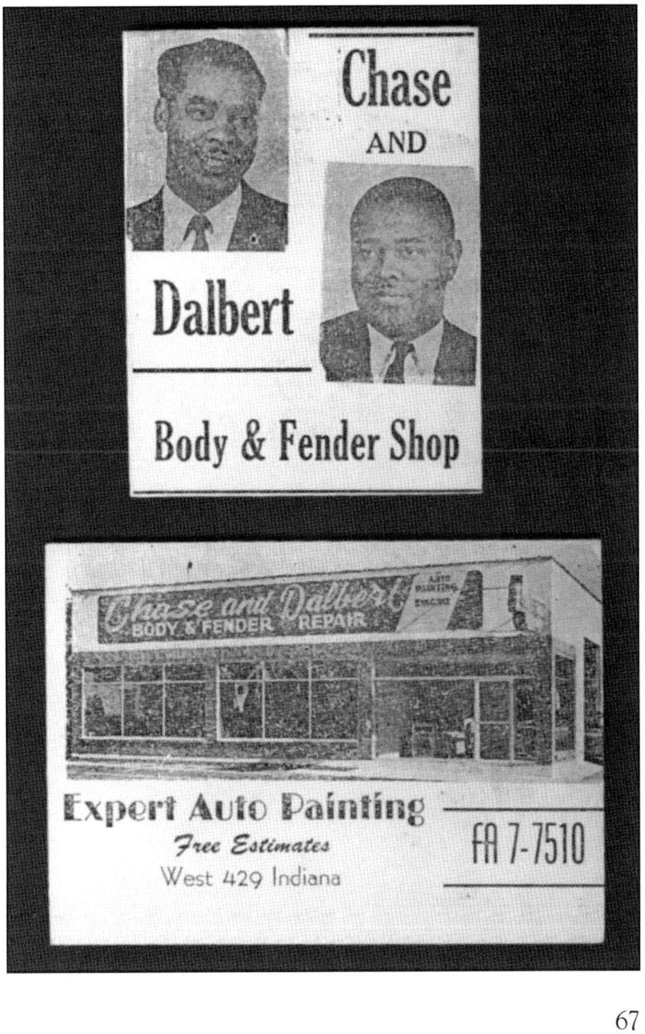

There have been many black entrepreneurs who opened their own businesses in Spokane, some of whom already have been mentioned. This *c.* 1950 photograph is of the Chase and Dalbert Body and Fender Shop, a very successful business run by James E. Chase and Elmo Dalbert. These two friends who came to Spokane on a freight train became very valued citizens of Spokane.

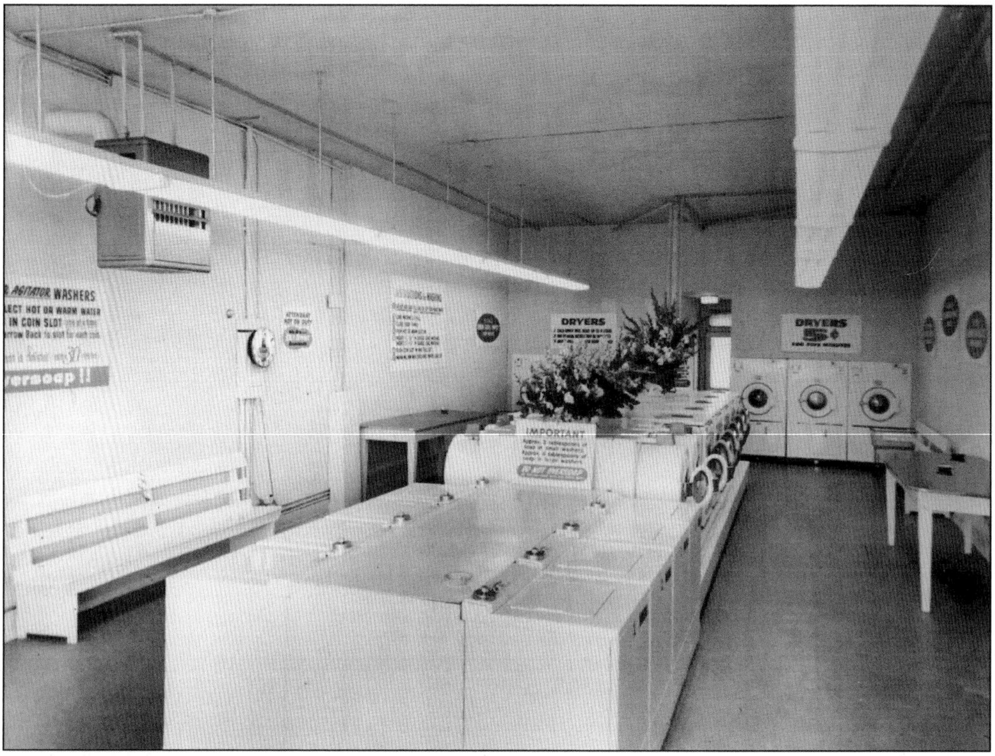

The Freeman Laundry was located at 207 East Third Avenue and was built by Clarence Freeman Construction Company. Freeman and his wife, Frances, had many enterprises in Spokane. The Merlin Apartments, on Second Avenue, was among them. The apartment building was sold in 1951. Clarence and Frances Freeman were very active in the city and were members of Bethel AME Church. This photograph was taken in 1950.

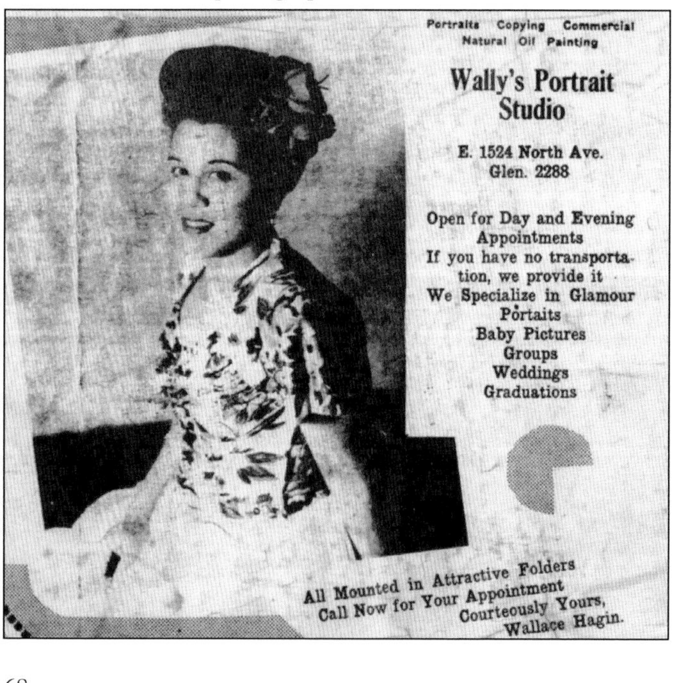

Wally's Portrait Studio was at 1524 East North Avenue. The young lady photographed for this 1950s advertisement is Francida Burnette. Wallace R. "Wally" Hagin has been a familiar face in all the events of the black community. Whenever something was going on, Hagin would be there with his camera. He went on to accomplish much more in photography and in the music world.

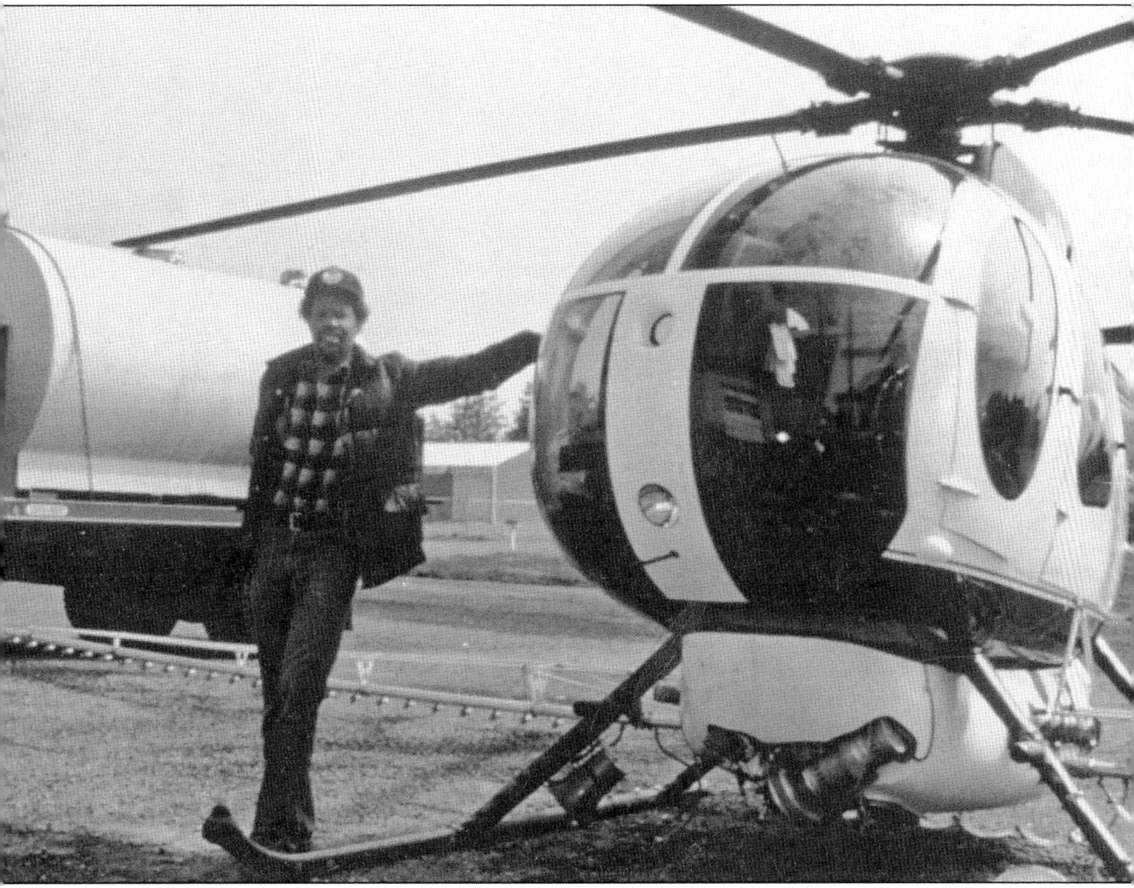

Clifford Richey and his family came to Spokane in the 1950s. He learned to operate a helicopter in the military and later opened Richey Helicopter Service. Tragically, Richey and KREM news reporter Gary Brown were killed while covering a Bloomsday run in Richey's helicopter. The Bloomsday run is an annual ritual that is usually covered by news reporters. People from all over the United States and the world come to Spokane to compete in the race. Thousands of people take to the streets for this exciting race, and some come to walk or push strollers or just to see if they can make it up "Doomsday Hill," one of the steepest grades in the city. There is also a wheelchair competition. Those who finish the race, no matter what their time is, receive a Bloomsday T-shirt for being in the race. There are cash prizes for the "serious" runners and, of course, trophies.

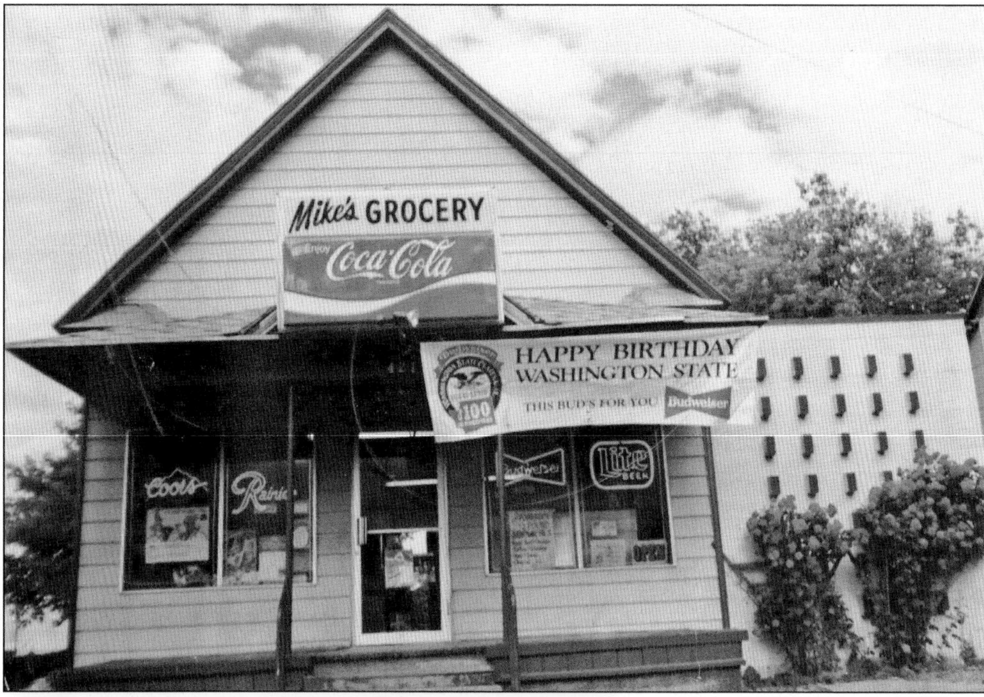

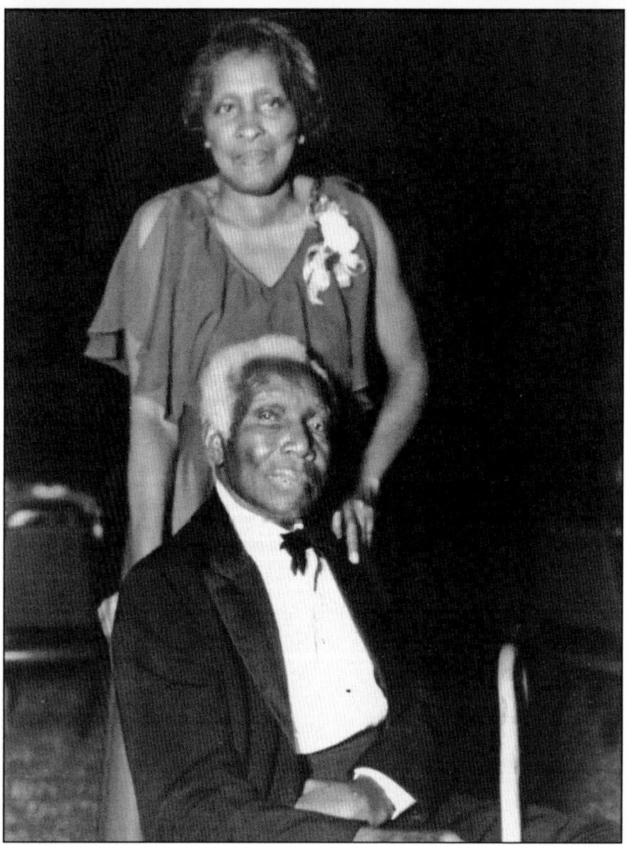

Mike's Grocery, 421 South Cowley Street, was founded by Mike A. Stephens in 1963. He was felled by a disabling stroke in 1968, and then his wife, Emma, became manager. Stephens passed away in 1986; however, his spirit of friendly service and customer satisfaction was carried on by his family. This is a photograph of the store in 1989, heralding the centennial of Washington state.

This photograph is of Mike Stephens and his wife, Emma. Stephens was perhaps best known for his undaunted zest for bringing a smile to the faces of all he came in contact with—young or old, black or white, rich or poor, whatever their position in life. His store, Mike's Grocery, is occupied by another business at this writing.

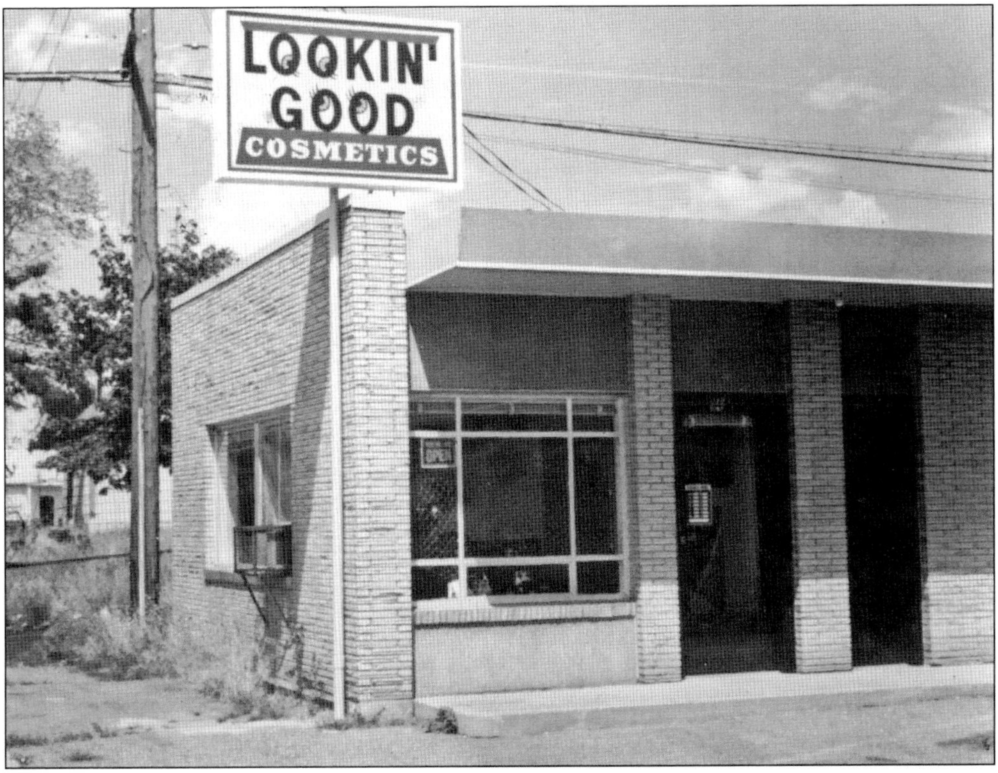

This is Lookin' Good Cosmetics around 1978, opened when there was no place to buy cosmetics for "people of color" in Spokane. Julie (Williamson) Serquinia decided to remedy that. She ordered products from major cities and opened her own shop. She and Debbie Lentz (hairstylist) had a successful business. This shop was located on Sprague Avenue but was later moved into downtown Spokane.

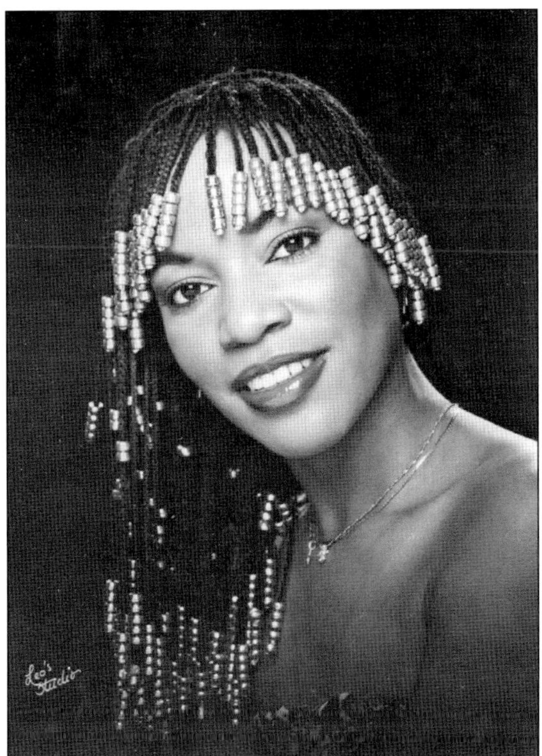

This photograph is of Julie (Williamson) Serquinia, owner and founder of Lookin' Good Cosmetics. The shop held a contest for "Beauty of the Week." The one who was chosen had her photograph taken at Leo's Photo Studio, and it was featured in the window of Lookin' Good Cosmetics for a week. Many lovely ladies graced the window of the shop. (Courtesy of Leo's Photo Studio—Andy McAlpin.)

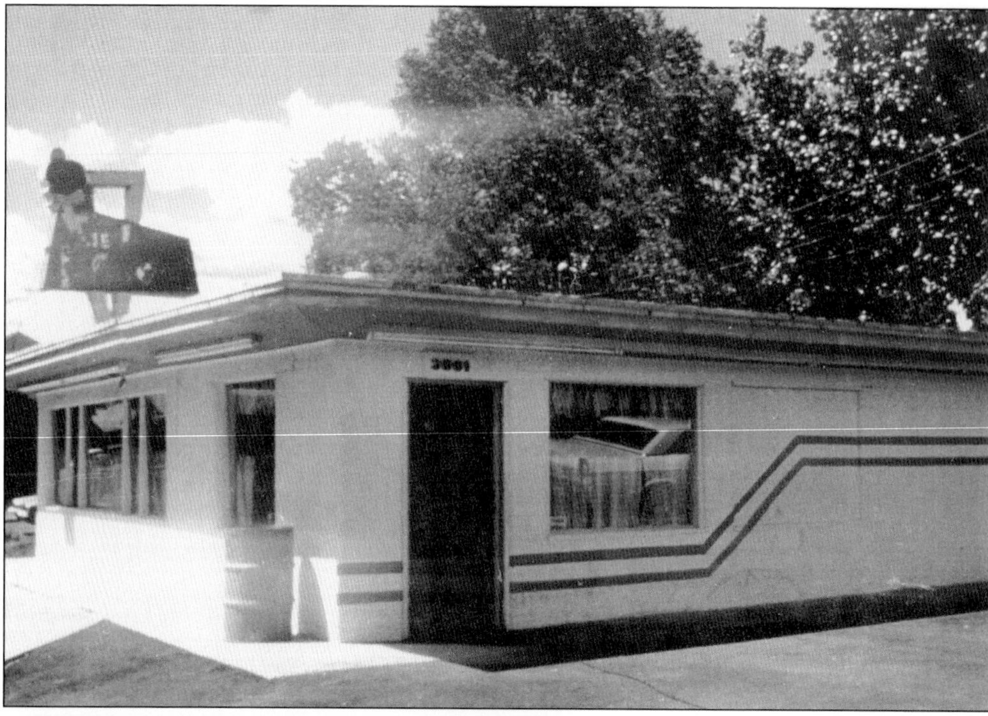

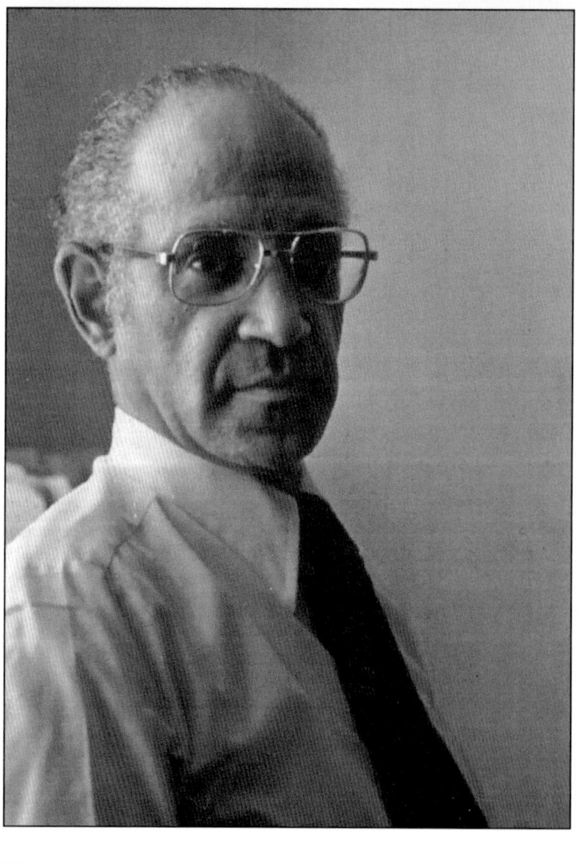

This is the O'Neil Vincent Restaurant, a soul food restaurant and then an ice cream parlor. The same block housed Lil' Bit of Philly, owned by James Whitsett, and Rainbow Gallery, moved from downtown by owner Jennifer (Williamson) Roseman. Another black business was Empire Ford, owned by Nate and Roberta Greene. Black businesses at this writing include Larry's Barber and Styling, Chicken N' Mo, Salon East, and Gifted Hands.

Donald Rose, CPA, had an office in the Paulsen Building in downtown Spokane. Spokane newspapers reported he was the first to pass the CPA exam on the first try. Rose has two daughters in Spokane, Kim and Tina. He was formerly married to Francelle Rose. He passed away May 2, 2008.

Eight

Sports and Athletes

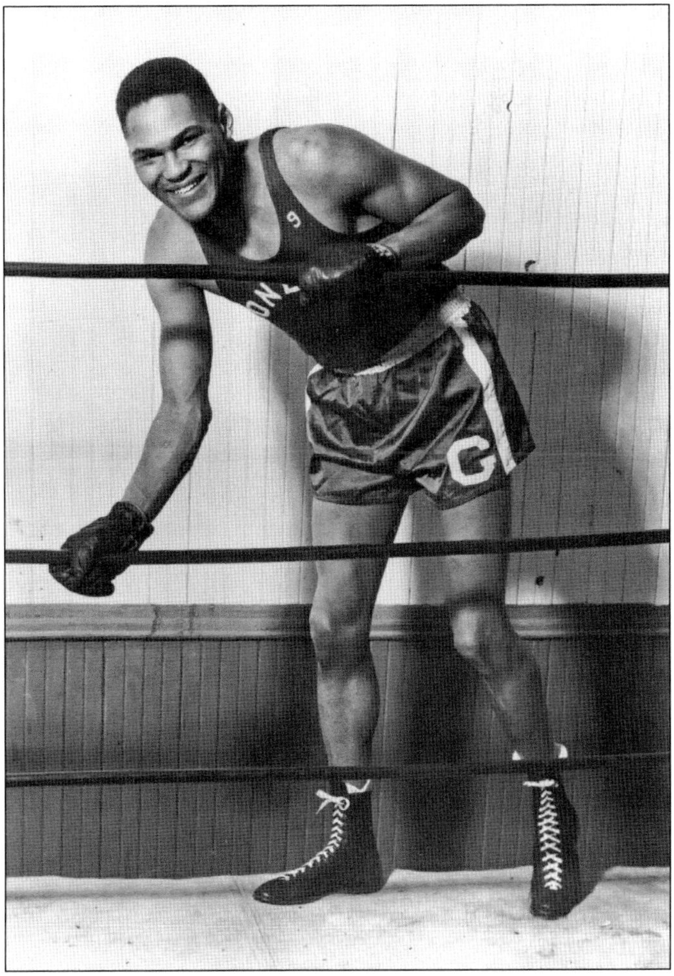

It is impossible to name all the outstanding African American athletes cheered by Spokane: Buck Pierce Campbell, Henry "Hank" Burnette, Toby Gibson, Maury Wills, Bump Wills, Dory Reeves, Michelle Williams, and more. This April 14, 1950, photograph of Carl "King Carl" Maxey was taken when he was a student at Gonzaga University Law School. Maxey was undefeated in all of his college boxing matches for two years.

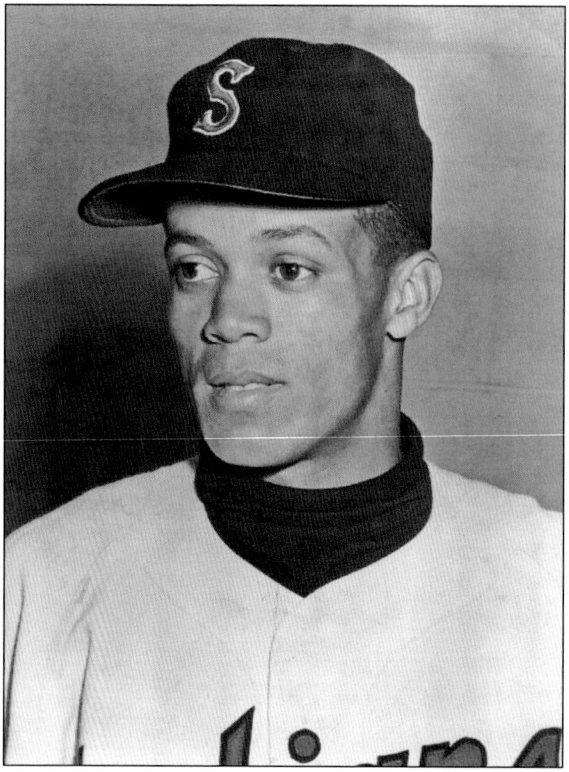

This photograph appeared in a Centennial Tribute to Northwest Black Pioneers sports exhibit, extending congratulations to Spokane's Maury Wills for a brilliant baseball career as a player, coach, manager, and radio and television broadcaster. During his career he stole 100 bases, breaking the Major League record in 1962. The sports exhibit for the Centennial Tribute was compiled by William Gaskins Sr. in 1989.

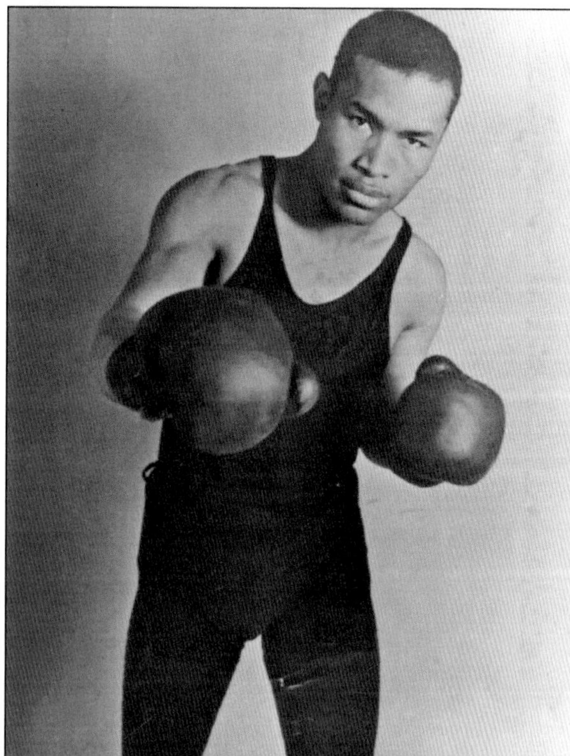

Professional boxer "Tiger Jack" Fox (John Linwood Fox) was the first to knock out Jersey Joe Walcott (eighth round, May 22, 1937). In 1939, weeks after a near fatal stab wound, Fox was a 3-to-1 favorite over Melio Bettina for the Light Heavyweight World Title but lost. Born in 1907, this Inland Empire Hall of Fame member passed away in 1954. The photograph is from the 1930s.

This is Bump Wills, who moved to Spokane with his parents, Mr. and Mrs. Maury Wills, and was a 1970 graduate of Central Valley High School. He was a superior performer on the Central Valley baseball team and later attended Arizona State University. In 1975, he was drafted by the Texas Rangers Baseball Club. After an outstanding Minor League career, he was promoted to the Texas Rangers Major League team.

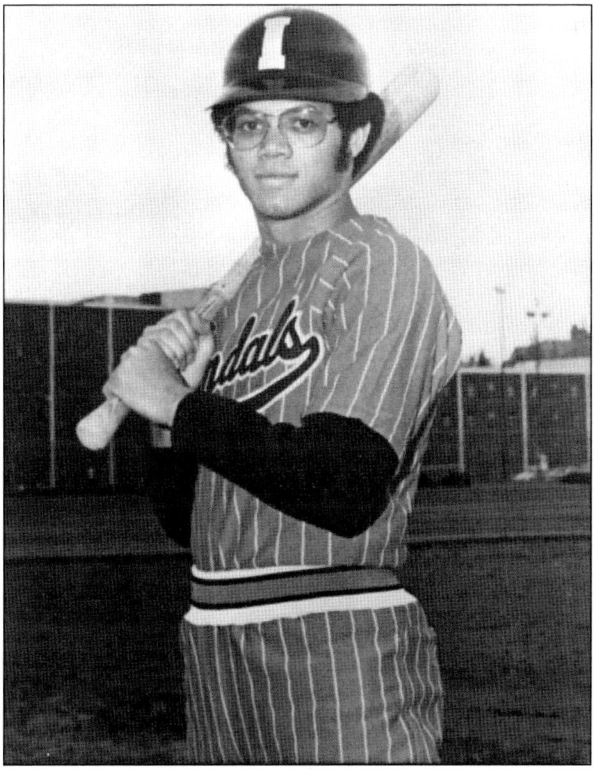

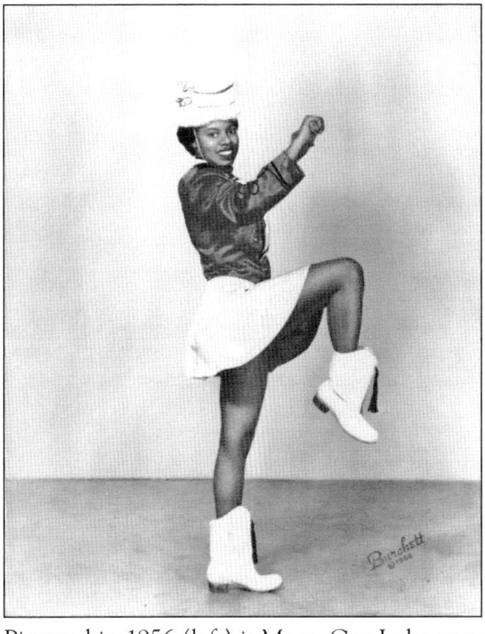

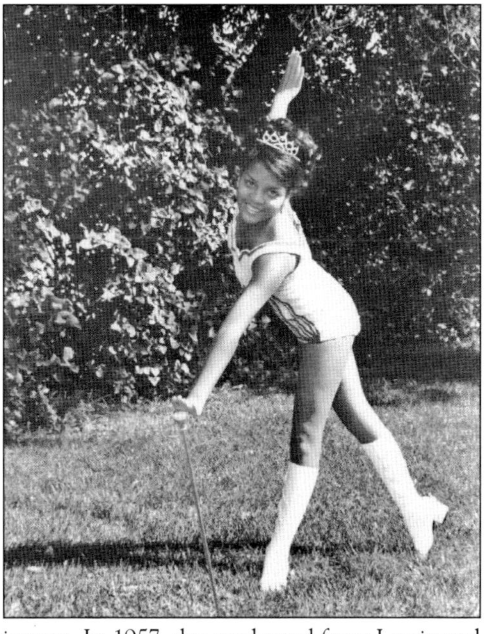

Pictured in 1956 (left) is Mona Gay Lake as a majorette. In 1957, she graduated from Lewis and Clark High School. As a student at Washington State University in Pullman, Washington, she was the only black woman on campus for an entire semester. Pictured in a 1968 photograph (right) is Sandra L. Freeman, who began twirling at the age of eight. She won honors including Miss Majorette (1968–1972).

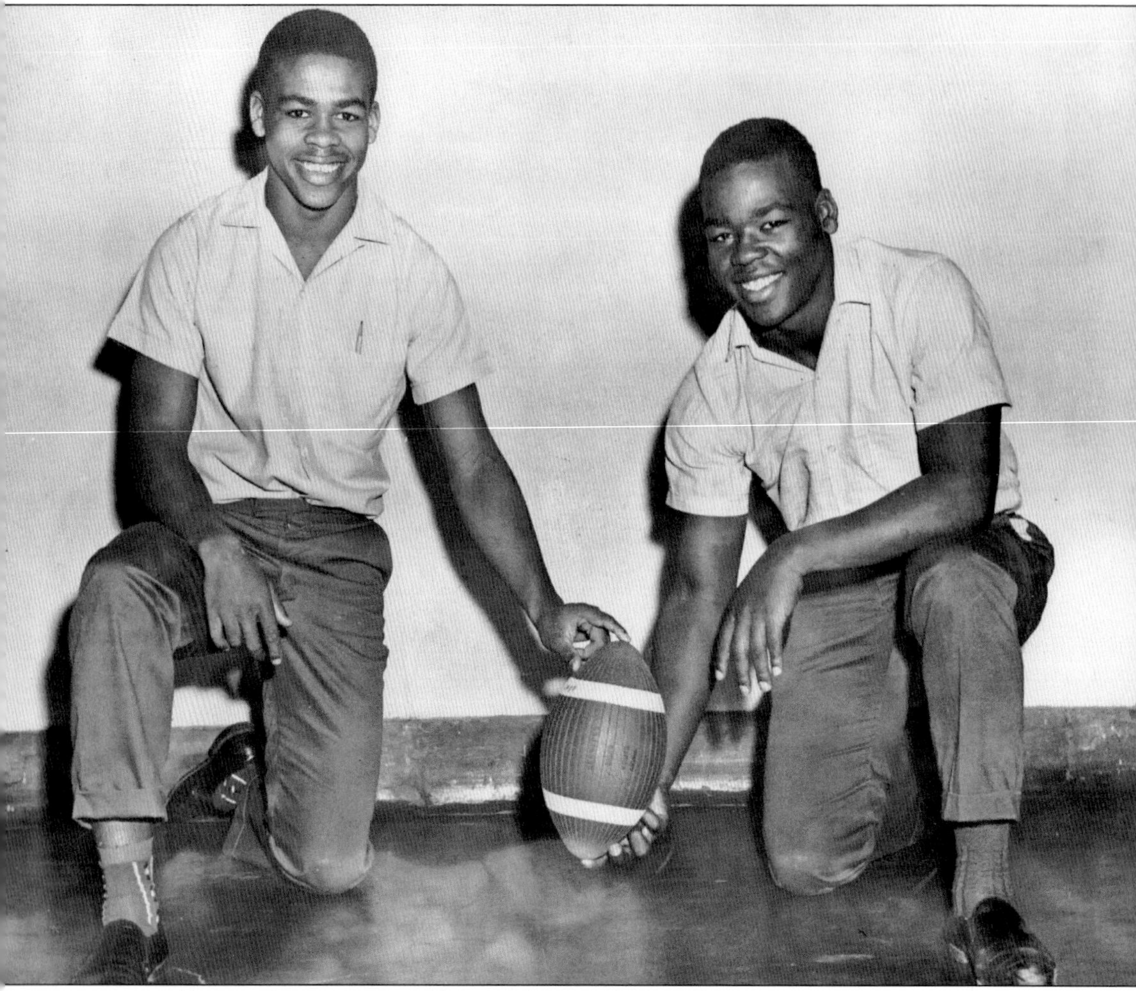

Pictured here in the 1960s are William Gaskins Jr. (left) and his brother Walter L. "Wally" Gaskins. They are the sons of Helen and William Gaskins Sr. After a prestigious college football career, William Jr. was drafted by the Canadian Football League and played professional football for two years with the Calgary Stampeders as defensive halfback. Bill's career ended with the Calgary Stampeders when he was sidelined by injuries. He is currently a pharmacy manager at Pullman Memorial Hospital, Pullman, Washington, where he resides with his wife, Felicia Gaskins, and daughter Helen Washington. Wally Gaskins also was an outstanding athlete and an impressive fullback. He broke and set many records in his high school career. After an illustrious college football career, in 1989, Wally Gaskins was entering his 10th season as a San Jose coach. Teaching young athletes is his fondest dream of success. Wally and his son Walter Erik Gaskins reside in San Jose, California.

Spokane native Toby Gibson managed one of the longest strings of knockouts (12) in boxing history by an amateur bidding for an Olympic medal. His record included Pacific Northwest Middleweight Champ, Inland Empire Champ, National Junior Amateur Athletic Union (AAU), National Senior AAU Champ, Final Olympic Trials, and Olympic Games (first round). He was called the best Olympic boxer since Cassius Clay by New York writers at the Olympic Trials. This photograph is from the 1950s.

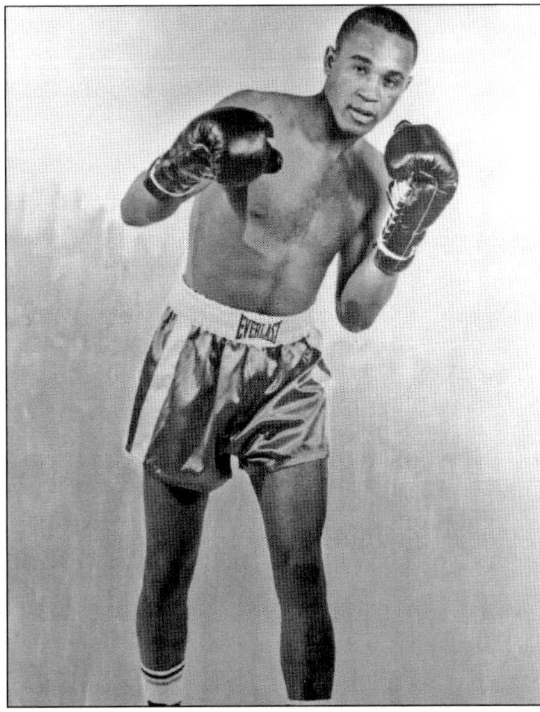

Buck Pierce Campbell, born in Spokane in 1906, was a star athlete at Lewis and Clark High School in basketball, track (javelin), and baseball. He played for Oscar Levitch's basketball team, the Sparklers, and was the first black to play in the Spokane Baseball League. This photograph is dated March 23, 1928.

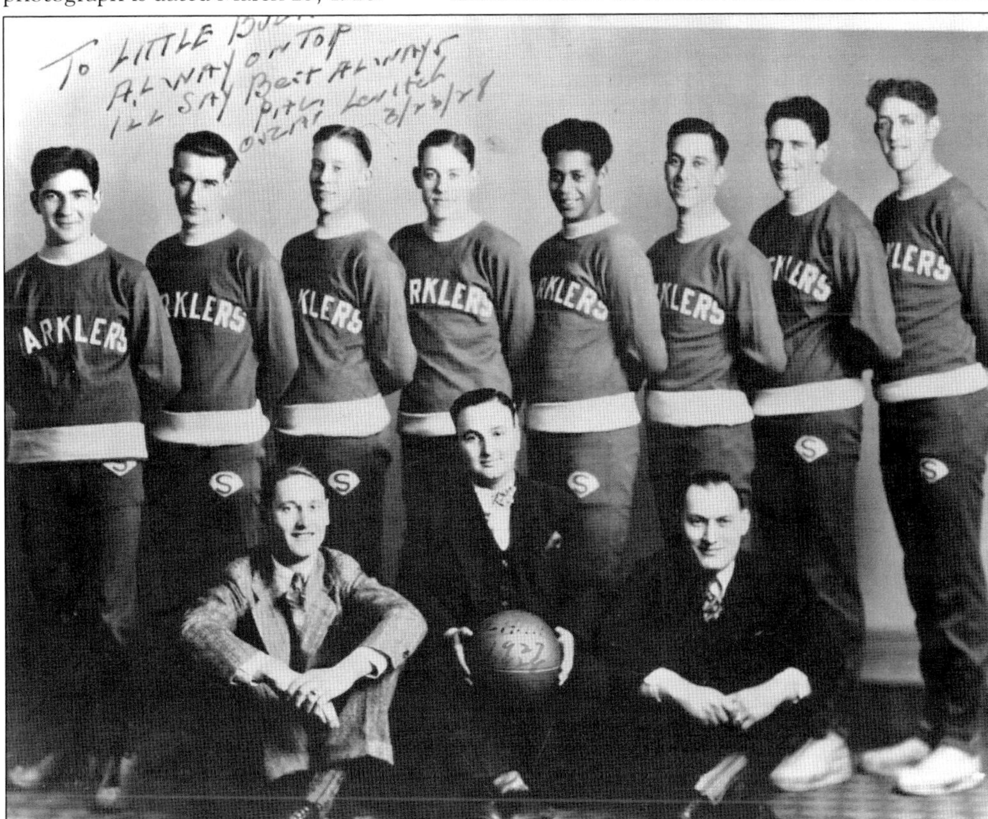

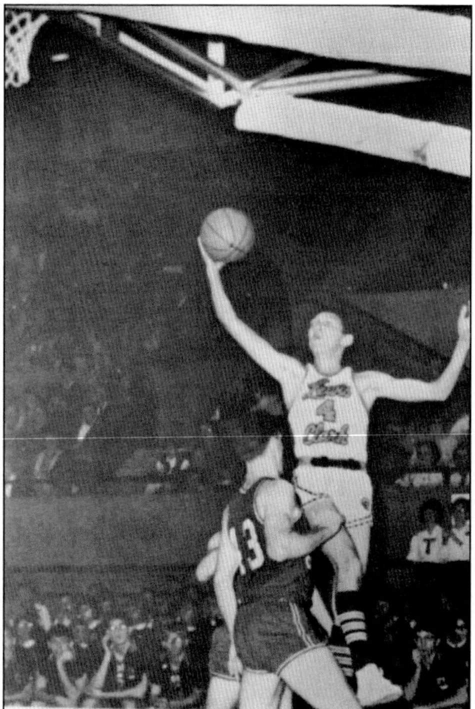

Bill Maxey, All-Regional Second Team, made many steals as a Junior

William ("Bill") Maxey, son of Carl and Ninon Maxey, excelled in sports at Lewis and Clark High School (1964–1967). He made the All-Regional second and first basketball teams (1966 and 1967, respectively) and the All-City second and first baseball teams (1966 and 1967). Bill played football for two years at the University of Oregon and graduated from Gonzaga Law School. He is a partner in Maxey Law Offices.

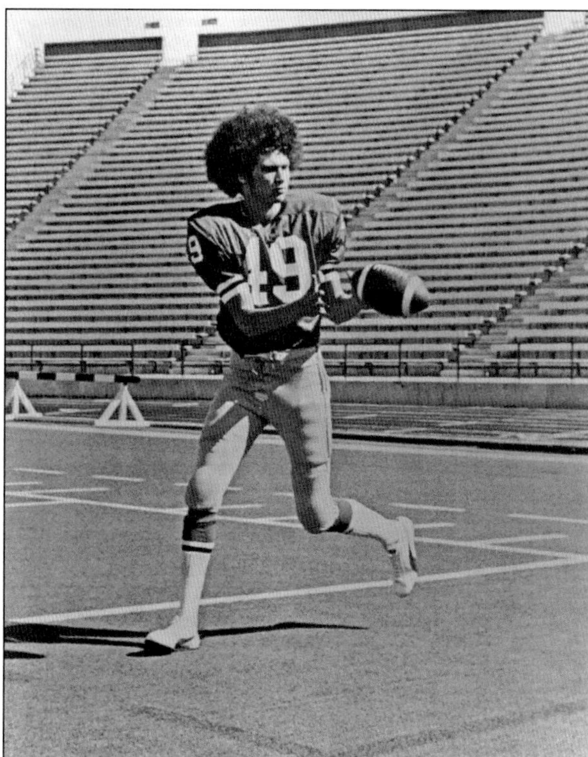

Another Maxey son, Bevan, also was a star athlete, playing varsity football and basketball at Lewis and Clark High School (1972–1975). He made All-City second basketball team (1975), "team inspirational" (1974–1975), and All-City first baseball team (1974). He played football at Washington State University and was "most inspirational player" (1980). Bevan graduated from Gonzaga University Law School in 1983 and is a partner in Maxey Law Offices.

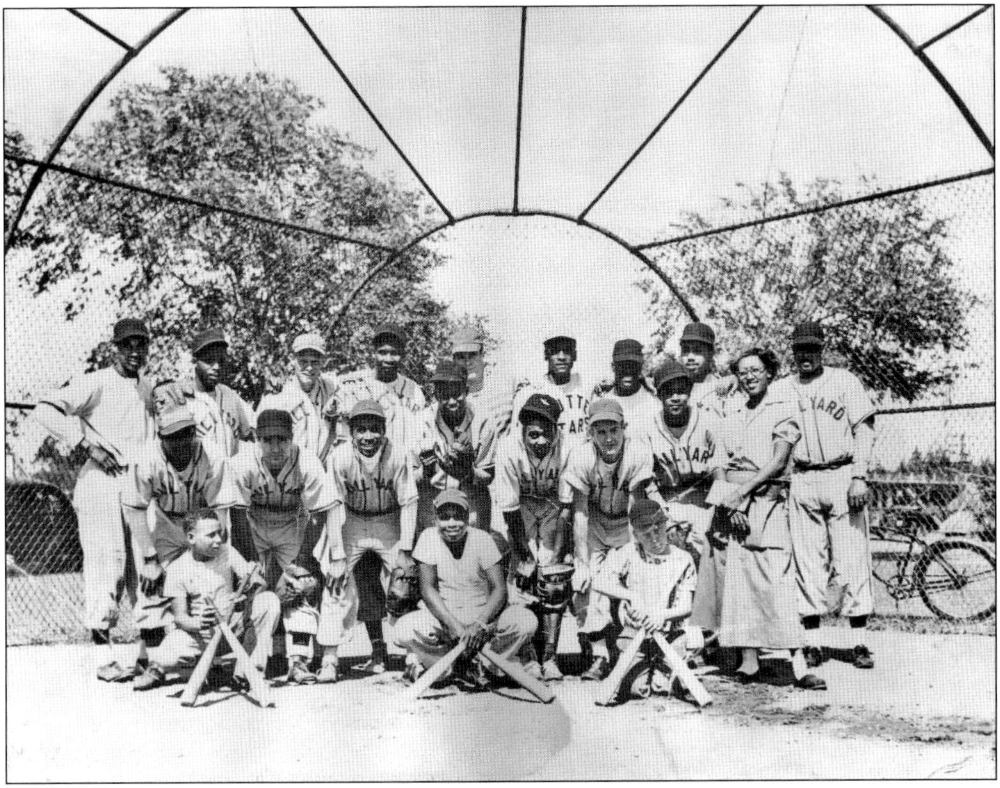

This is the Hillyard Stars baseball team around 1950: from left to right, (first row) Sonny Burnette, Oliver Gibson, and unidentified; (second row) "Hank" Burnette, Al Casseto, Nick Sharpley, Idaho Davis, Odell Kennard, unidentified, James Sharpley, and Verna Sharpley; (third row) Bill Coleman, Sam Minnix, ? Smith, James Hopson, three unidentified, and Duane Watts. Players were residents of the North Side, where Hillyard is located.

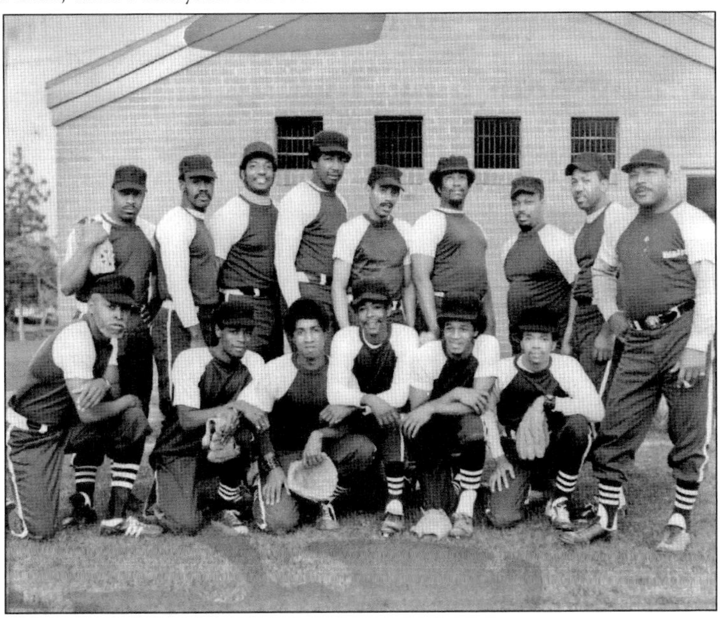

Sam Willis, coach, is pictured with his baseball team in the mid-1970s. He formed the team because he enjoyed working with young people. These young men were extremely fortunate to have Willis as somewhat of a mentor. Willis believed in giving back to the community. This is just one of his many projects. When Willis passed away, many came to pay their respects, young and old, black and white. (Courtesy of Larry's Barber & Styling.)

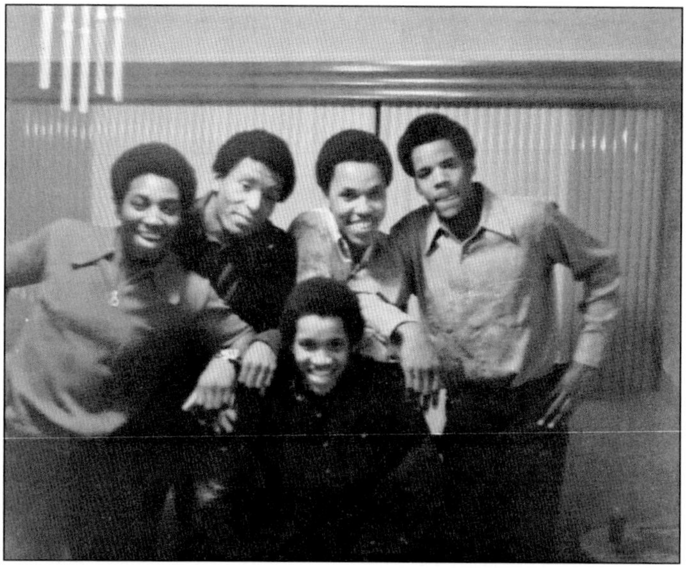

"The Fantastic 5," pictured here from left to right, are (standing) Ronald Owens, 100- and 220-yard dashes; Archie Grant, the football star; James Williamson, 220- and 440-yard dashes; Sid Lofton, 110-yard high hurdles and the high jump; and (seated) Bobby Sepolen, long jump and the 330-yard hurdles. Sepolen, Lofton, Williamson, and Owens ran the 880-yard relay. In 1971 in Seattle, they won the state championship for Ferris High School.

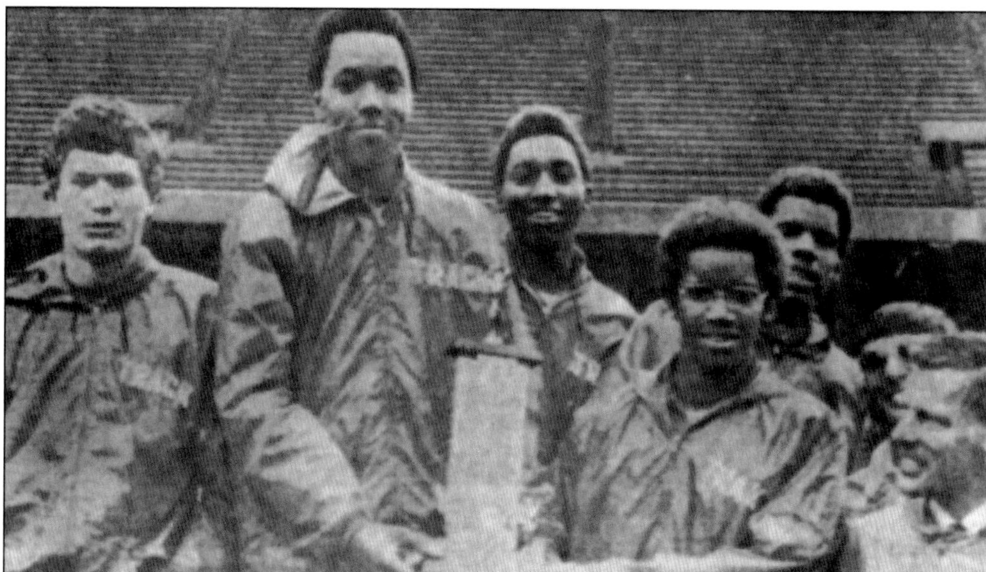

Saxons' State Champion Delegation
Caviness, right, with Eddy, Williamson, Owens, Sepolen, Lofton.

This is the Ferris Saxons' state champion delegation in 1971. Archie Grant Jr. (also in the "Fantastic 5" photograph above) is the son of Archie Grant Sr. and Hazel Grant. Grant attended Lincoln Elementary School, Libby Junior High, and Ferris High School. He earned All-City honors as a running back during his junior and senior years and graduated in 1972. He also played football at Spokane Falls Community College.

Nine

African American Families

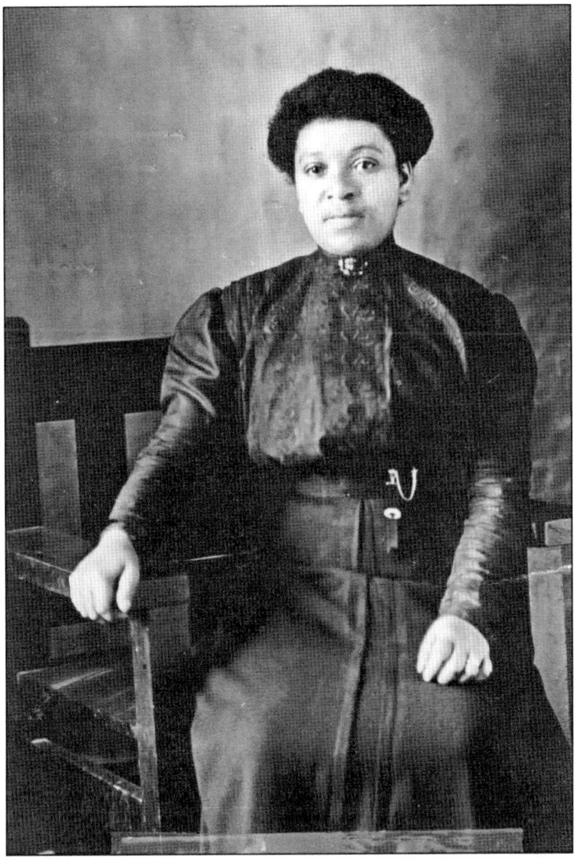

This is Alice Breckenridge, who came to Spokane in 1899 with her husband John's parents, Henry and Lucy Breckenridge. Alice and John had one daughter, Emma, and a son, Abner, was born soon after in July 1899. Alice and John divorced May 16, 1909, and she later married James Hill. The boys, by then three of them, took the name Hill; Emma remained a Breckenridge. This photograph is from around 1910.

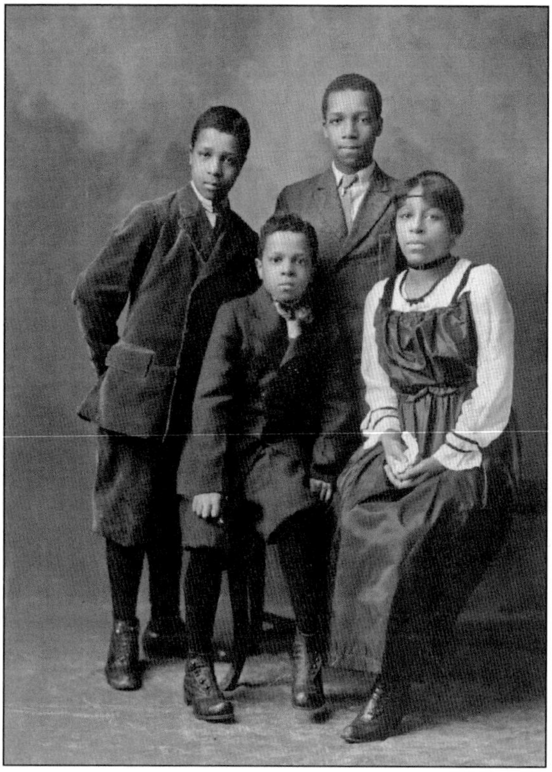

Pictured here around 1912, the Breckenridge children are, from left to right, (seated) Elbert and Emma; (standing) John Jr. and Abner. They are grandchildren of Henry and Lucy Breckenridge, who came to Spokane in 1899 from Roslyn, Washington. They grew up in Spokane and then moved away. Abner returned to Spokane in 1934 with his family. Alice, their mother, remained in Spokane until her death in 1927.

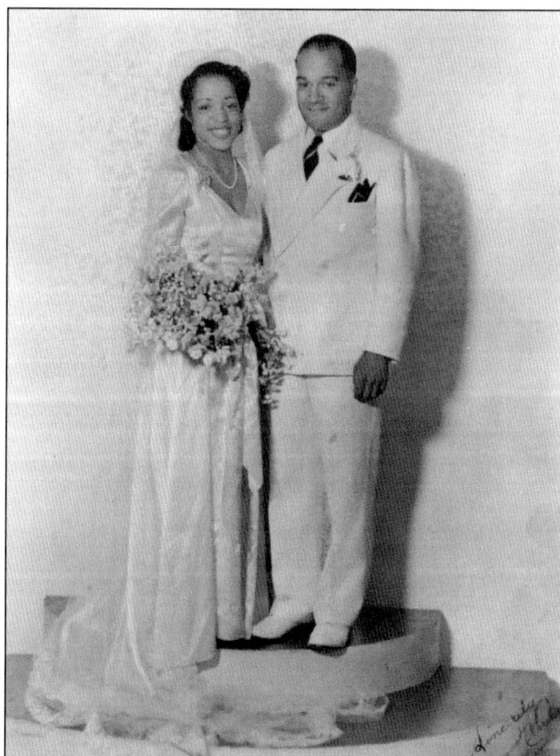

This photograph is of Clarence Freeman and Frances Mitchell, who married at Bethel AME Church. The bride made a lovely picture in her white satin wedding gown. The bridesmaids were Willabelle Thomas and Mrs. Oliver Johnson. Ushers were Elmo Dalbert, James Chase, William Tucker, Oliver Johnson, and Harold Freeman. The bride was a graduate of Lewis and Clark High School. The groom attended Gonzaga University.

Clarence T. Freeman Jr., son of Clarence and Frances Freeman, graduated from Lewis and Clark High School. He was the first black student to be named concert master and also to be in All-State Orchestra. He graduated as a dentist from Washington State University, becoming the first black and the only "Spokane grown" person from the state of Washington to do so. This photograph dates to around 1960.

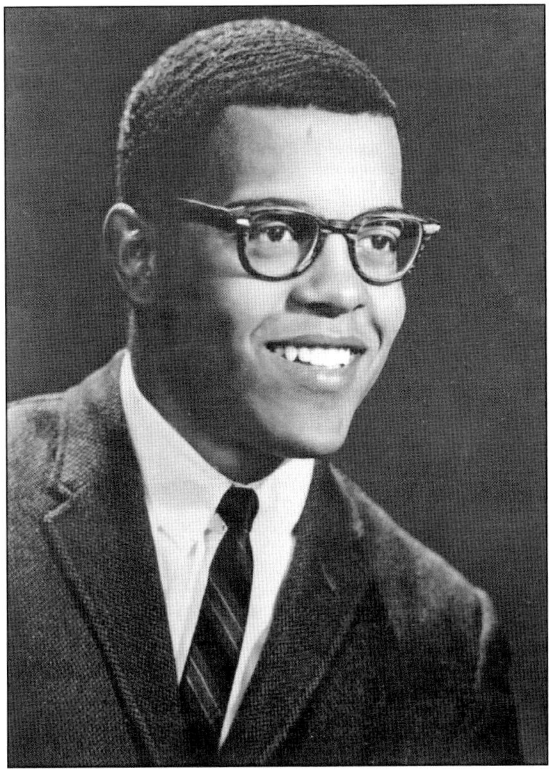

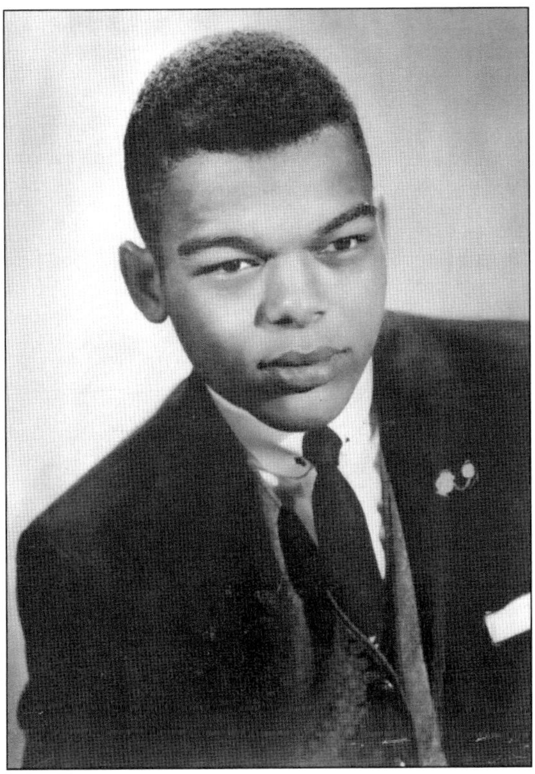

Frederic J. Freeman, pictured in 1963, is a Lewis and Clark High School graduate and was the first black officer of the Signal Corps to command the computer division of the Pentagon. He also set up a statewide computer system for major banks. His sister, Sandra L. (Freeman) Sinclair, a Lewis and Clark graduate and transportation coordinator for Boeing in Seattle, is pictured in the "Sports" section of this book.

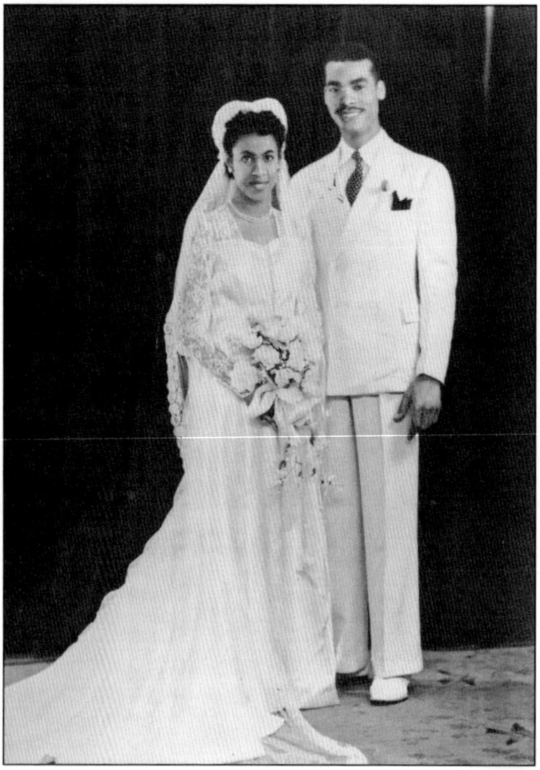

Eleanor Elizabeth Barrow and James E. Chase were married April 10, 1942. Eleanor is a descendant of the Barrow family, longtime Spokane residents. Her parents are Charles and Olive Barrow. Eleanor, a soloist, performed many concerts and sang at many venues. Chase was a partner in Chase and Dalbert Body and Fender. They had one son, Roland. This photograph is from April 10, 1942.

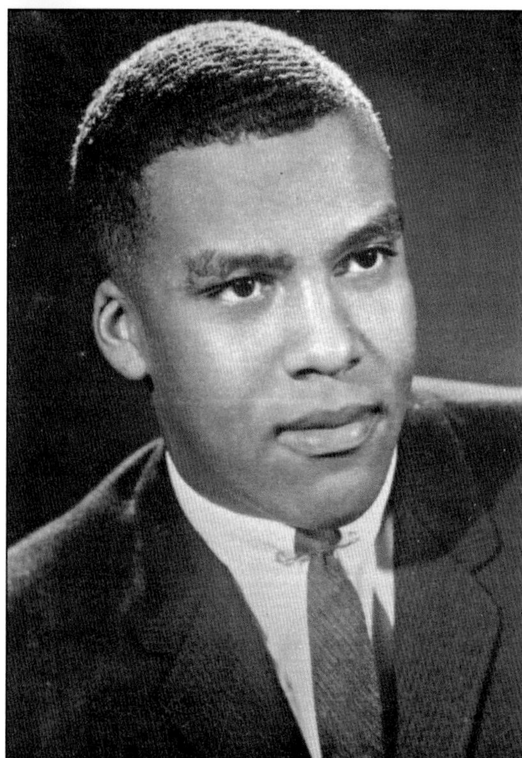

Roland Chase was born in Spokane to James and Eleanor Chase on May 8, 1943. He was named after the great tenor Roland Hayes. Roland Chase graduated from Shadle Park High School in 1961. He has served as a bailiff in both the Spokane County Courthouse and the courthouse in Medical Lake. He has three children. Roland Chase married his current wife, Susan, on May 13, 1987.

This *c.* 1940 playbill is for the concert of Roland Chase's namesake, Roland Hayes, tenor. The photograph was taken from the *New York Sun* newspaper, November 27, 1939. It reads, "Whitworth College Sponsors Roland Hayes." The concert was held at First Presbyterian Church, Fourth Avenue and Cedar Street, Saturday, January 25. What is truly unbelievable is the fact that the tickets were only $1.10.

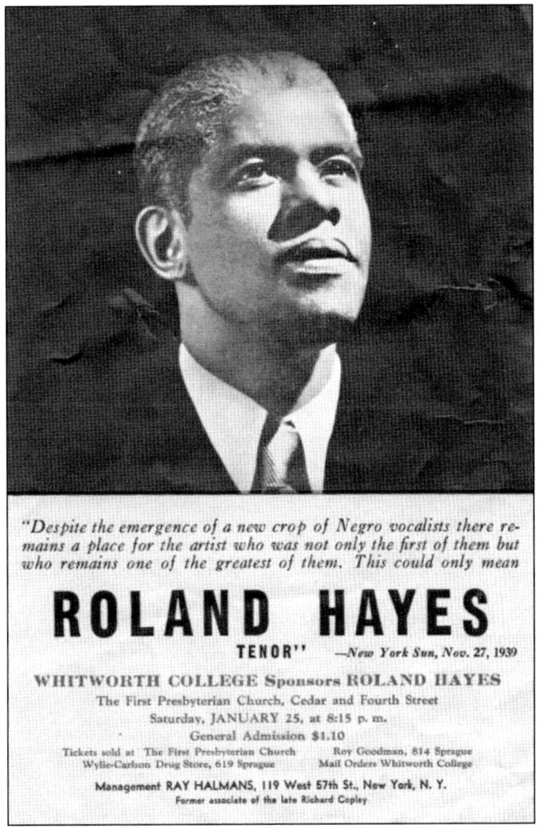

The Lipscomb family, pictured here around 1918, included Isabelle Lipscomb surrounded by daughters Ruth, Baley, and Oney. The Lipscomb family came to Spokane in 1905 and lived in a house built by the girls' father at 1632 West Main Street in Peaceful Valley. Mack Lipscomb was a stonemason who worked on many Spokane buildings. The seven Lipscomb girls were known for their beautiful singing voices.

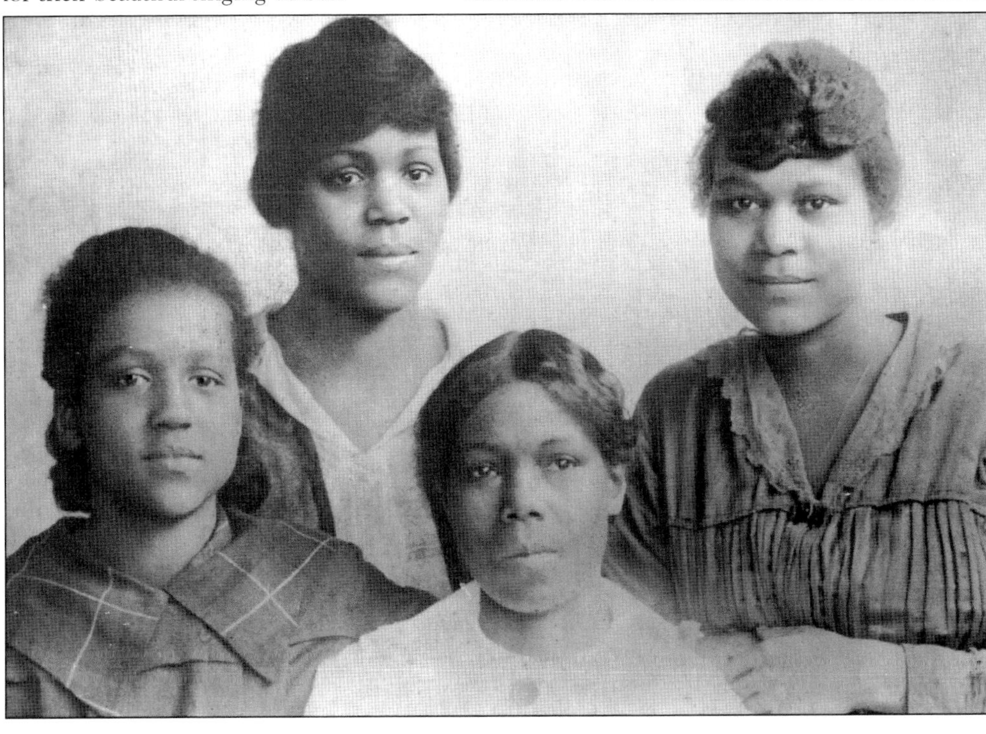

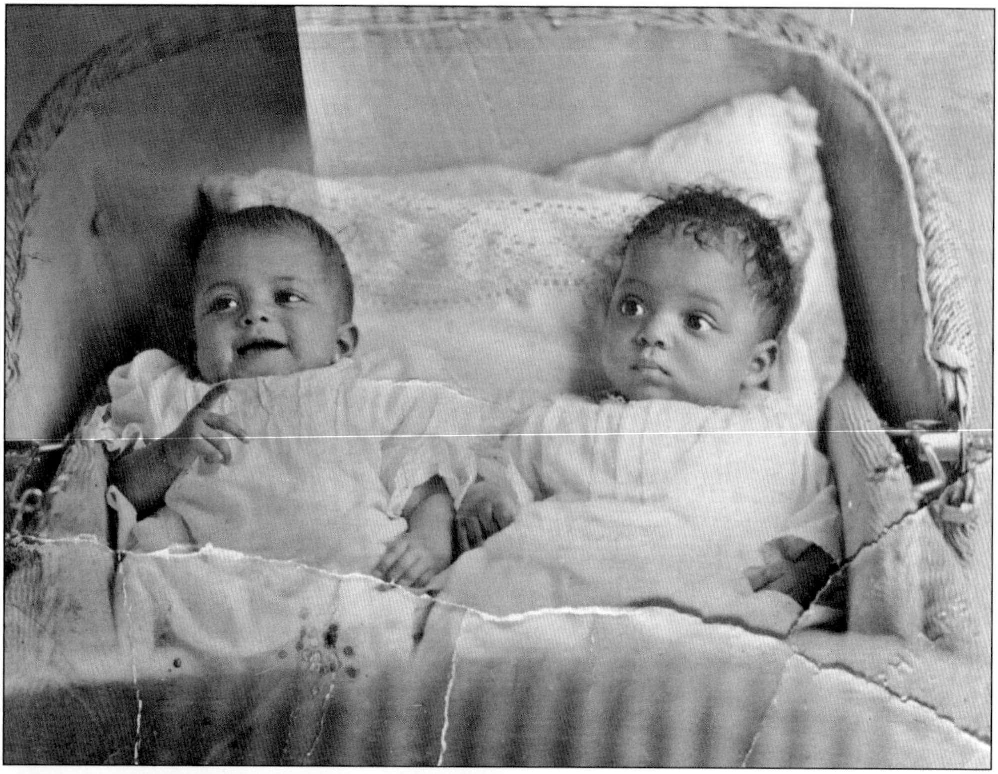

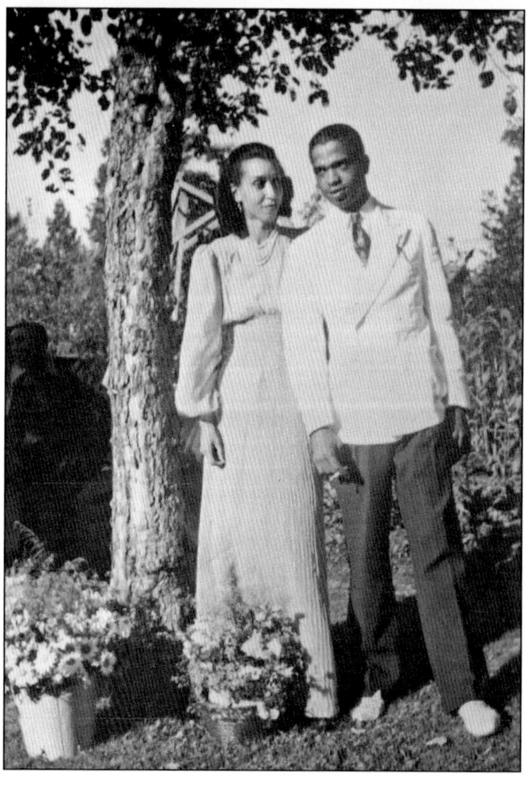

Shown here are the first African American twins born in Spokane and in the state of Washington. Mildred Louise (Nichols) Elliott (left) and Louis Patrick Nichols (right) are the children of Marie (Nichols) Maley and Louis P. Nichols Sr. After Marie Maley graduated from nursing school in Atlanta, they moved to Spokane about 1920. Her other two children are Frances Nichols Scott and Ruth Nichols.

This is Willabelle and William Tucker at their c. 1937 wedding at the home of Wayland and Willa Boot. The Boots lived at 1519 North Washington Street in Spokane. Their families were black pioneers in Spokane, and they chose to reside here also. The Tuckers had four children: Neil, Steve, Kathleen, and Richard. Willabelle Tucker passed away December 31, 2005. She was 88. William Tucker preceded her in death.

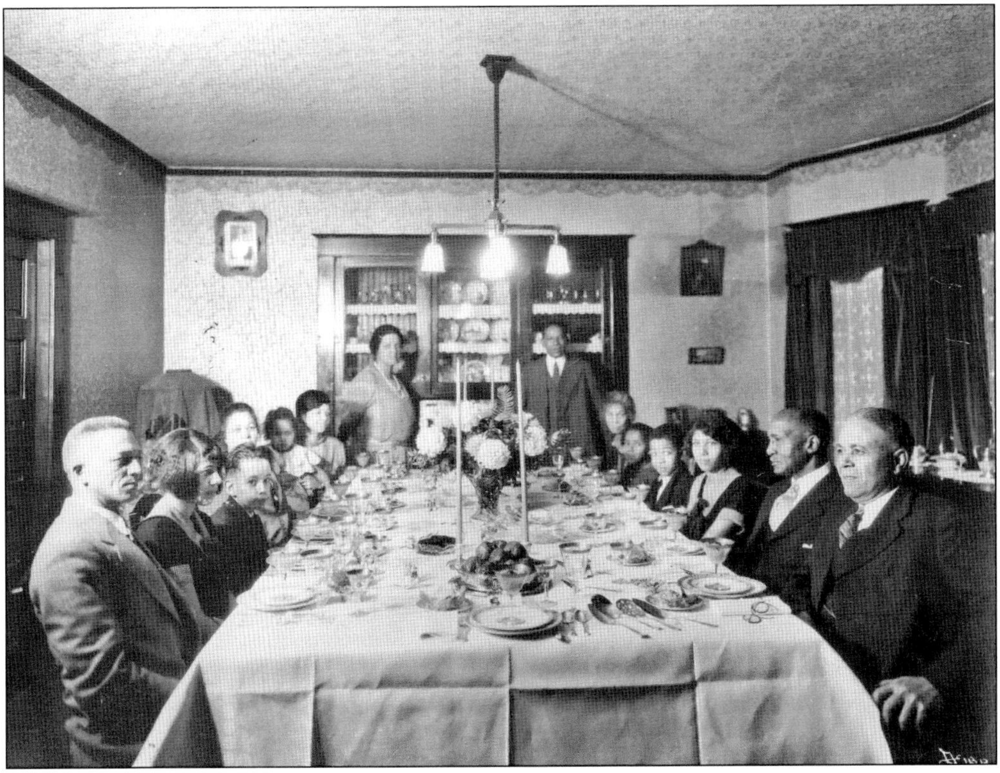

This 1927 photograph was taken at the home of Mr. and Mrs. E. C. Williamson. Many Spokane pioneers are pictured here. They are, from left to right, Mr. Derek, Gwendolyn Derek, Buddy Williamson, Mrs. Derek, unidentified baby, Mrs. Williamson, Emerson C. Williamson, Mrs. Perkins, Fred Rosa, Jack Holsclaw, Gwenivere Derek, Alfred Perkins, and Mr. Holsclaw. Williamson was honorably discharged from the army and stayed in Spokane.

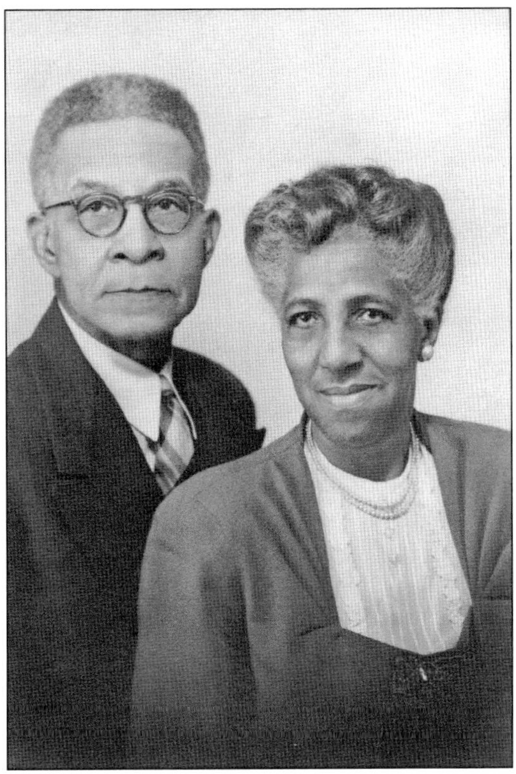

This is a photograph of Charles and Olive Barrow, longtime residents of the African American community of Spokane. They are the parents of Eleanor and Kirk Barrow. Charles Barrow was the founder of the *Citizen*, a local black newspaper. This newspaper reported all that was going on with black people in the community. This photograph was taken in 1947. (Courtesy of MAC/EWHS MS 159-814.)

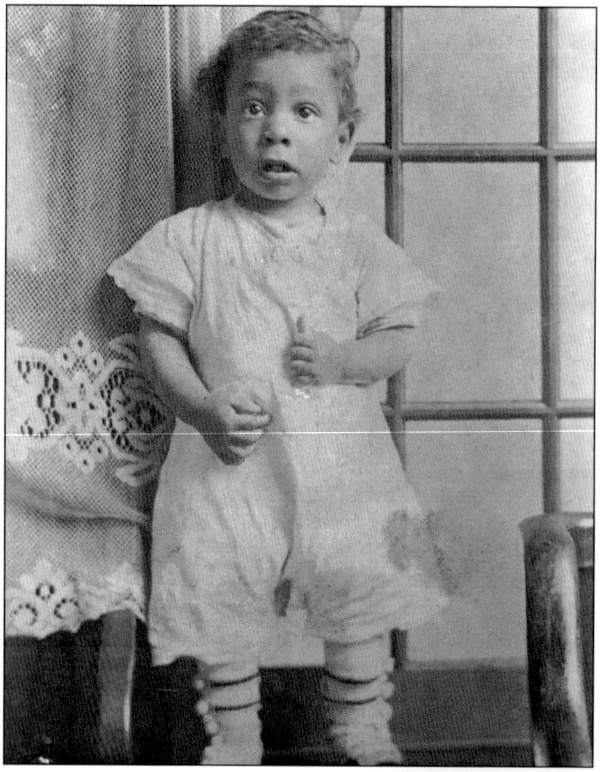

This photograph is of Wallace H. Hagin around 1920. His parents, Irene and Wallace Hagin Sr., came to Spokane from Great Falls, Montana. His grandmother, "Grandma Fagin" as he called her, was born into slavery in Georgia. She was a longtime resident of Spokane. "Wally" Hagin became somewhat of an icon in the Spokane community, which is explained in the last chapter of this book.

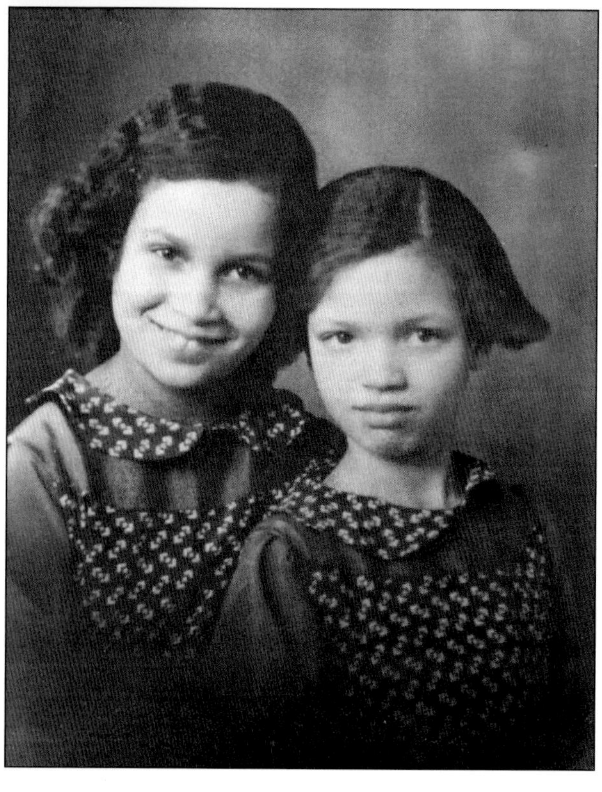

The children pictured here in Spokane around 1930 are Lillian Frances (Stokes) Mitchell, left, and Gloria (Stokes) Murphy. They are the children of Lillian and Frank Stokes. The Stokes family were longtime residents of Spokane. Both parents have passed away, as has Lillian Frances. Gloria Murphy, at this writing, is still a resident of Spokane.

The children in this *c.* 1938 photograph are (standing) Lewis Strong and (seated) Charlotte Strong and Robert "Bobby" Strong. They lived across the street from Bethel AME Church when it was at Fifth Avenue and Pine Street. As teens, they had great parties at their house, lots of food, and the latest records for dancing. One of the favorite records was Nat "King" Cole's *For Sentimental Reasons.*

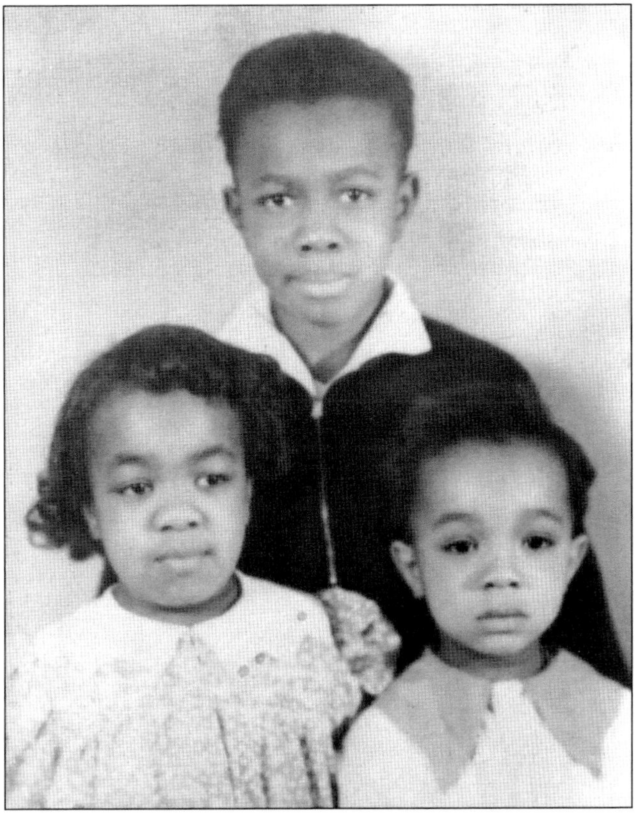

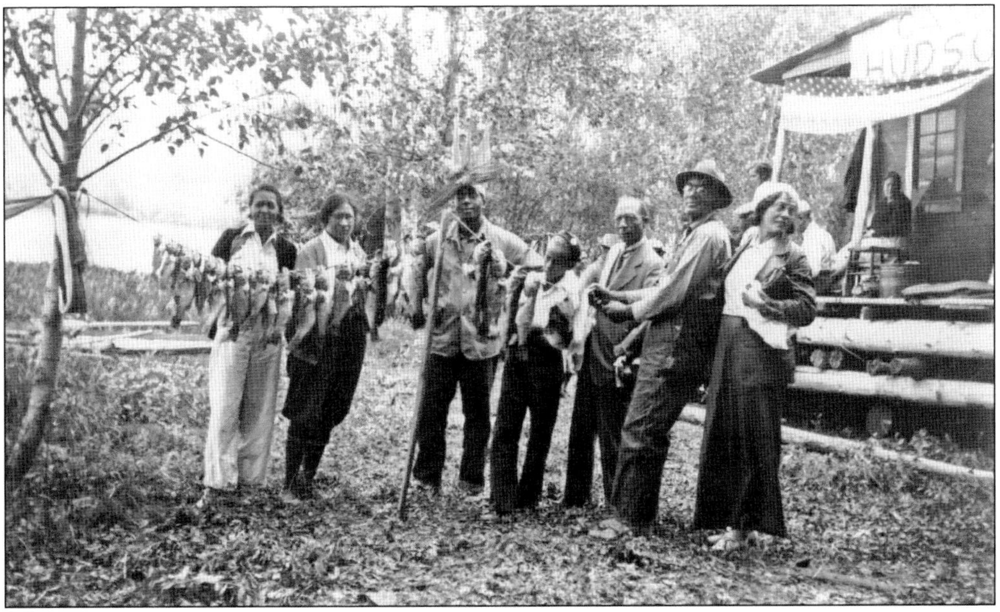

This 1930s photograph was taken at the homestead of the King family in King Valley, Idaho; however, some of those pictured were residents of Spokane. This area was officially named King Valley after the King family. Pictured from left to right are Willa Boot (Lipscomb), her sister Ruth Lipscomb, two unidentified, Jim Loupe, his cousin Bill King ("Bud"), and Bill's wife, Clara King.

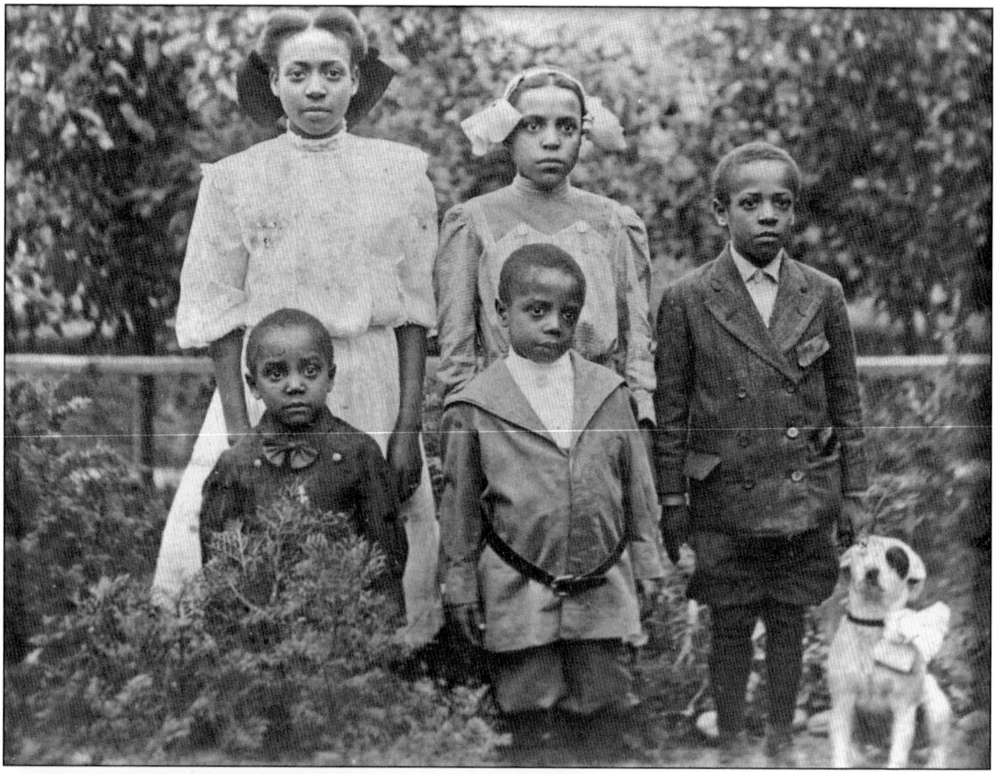

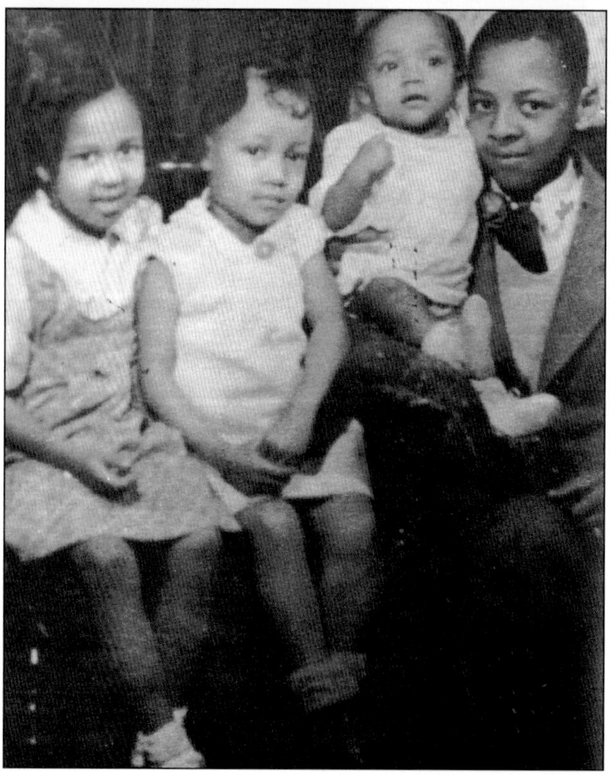

This is a favorite photograph. Pictured from left to right are (first row) brothers Jack and Clayborne Lipscomb; (second row) Ethyl King, Catherine Edmonson, an unidentified boy, and their dog. It looks like it is from the "Our Gang" series. This photograph has no date, but because of the way they are dressed, it probably was taken around 1930 in Spokane.

Pictured here are the Hill children, from left to right: Mary Emma Hill, Jerrelene Hill, and Lillian Hill, held by brother Alfonse Hill. Abner (Breckenridge) Hill married Hester Warfield in 1923 in Chicago. They returned to Spokane with three children. Later they had six other children born in Spokane. Lillian Hill was the first. This photograph was taken at their home on the north side of Spokane in 1936.

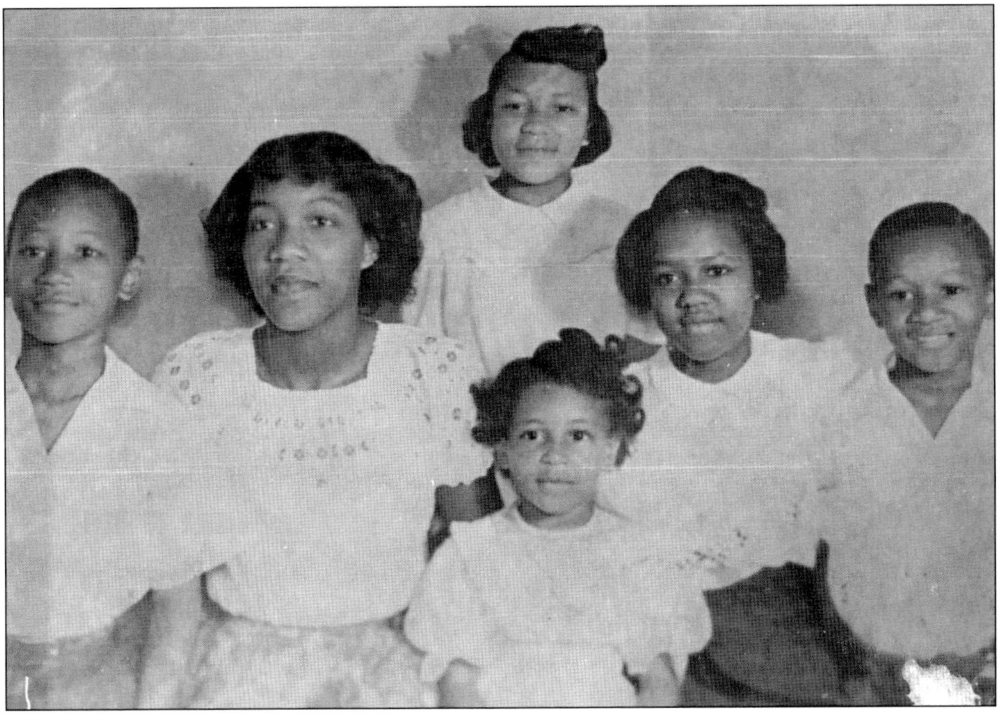

This c. 1945 photograph shows the rest of the Hill children, from left to right: (first row) Sharon Anne; (second row) Abner Warfield, Lillian Eva, Louise Elizabeth, and Joseph Louis; (third row) Vada Mae. This family grew up in Spokane. They are the descendants of Henry and Lucy Breckenridge, their great-grandparents. Henry was killed when he fell down a well in Spokane in 1906. Lucy passed away in 1940 in Spokane.

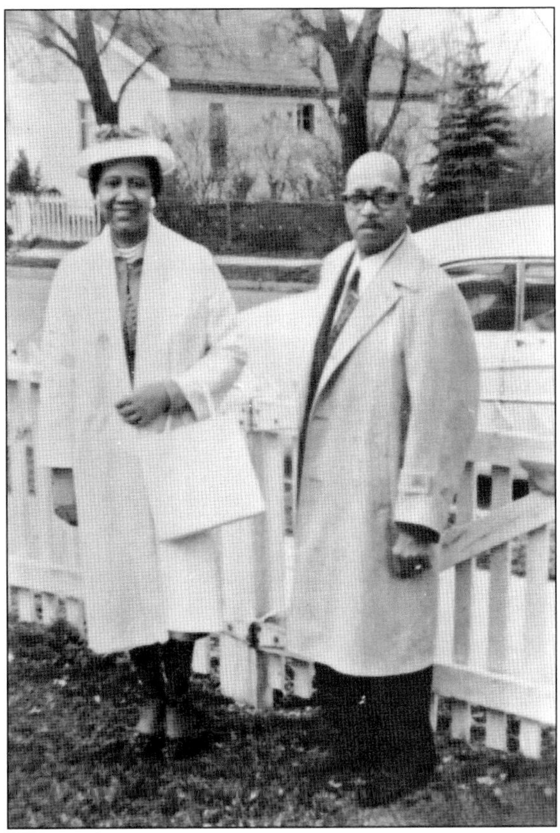

This 1950s photograph is of Spokane native Abner (Breckenridge) Hill and his wife, Hester Anne. It was taken in front of their home at 407 East Broad Street. Abner became a Pullman porter. In Chicago, he met and married Hester Warfield. Returning to Spokane, they moved into his mother Alice's home and raised their family there. Alice Breckenridge passed away in 1927.

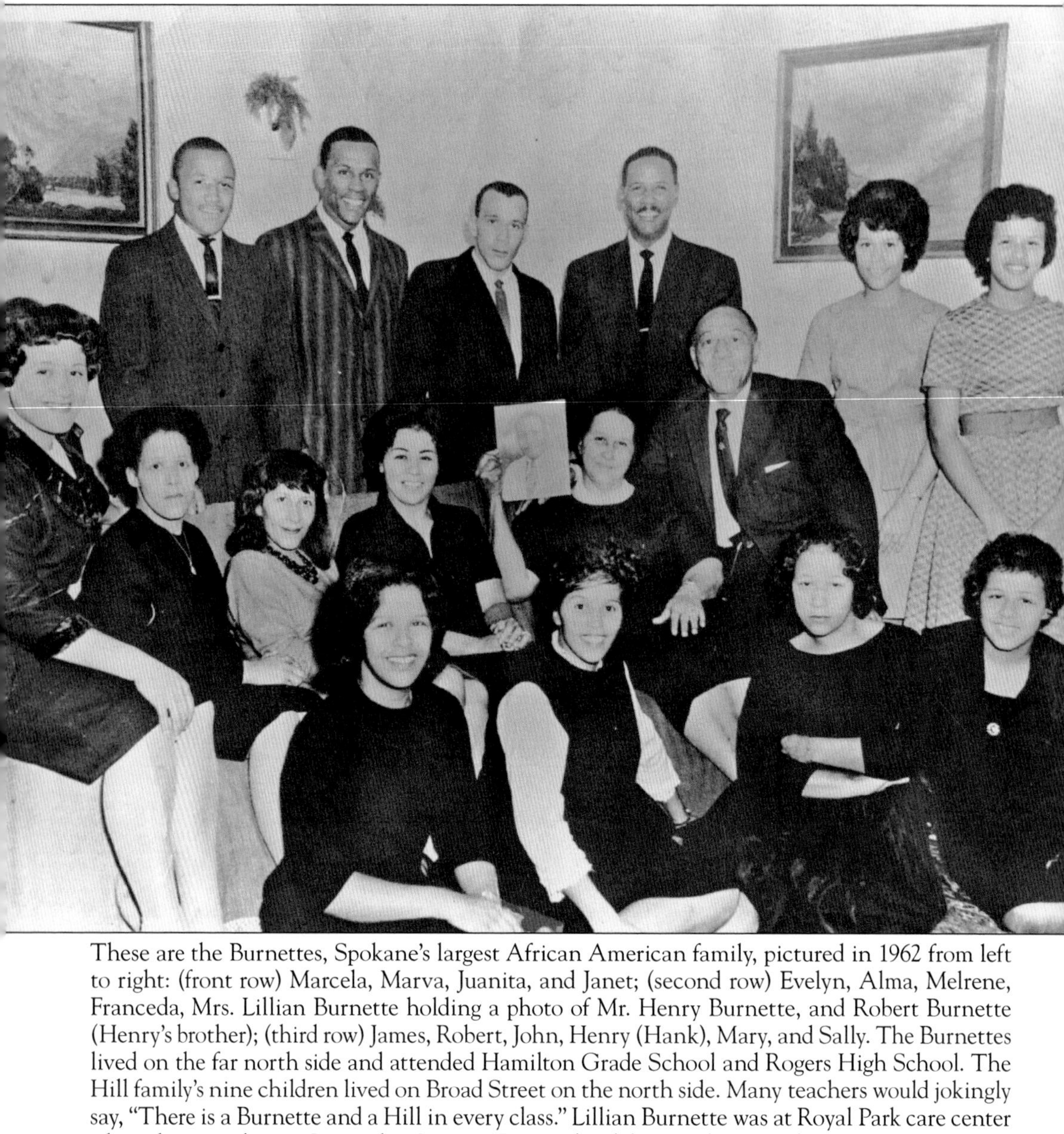

These are the Burnettes, Spokane's largest African American family, pictured in 1962 from left to right: (front row) Marcela, Marva, Juanita, and Janet; (second row) Evelyn, Alma, Melrene, Franceda, Mrs. Lillian Burnette holding a photo of Mr. Henry Burnette, and Robert Burnette (Henry's brother); (third row) James, Robert, John, Henry (Hank), Mary, and Sally. The Burnettes lived on the far north side and attended Hamilton Grade School and Rogers High School. The Hill family's nine children lived on Broad Street on the north side. Many teachers would jokingly say, "There is a Burnette and a Hill in every class." Lillian Burnette was at Royal Park care center when she passed away September 7, 2002. During her lifetime, she was a homemaker, caterer of parties on the South Hill, foster grandparent at Lakeland Village, and receptionist at Northeast Neighborhood Center, plus so many more things for others than it is possible to put on paper.

Thelma Weiseger and her husband Ben, left, are pictured with Levi and Sarah Gardner and their daughter Antoinette. Thelma is the daughter of Rev. Emmett B. Reed, former pastor of Calvary Baptist Church. She was church pianist and choir director at one time. Thelma has a brother, Emmett Reed Jr. This photograph was taken around 1962.

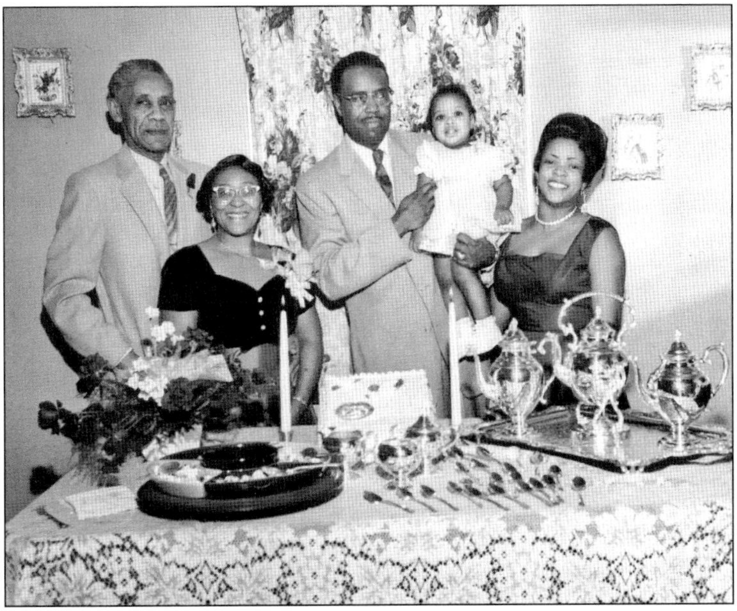

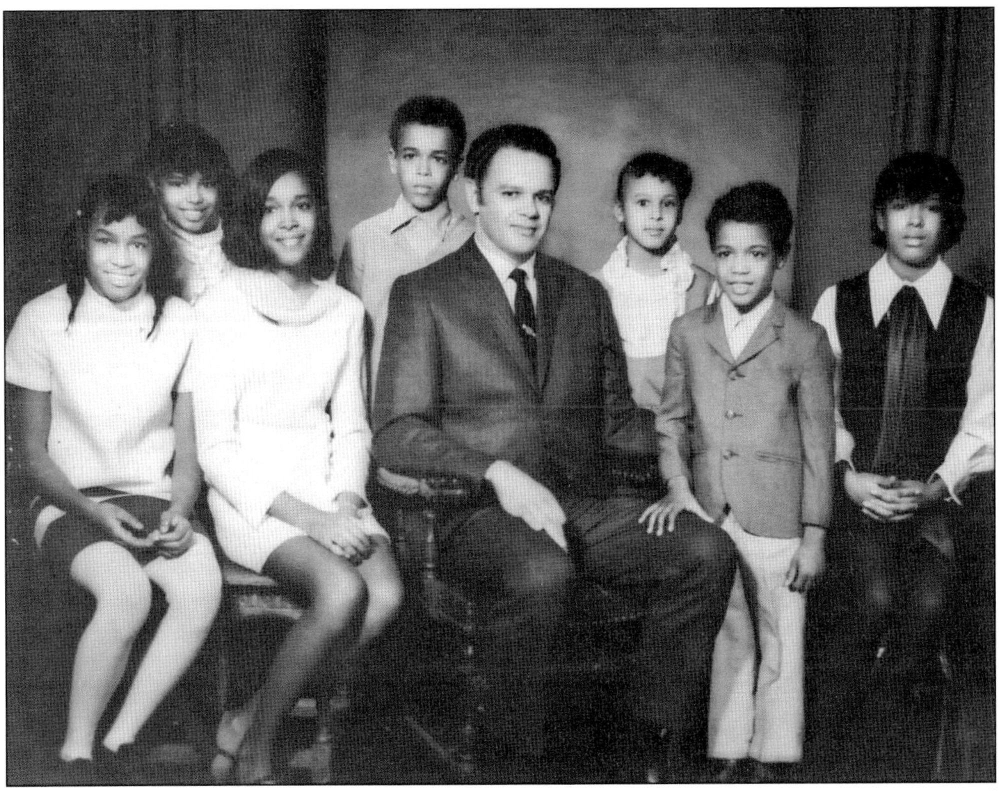

Dr. Charles Hopkins is shown with his family. Formerly of Spokane, he had once been married to Gloria Dixon of Spokane. Pictured from left to right are (first row) Theresa, Linda, Charles, Lance, and Yvonne; (second row) Carole, Charles III, and Cheryl. Dr. Hopkins, a well-known Chicago heart surgeon, was tragically killed in an auto accident in Chicago. This photograph was taken in 1969. (Courtesy of Carole (Crowder) King.)

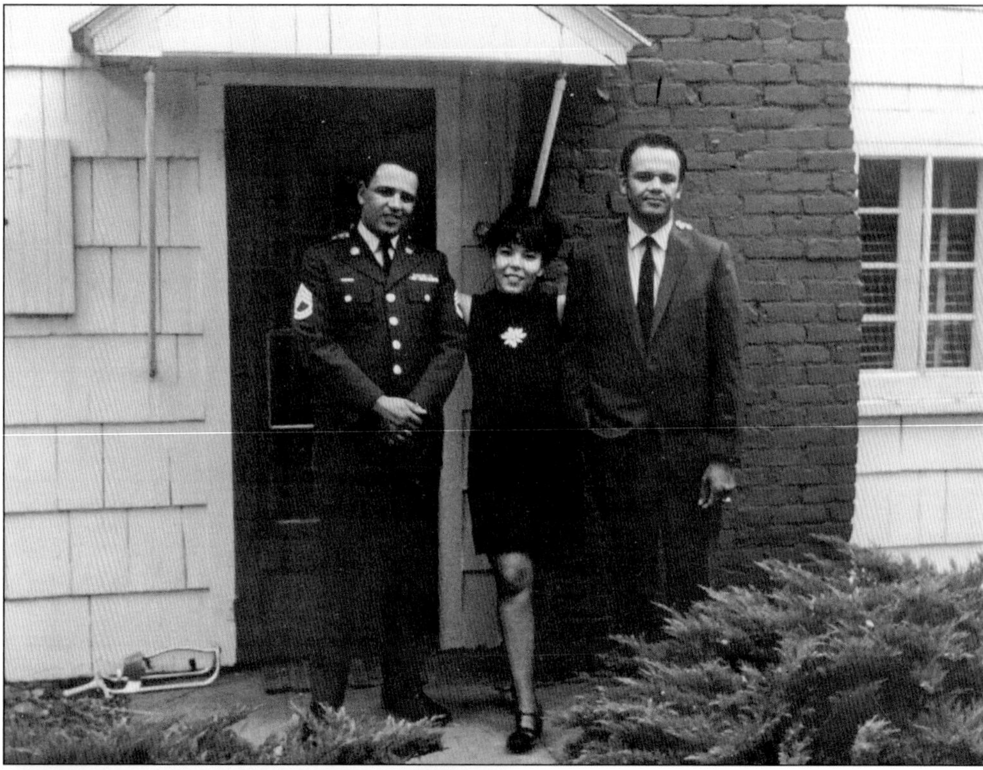

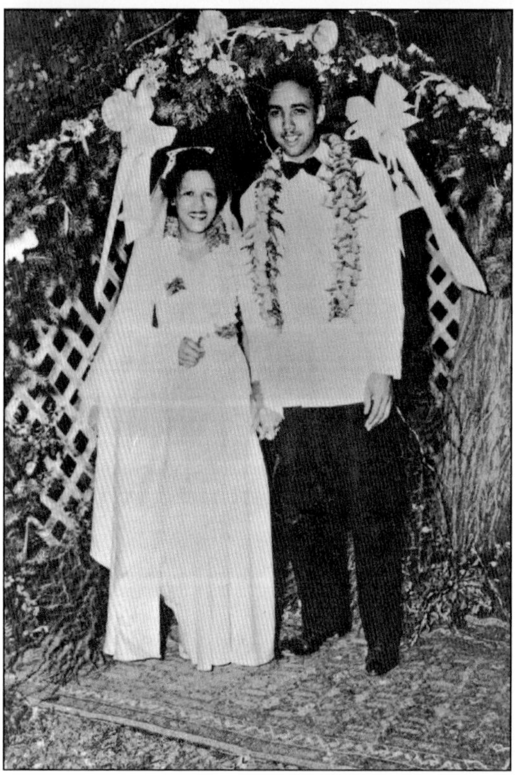

This c. 1960 photograph is of Chester Hopkins (in uniform) and Charles Hopkins—sons of John Hopkins Sr. and Katrina (Hopkins) Crowder—and Carole Ann Crowder, daughter of Katrina Crowder. They and their brother Donald grew up in Spokane, attending schools here. Carole Crowder is married to well-known Seattle architect Donald King, who designed the building for the Northwest African American Museum in Seattle. (Courtesy of Carole (Crowder) King.)

Alma and DuWayne Watts were married in August 1951. Born in Spokane, the bride is the daughter of Henry and Lillian Burnette and graduated from John Rogers High School in 1947. DuWayne is a longtime Spokane resident. The Wattses have three sons, Michael, Alan, and Steven, and three daughters, Patricia Watts (deceased February 10, 2007), Delores "Dee Dee" Grant, and Susan Poindexter. Alma passed away June 18, 1998. (Courtesy of Delores "Dee Dee" Grant.)

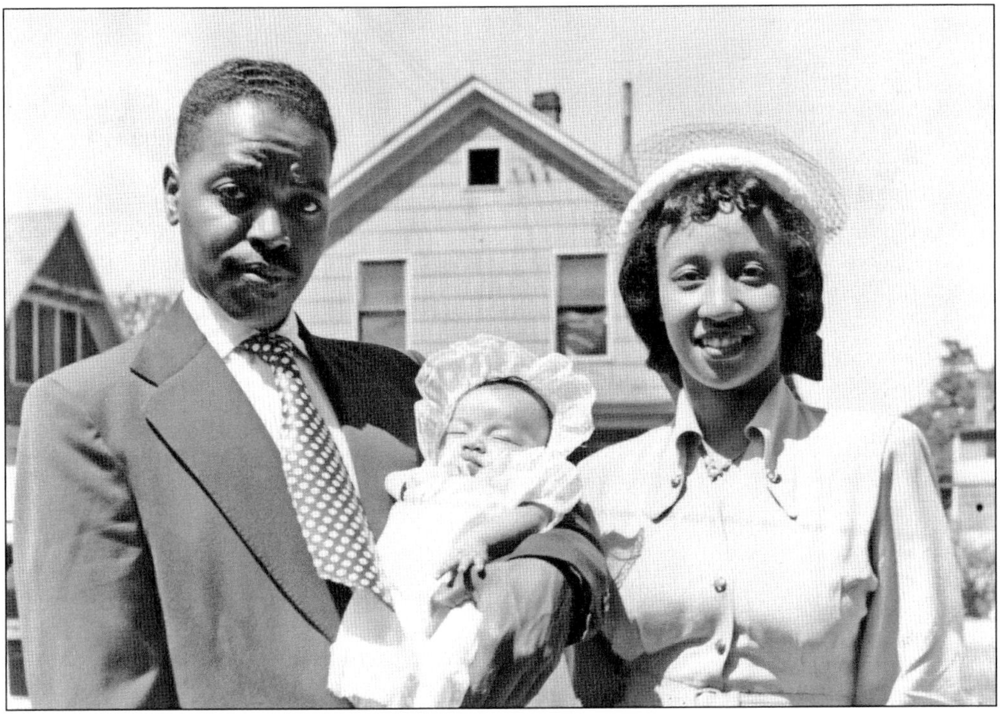

This 1951 photograph was taken at Bethel AME Church after Sunday service. Pictured are Sam and Jerrelene Williamson with baby daughter Annette. The Williamsons had four other children: Jennifer, James, Sam Jr., and Julie. All of the children graduated from Spokane schools and some of them still reside in Spokane.

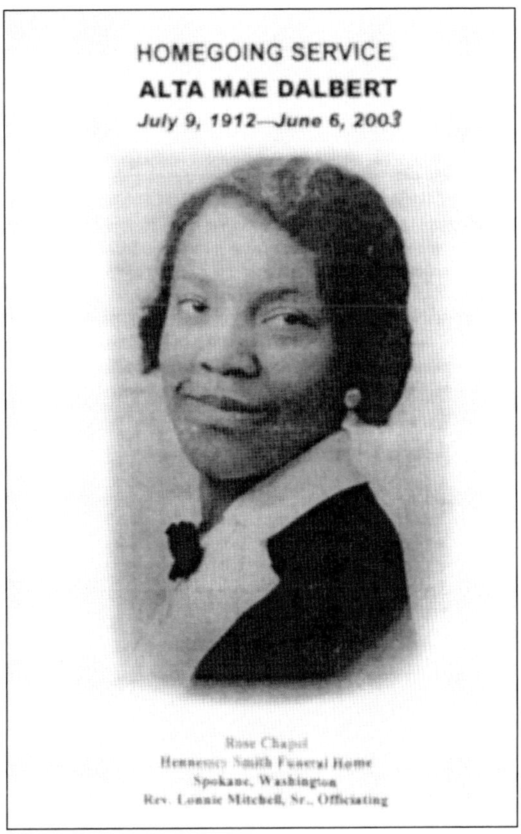

This is Alta Mae Dalbert, wife of Elmo Dalbert. She was born July 9, 1912, in Centralia, Washington. Alta was part of the Spokane community for 70 years and was a member of the Bethel AME Church, Eastern Star, and Wednesday Art Club. She passed away June 6, 2003. Elmo passed away May 29, 2006. They had one grandchild, Francell, who married Adam Daubert. The memorial photograph is from around 1930.

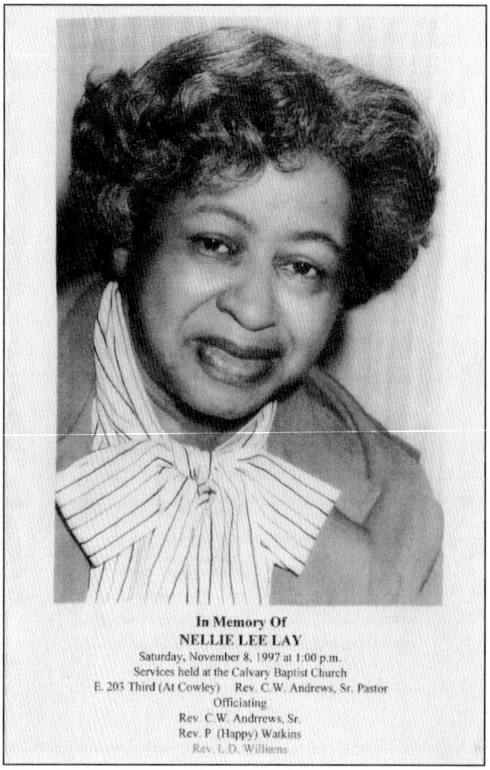
In Memory Of
NELLIE LEE LAY
Saturday, November 8, 1997 at 1:00 p.m.
Services held at the Calvary Baptist Church
E. 203 Third (At Cowley) Rev. C.W. Andrews, Sr. Pastor
Officiating
Rev. C.W. Andrrews, Sr.
Rev. P. (Happy) Watkins
Rev. L.D. Williams

Nellie Lay was born in Yakima, Washington, December 20, 1928. Her parents were Edward Green Jones and Emmetta Mae Jones (daughter of Rev. Emmett B. Reed). Lay graduated from Yakima High School and married Alvie Allen. They divorced, and Nellie married Doyle Lay. Mother of five, she was one of the first directors of the Eastside Neighborhood Center and was active in the community. She passed away October 31, 1997.

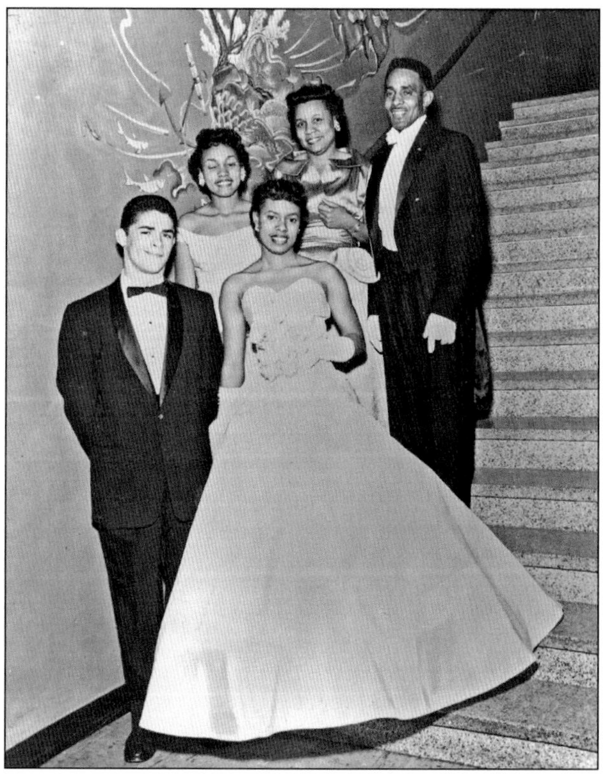

The Sylvester Lake family of Spokane is shown in this photograph taken in 1957 at the Rhinestone Club's Debutante Ball in Seattle. Shown in the rear on the steps are Pauline Lake and her husband, Sylvester Lake. A step in front is Sylvia Lake, their daughter. In the very front are Mona Lake and escort Carver Gayton, both of Washington State University.

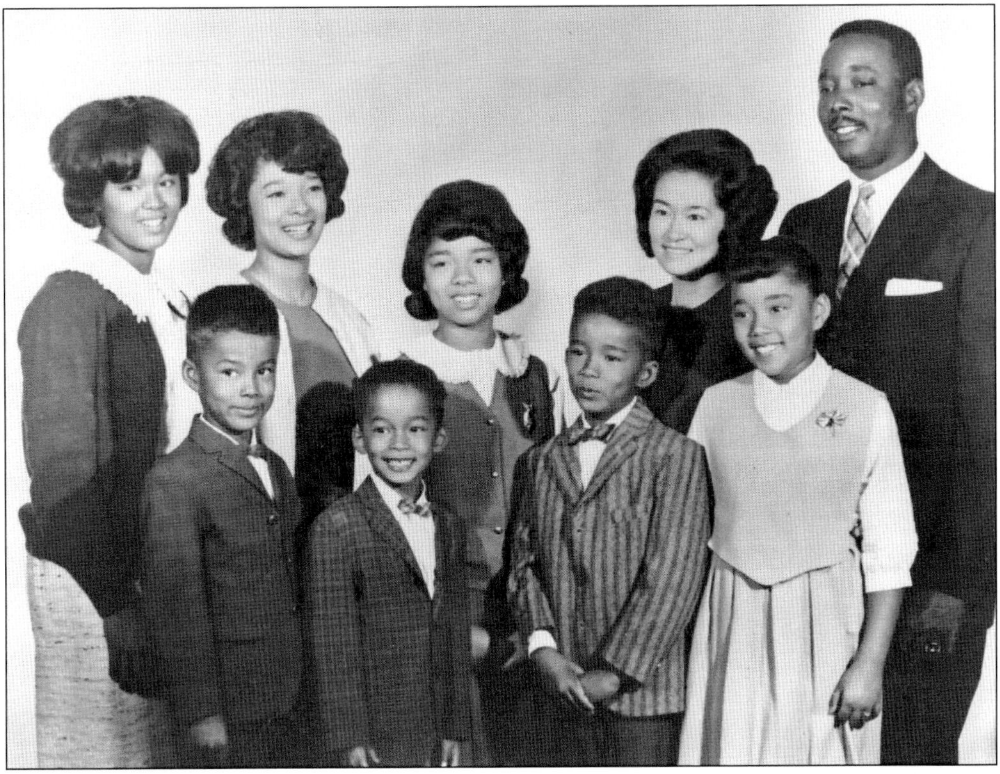

Clarence West came to Spokane in the military at what is now Fairchild Air Force Base. He met and married Marianne (born Fusaye Sumihiro) in Spokane. Family members pictured here are, from left to right, (first row) Allen, Masami (Charles), Clarence Jr., and Patty; (second row) Mary, Linda, Ella, Marianne, and Clarence Sr. Clarence passed away April 30, 2004. Marianne passed away April 11, 2006. This photograph is from around 1960.

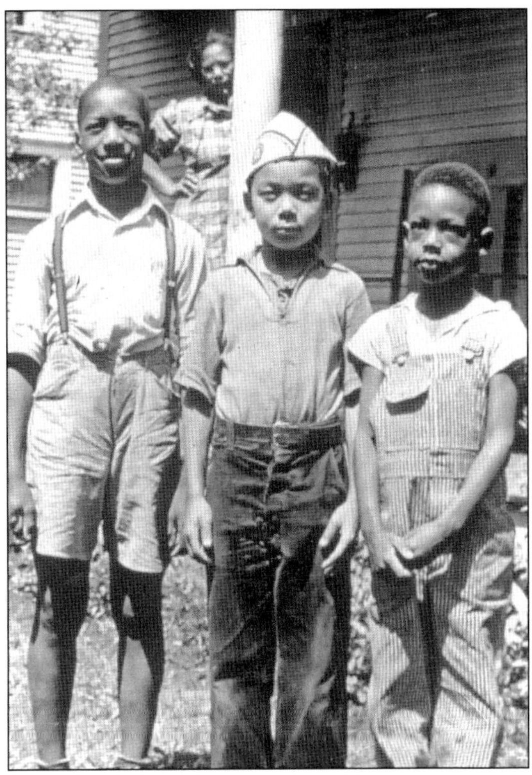

Sidney Breckenridge of Tacoma (center) is in front of the Booker T. Washington Community Center. Roy Smalley is on the left. The boy on the right is unidentified. Sidney was raised by Mary (Breckenridge) Hunt in Tacoma but spent many of his summers in Spokane. Rosa D. Malone is in the background on the steps of the center. This photograph is from about 1940.

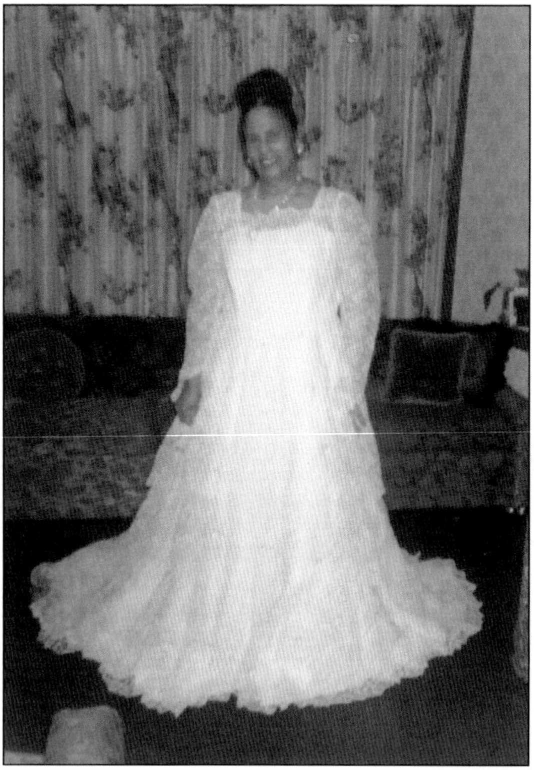

Willie Ann (Bangs) Earthman is Spokane's centenarian. Born in Pascagoula, Mississippi, on July 13, 1908, she has been a Spokane resident for more than 60 years. She is a member of Bethel AME Church. She met her husband, James, in Spokane, and they married in 1935. The Earthmans had two children, Arealous ("Ace") and Arneathea (deceased). James passed away in 1985. This photograph is from around 1960.

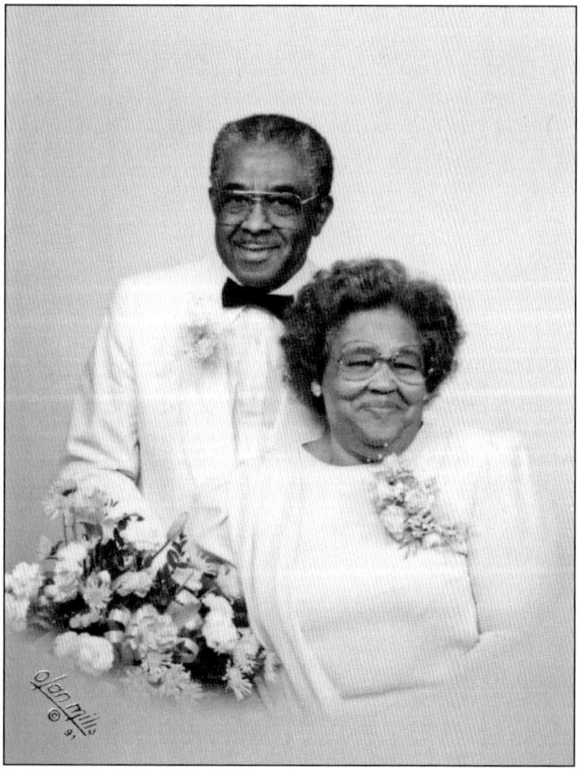

This is William and Helen Gaskins on their 25th wedding anniversary. The Gaskins were members of the Centennial Tribute to Northwest Black Pioneers. William worked for and retired from the Bon Marche department store. Helen loved to cook and care for her family. Their sons are William Jr. and Wally Gaskins. Helen Juanita Gaskins passed away July 17, 2007. This photograph is from about 1967. (Courtesy of Olan Mills Photo Studio.)

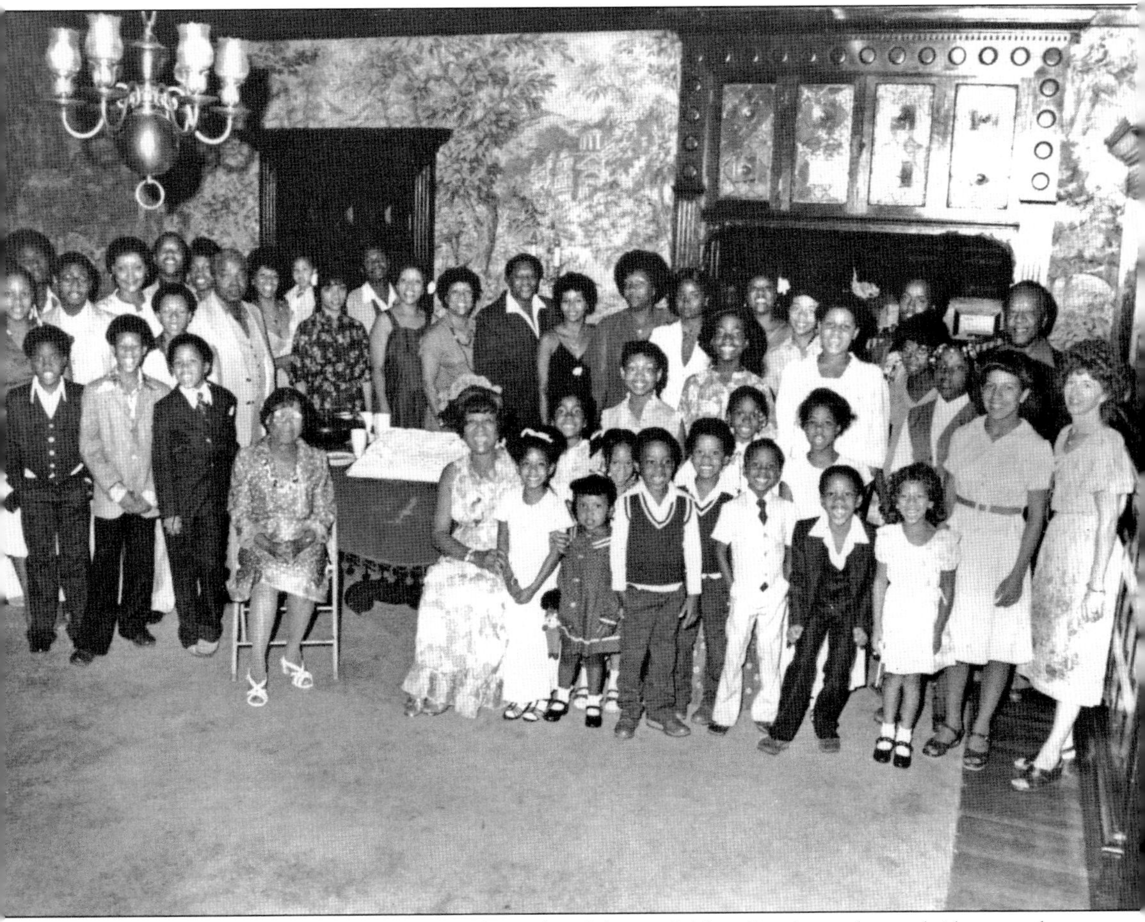

The descendants of Henry and Lucy Breckenridge, John and Alice Breckenridge and Abner and Hester Hill, all lived in Spokane at one time; however, they left to find work and raise their families in other parts of the United States. Some went to California, Seattle, and other destinations, but somehow their hearts were always connected to the place where the Breckenridges first came in 1899. This is the last photograph of Hester Hill and Mary Breckenridge with the family. This image shows a reunion of the Breckenridge descendants lined up at the Glover Mansion in Spokane in 1980. Seated in front are Mary (Breckenridge) Hunt, daughter of Henry and Lucy Breckenridge, at left, and Hester Ann Hill, wife of Abner (Breckenridge) Hill, who was born in Spokane and lived most of his life there. The Breckenridge descendants represented are the Hills, Williamsons, Carters, Lillys, Briscoes, Rosemans, Johnsons, and Martins.

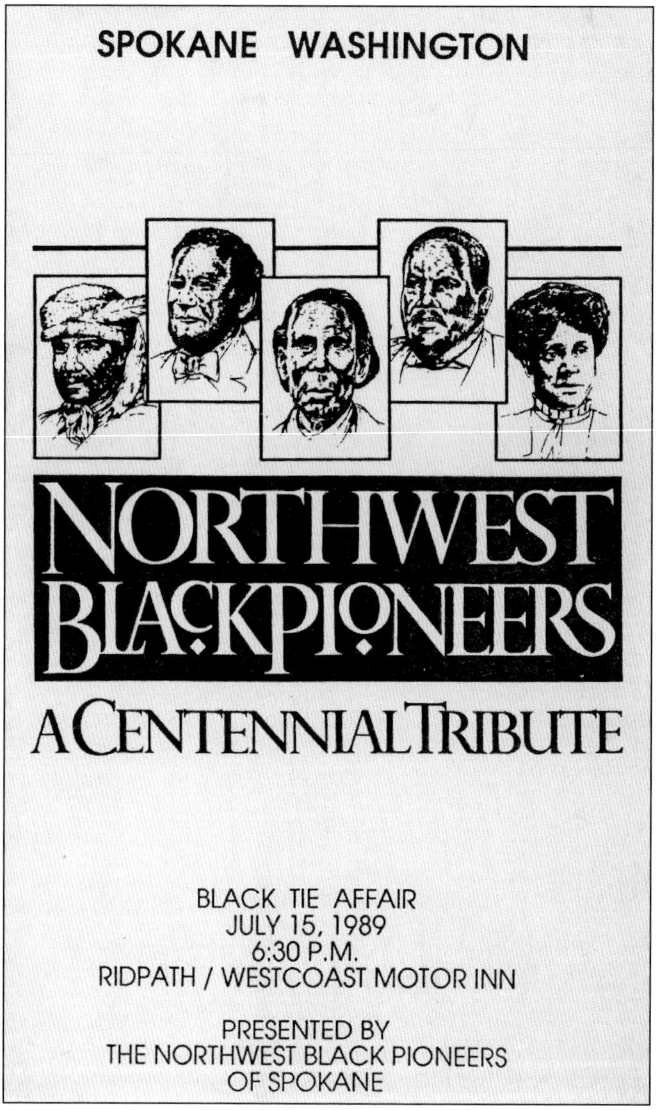

This ad is for the Centennial Tribute to Northwest Black Pioneers in 1989. There are many faces beyond the photographs in this book that are in the "memories of my mind:" Russlynne Hagin, the Bass family, the Kenoleys, the Carpenters, the Martins, Sybil Stafford, Jeanine, Beverly, and Katherine Turner, Edna, Julia and Harvey Potter, Ellis Casson, Leroy Wilson, the Solomons, the McNabbs, the Grubbs, Carl and Sarah Jones, the Bernestiens, the Montgomerys, the Dunns, Selma Clark, the Bangs, the Wellingtons, Flexian and Bailey Pierce, the Sartos, the Postons, the Hamms, Elaine Cleveland, Peggy Parker, J. J. Johnson, Helen Johnson, Cora Teel, Harold and Bea Freeman, the Hudsons, the Jacksons, the McHenrys, the Williamses, Bernice and Shirley Adams, Lydia Ann Henry, the Chapmans, the Mooreheads, the Dillards, the Caldwells, the Andersons, the Sharpleys, the Gibsons, the Dixons, the Brazils, the Bridges, James Hopson, "Idaho" Davis, Helen Davis, the Joneses, the Wilsons, Rev. C. E. Hamp . . . The memories of my mind go on and on. Those who are not mentioned are not forgotten.

Ten

NOTABLES

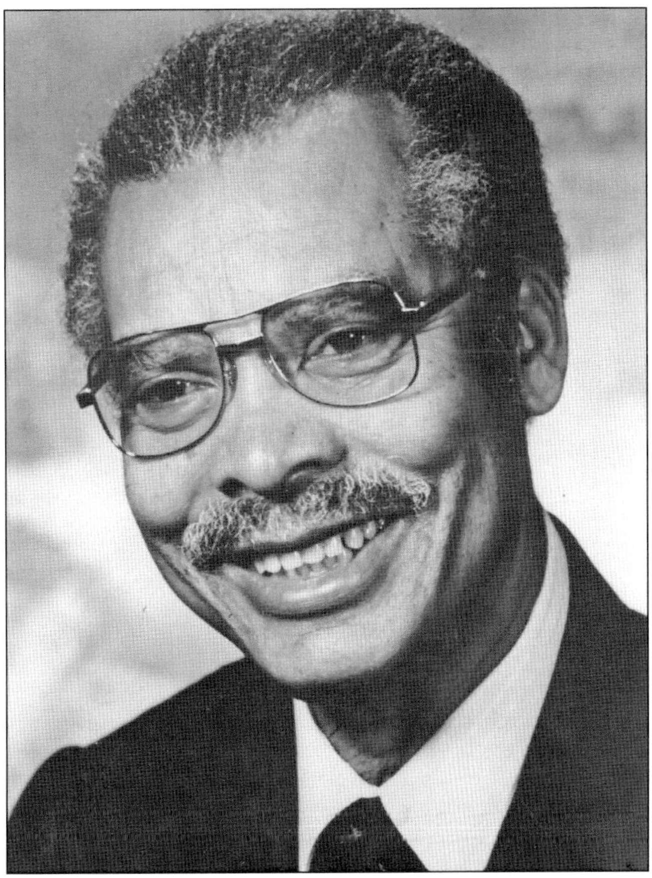

James Edward Chase, Spokane's first African American mayor (1981–1985), came to Spokane in 1934 on a freight train with friend Elmo Dalbert. Born in East Texas in 1914, he married Spokane girl Eleanor Barrow in 1942. He was president of the Spokane NAACP (1952–1970) and was grand master of Prince Hall Masonic Lodge for the state of Washington. James Chase passed away in 1987. This photograph is from the 1980s.

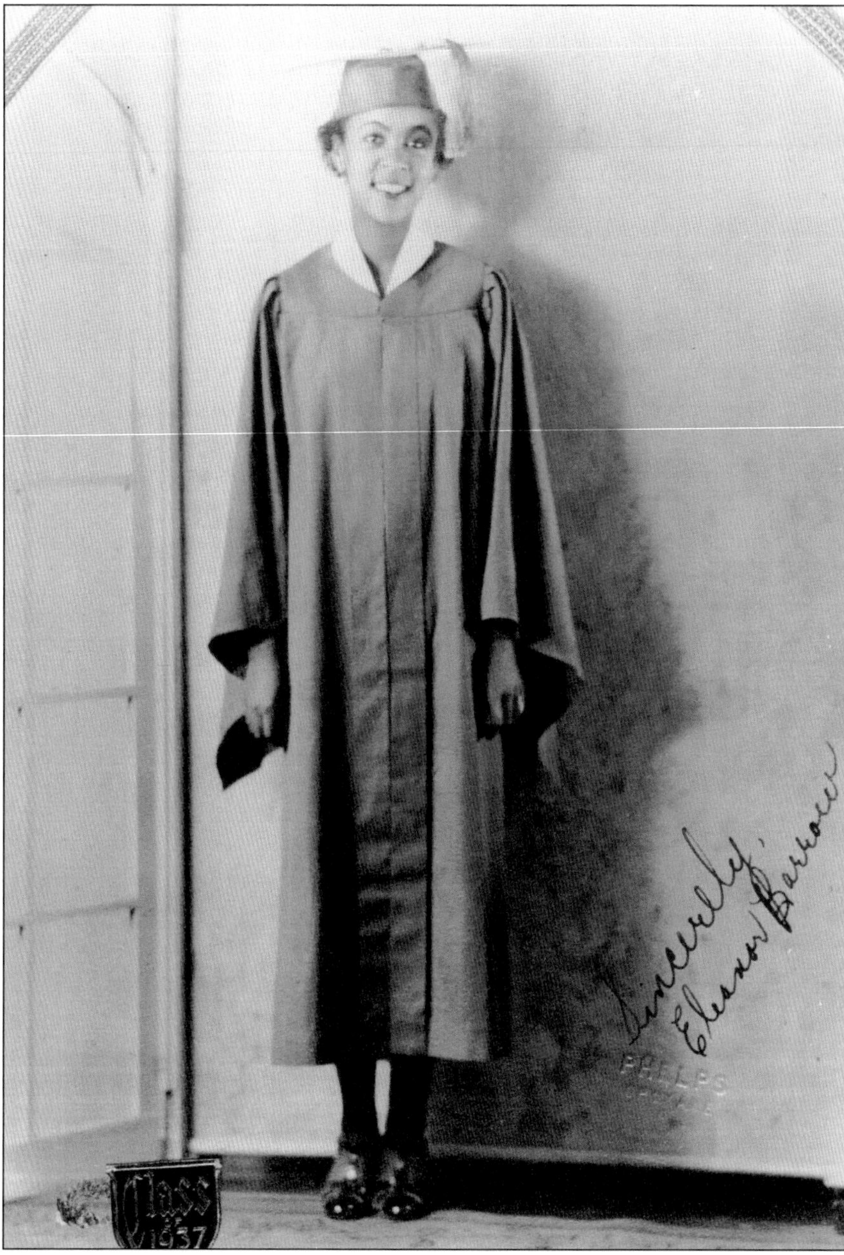

Eleanor Barrow Chase was a personality in her own right. She excelled in academics from grade school through Lewis and Clark High School and on to college and graduate school. She was featured in the magazine *Silhouette* in the February 1940 issue. The article tells about her accomplishments: "Outstanding in collegiate music circles of the Northwest is Eleanor Barrow, junior at Whitworth College, Spokane, Wa. As solo artist and piano accompanist, Miss Barrow will tour with the college quartet and choral groups. In addition, she is an expert typist, and was the first clerical worker at Booker T. Washington Community Center in Spokane." Eleanor Chase graduated magna cum laude from Whitworth College in Spokane with a degree in vocal music. Her beautiful voice was matched by her looks and personality. A women's facility in Spokane is named in her honor. Eleanor (Barrow) Chase, pictured here in 1937, passed away in 2002.

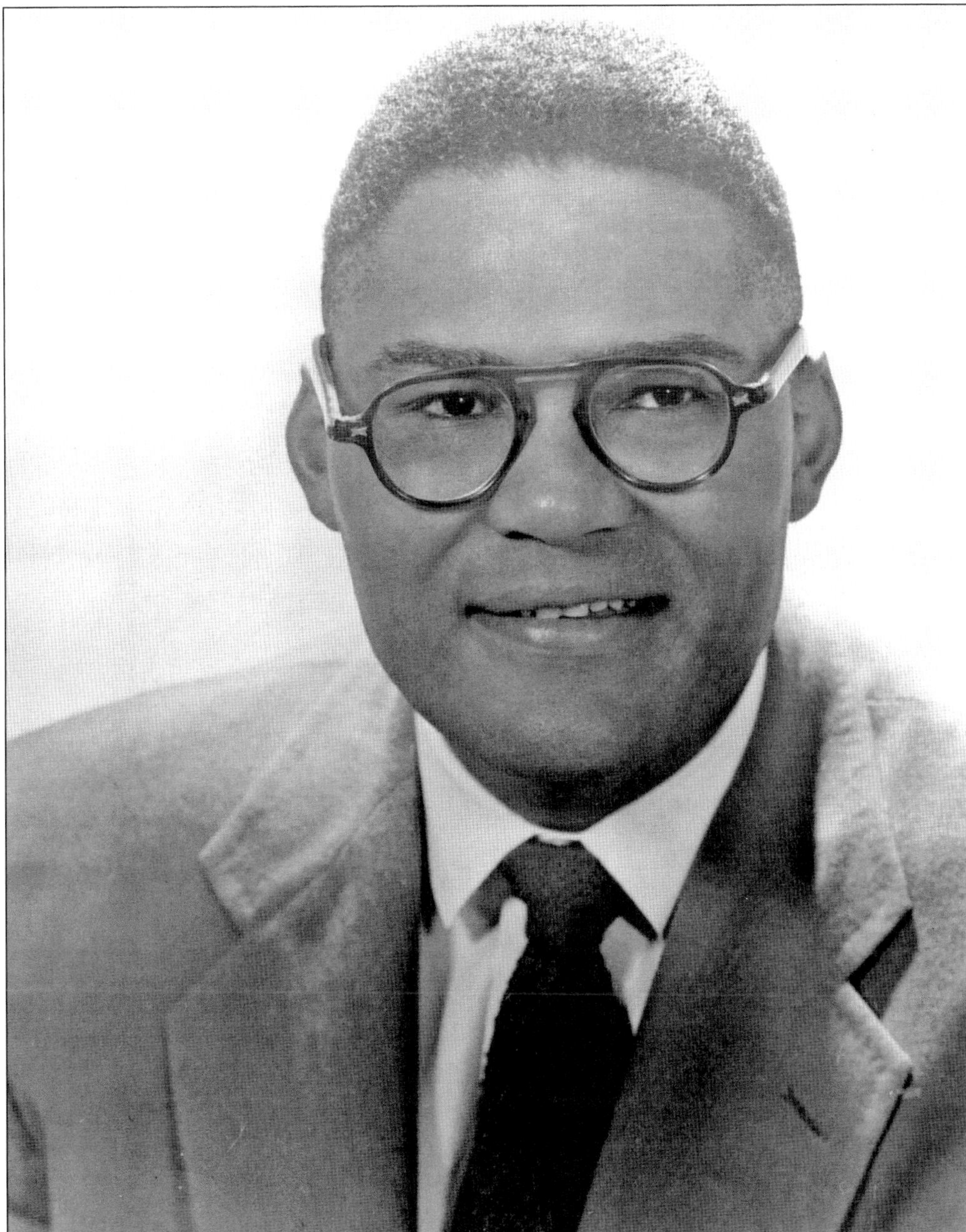

Carl Maxey was born in Tacoma on June 23, 1924, and was given up for adoption by his mother. Spokane residents Carl and Carolyn Maxey adopted him. He became an orphan after Carl Sr. abandoned his wife and baby and Carolyn died. Carl Maxey spent some time in the orphanage but later was rescued by Fr. Cornelius E. Byrne of the Sacred Heart Mission School. Maxey was an exceptional athlete and a good student. He decided, at age 21, to become a lawyer. Maxey was diligent in his pursuit of being a good attorney. Many African Americans went to him for legal advice and to hire him as their attorney. He was a cracker-jack attorney (as they say). He never backed down from a good old legal battle. When he came into the courtroom, he had the air of "Bring it on." This 1950s photograph is of Maxey when he graduated from Gonzaga University.

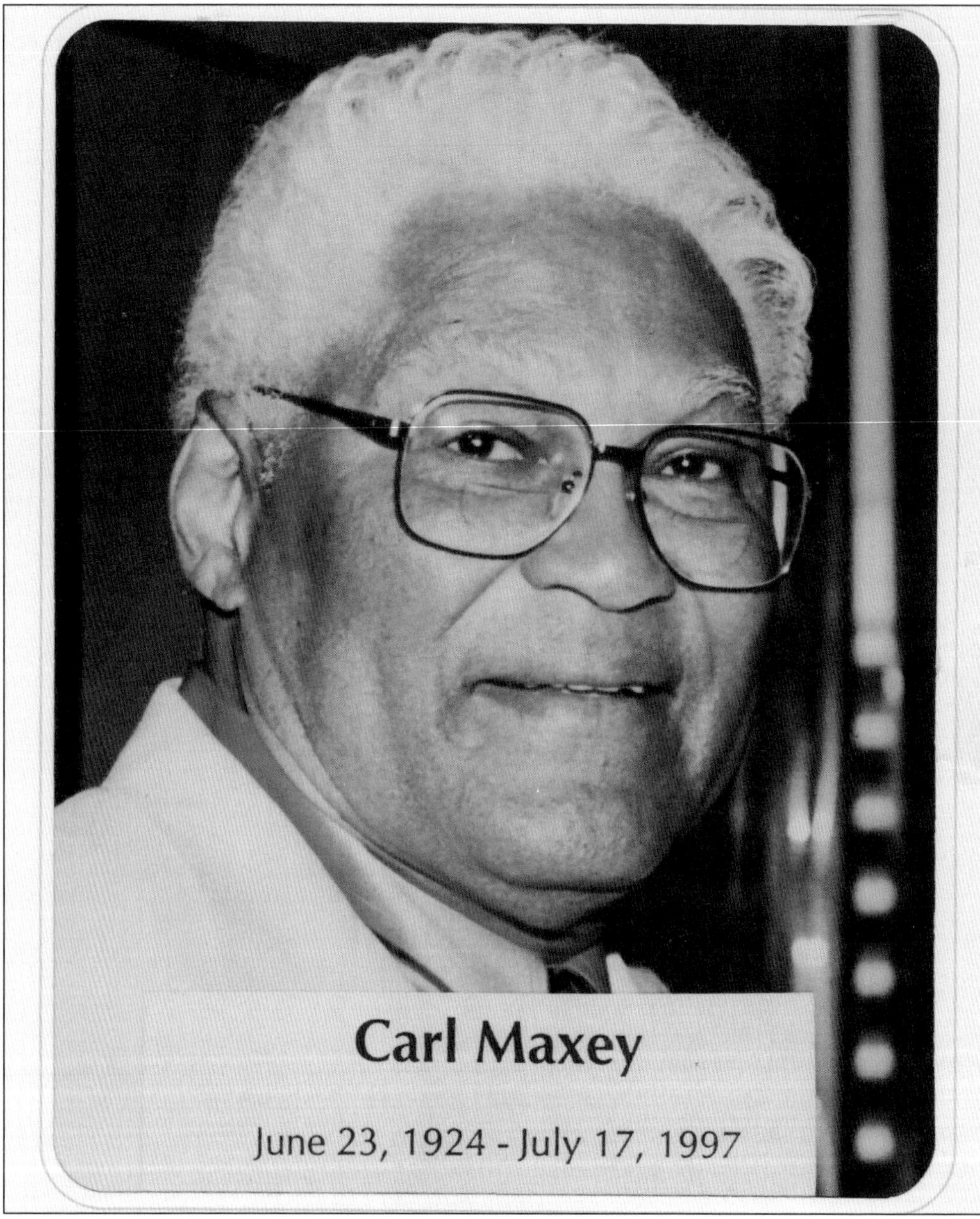

Carl Maxey made a big difference in the legal arena for blacks. An example was in 1961, when the Spokane School Board wanted to close Lincoln Elementary School, where students were primarily African American and Japanese, with some whites. The parents thought they were being discriminated against and went to Maxey with $100 from the PTA. Maxey was a little late to the school board meeting, and they had decided to close the school. When he walked in and sat down next to the parents, the school board went into a quick huddle and announced that they would not close the school that year. Maxey had not spoken, but he won the case. There is much more to be written about Carl Maxey, as Jim Kershner has done in his book, *Carl Maxey: A Fighting Life*. Carl ended his own life on July 7, 1997. The whole city mourned his passing, but black people had lost a hero. Maxey is survived by two sons, Bill and Bevan, and his wife Lou. This photograph is from around 1989.

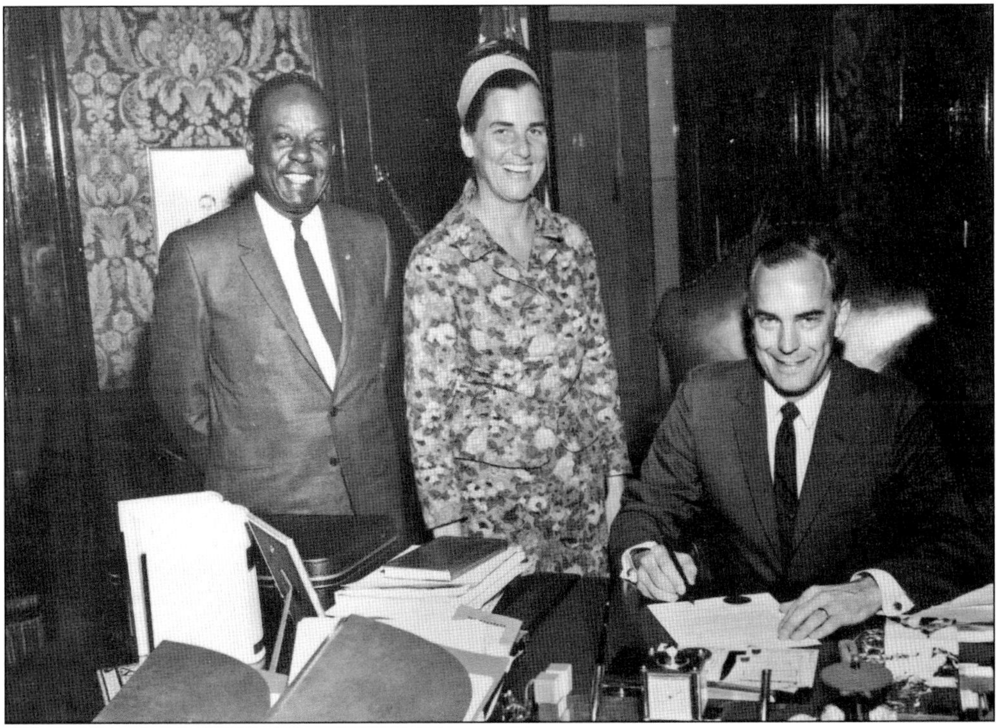

Eugene Breckenridge applied to teach in the Spokane School District, but despite his great credentials, the district said he was not qualified. Attorney Carl Maxey went to the school board and threatened an NAACP lawsuit. Breckenridge was hired. He later became president of the Washington State Council of the United Nations. He is shown with Norma F. Grant and Gov. Dan Evans in an October 26, 1968, photograph.

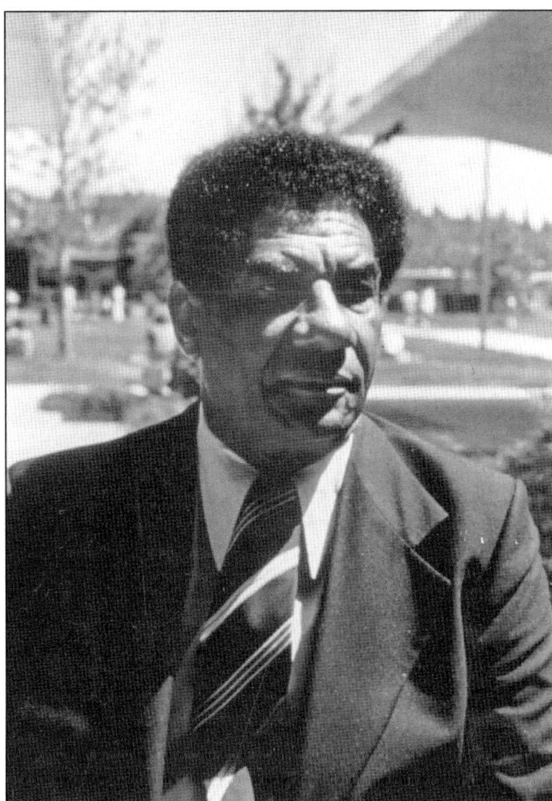

Orlando Fletcher was a social studies teacher at Lewis and Clark High School. The hiring of Eugene Breckenridge opened the door for other hires. Daisy L. Parker was the first black woman teacher in the Spokane schools, according to a 1955 *Spokesman Review* article; however, in the book *All through the Night*, Joseph Franklin wrote that Helen Dundee was the first black woman teacher. This photograph is from about 1978.

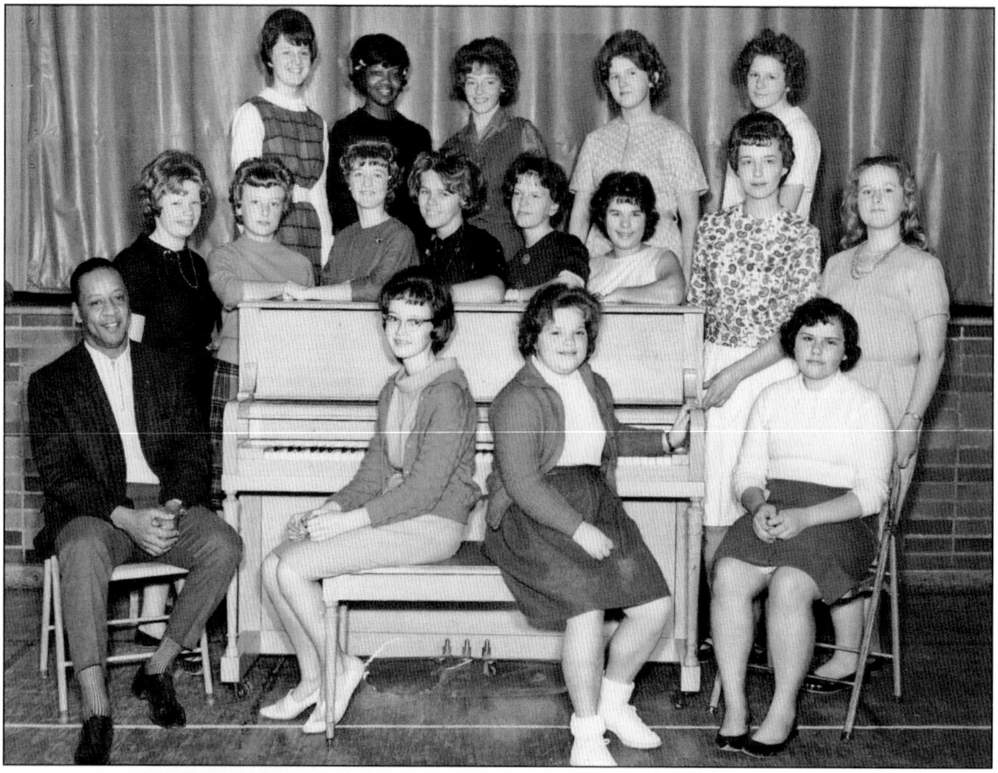

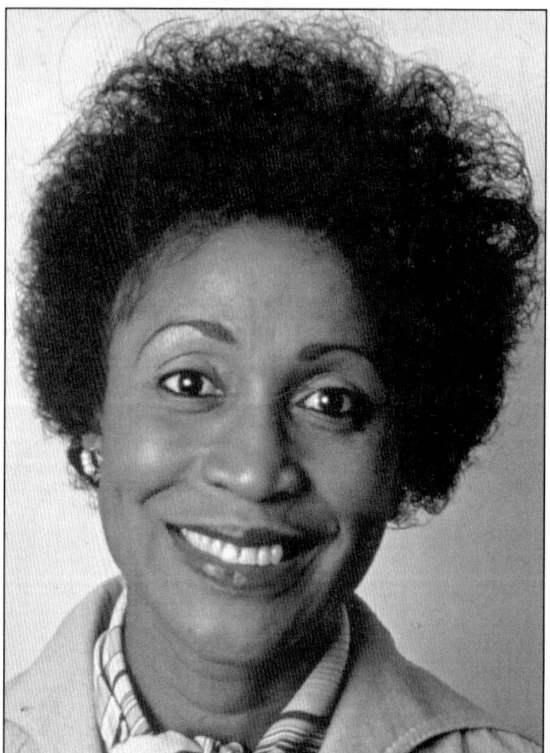

Pictured in the 1960s, Alfonse H. Hill was the first African American music teacher in the Spokane schools, teaching at Hamilton, Washington, and Emerson Elementary Schools and at Havermale and Glover Junior High Schools. Hill sang professionally and directed All-City Choir. He passed away December 18, 1999. He and his wife Gwen have two daughters, Angela and Erica, grandchildren Brandon and Savannah, and son-in-law Robert McDonald. Gwen Lucas is in the third row, second from left. (Courtesy of Gwen Hill.)

Educator Gloria R. Morris, shown in this 1980s photograph, came to Spokane in 1971 and later became the area's first black elementary school principal. She and her husband, Billy V. Morris, are the parents of Billy Jr., Vernon, and Cynthia. Spokane's first black high school principal was Wallace Williams, serving at John Rogers High School for 17 years. The first black woman member of the Spokane School Board was Joyce Bobb-itt.

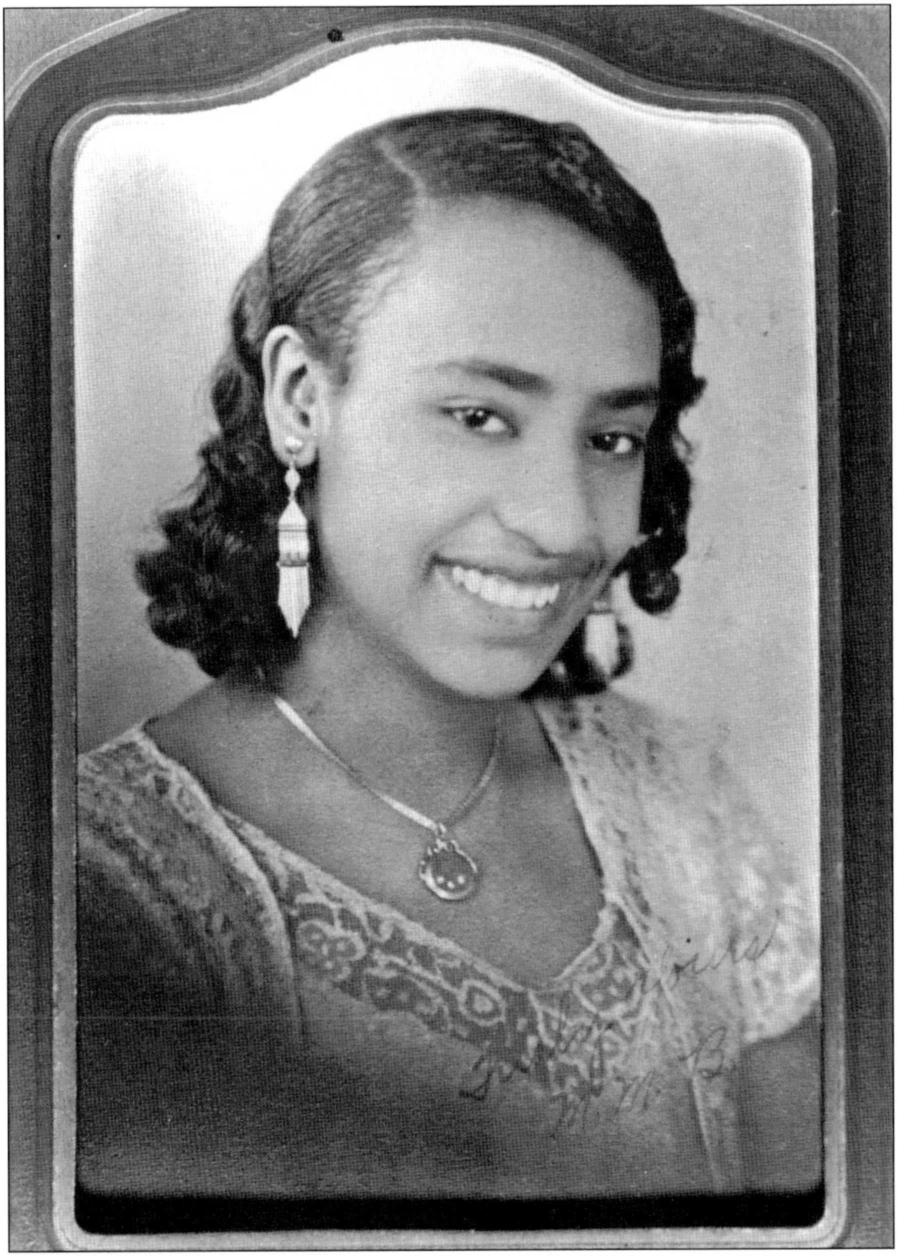

Marjorie Boyd Wellington came to Spokane to live with her grandparents, Mr. and Mrs. Henry Washington. She graduated from Lewis and Clark High School in 1932 and was the first black to graduate from Cheney Normal School (Eastern Washington University) in Cheney, Washington. More than anything else, Wellington wanted to be a black educator in the Spokane Public Schools system. However, weeks before graduation in 1935, a college administrator informed her that she was a "problem" because she was a black woman. He said he did not believe that Spokane was ready for a black schoolteacher. After being told that she would not be hired to teach, she married and worked in various day care centers in the area. Today Eastern Washington University gives the Marjorie Boyd Wellington Academic Excellence Award in her honor. This photograph is from around 1936.

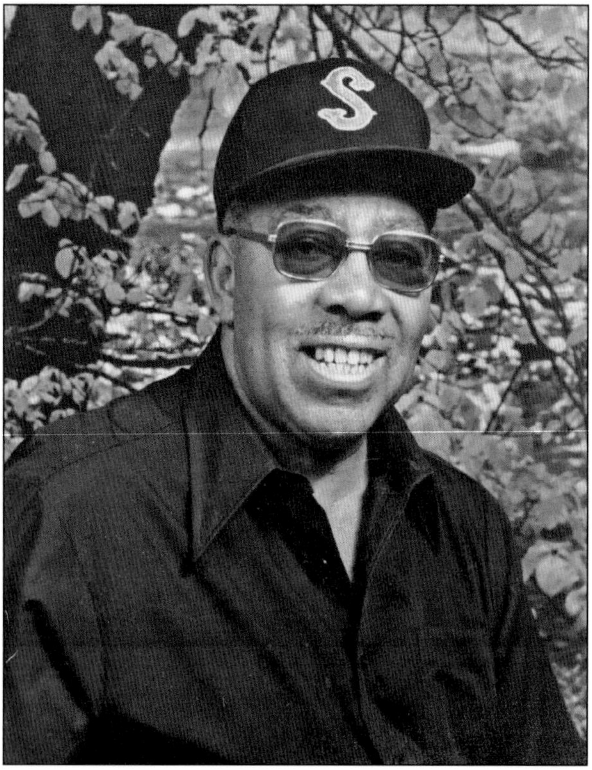

Wallace "Wally" Hagin was born July 4, 1915, in Great Falls, Montana. He attended Spokane's North Central High School and studied mortuary science at the University of Washington. A musician, aviator, and photographer, he was Washington's first African American licensed commercial pilot. Jerrelene Williamson helped Marsha Rooney at Spokane's Northwest Museum of Arts and Culture (MAC) collect 14,000 Hagin images. "Everything I have and everything I've done would have died with me if it had not been for Jerrie," Hagin said. Some of Spokane's African American history is included in the Northwest African American Museum in Seattle.

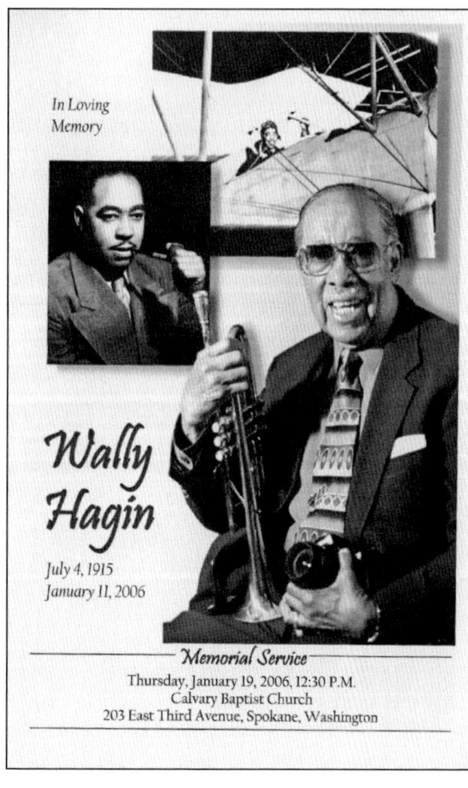

In Loving Memory

Wally Hagin

July 4, 1915
January 11, 2006

Memorial Service

Thursday, January 19, 2006, 12:30 P.M.
Calvary Baptist Church
203 East Third Avenue, Spokane, Washington

This program is from the memorial service for Wally Hagin on January 11, 2006. He is survived by his daughters, Wallene Boone, Los Angeles; and Donna Sherr, Miami; grandchildren Jamila Donaldson, Kamilah Boone, Geoff Sherr, Adam Sherr, Tracy Wellington, and Kendrick Fox; great-grandchildren Nicole and Jeffrey Donaldson; and good friends Pam and Randy Jolibis. He was preceded in death by his wife, Billie Hagin, and his son, Wally III.

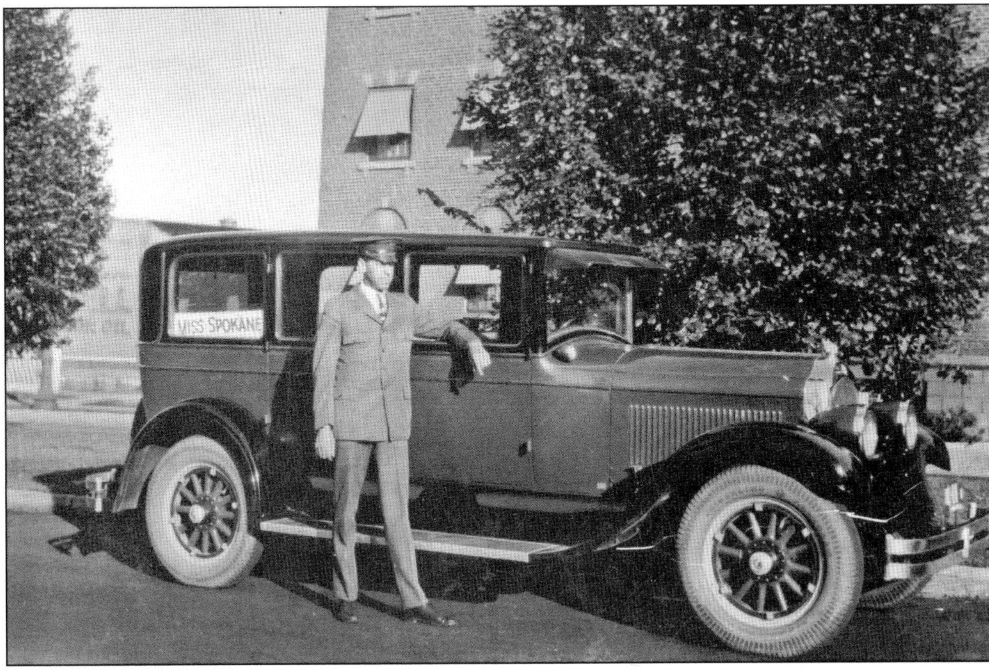

The Spokane Lilac Festival has been a longtime tradition in Spokane. Each year, the town gathers for festivities, fun, and a parade. Featured in the parade is Miss Spokane. Seen here in about 1930 is Wallace Hagin Sr., driver for Miss Spokane in the parade. The auto is a Willys Knight.

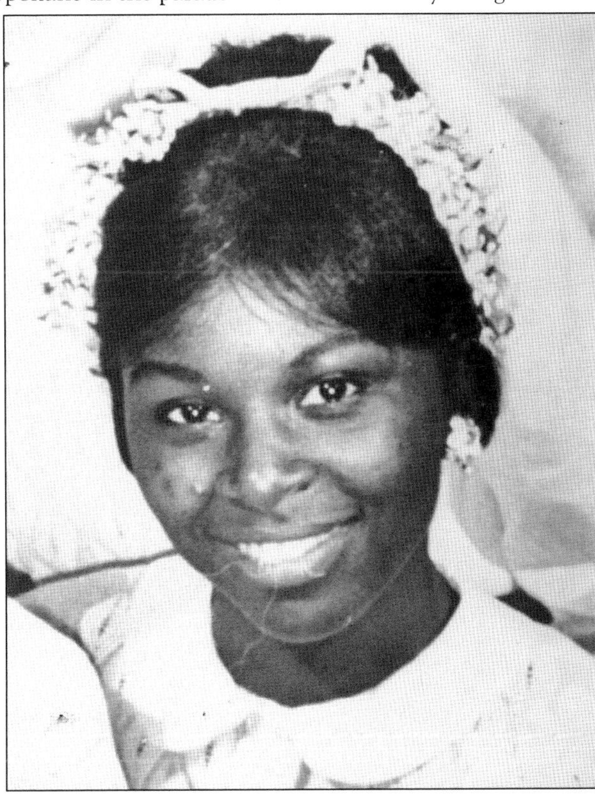

This lovely lady is Princess Gail Caldwell of Marycliff High School, the first "Negro" (as written in the newspaper) ever to be named a Lilac Princess in Spokane. She is the daughter of Mr. and Mrs. Jesse Caldwell. The account is from the *Spokesman Review* dated Wednesday, April 10, 1963.

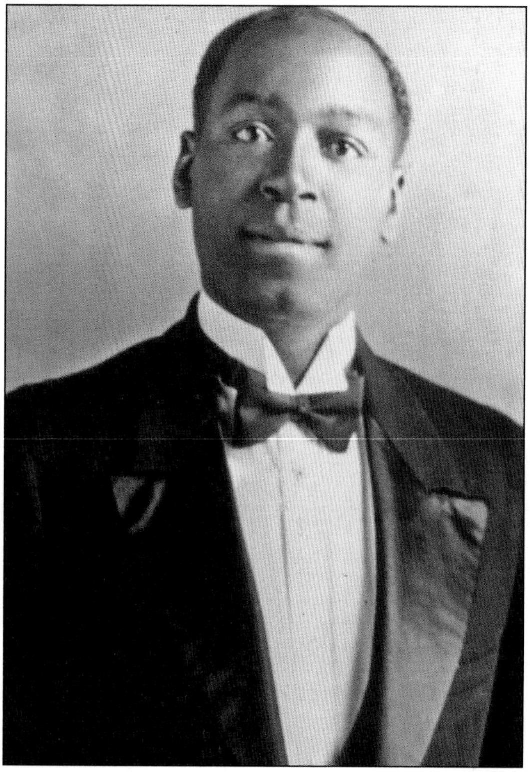

Earl Coates, born in Grand Junction, Tennessee, came to Spokane as a boy. Coates was a past master of the Masons. He was well known for his beautiful voice and toured throughout the Northwest and Canada in a quartet and as a soloist. He wrote the song, "I Have a Hard Time." This photograph is from around 1933.

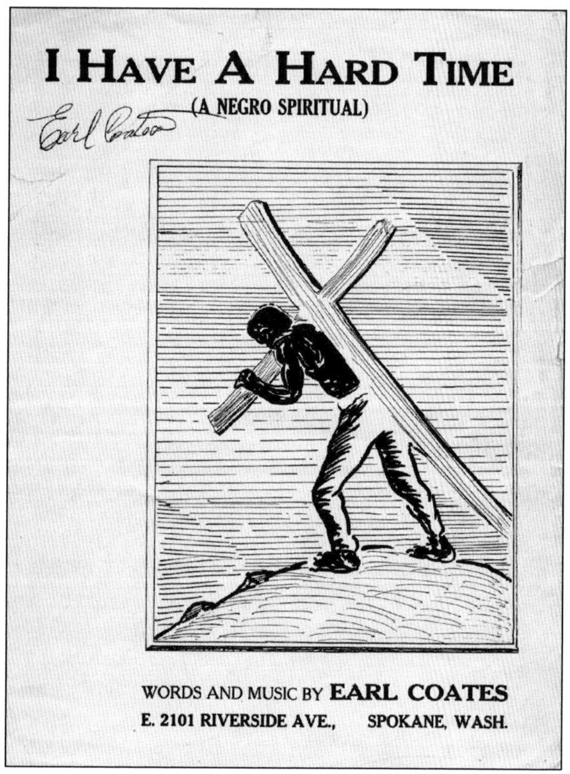

This is the sheet music for the song Earl Coates wrote. Some of the lyrics are: "I know the Lord's going to hear me pray—I have a hard time living in this old world; I sing and pray all along the way, I have a hard time living in this old world." The sheet music for this "negro spiritual" is from around 1933.

Shown here around 1939, Buck Pierce Campbell was born April 20, 1906, in Spokane to Benjamin and Daisy Campbell. He was a super athlete at Lewis and Clark High School and the first black to play in the Spokane Baseball League. Campbell attended Delaney College to study radio and television and was an engineer for NBC. He and his wife, Seletta, retired in Spokane. He passed away August 7, 1989.

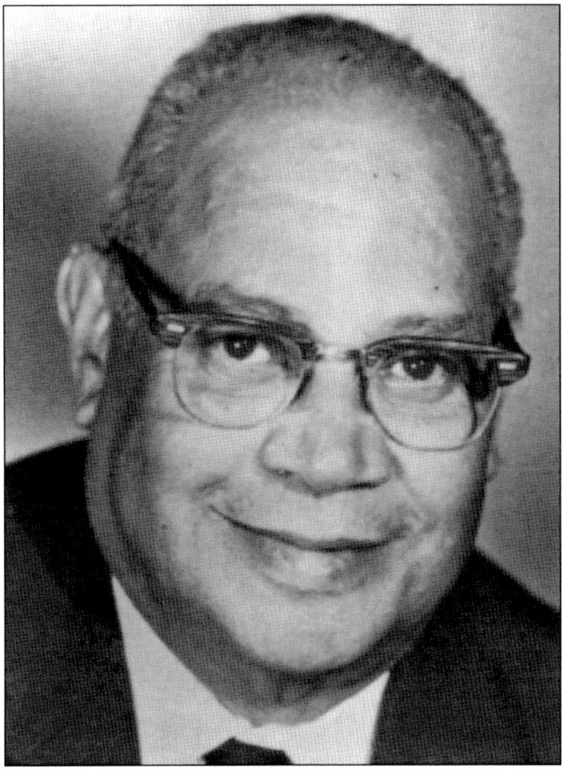

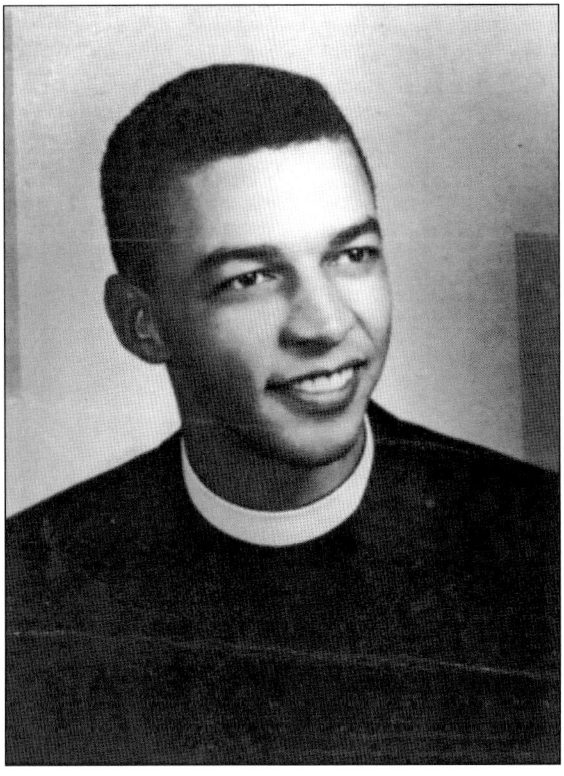

Fr. John Orville Hopkins was the first black priest ordained in Spokane's Catholic Diocese. Born in Missoula, Montana, he and his parents, John and Katrina Hopkins, moved to Spokane, and he graduated from Gonzaga Preparatory School as valedictorian. He was the first black person granted a doctorate in philosophy by Columbia University. Before his death from cancer in 1989, Father Hopkins, shown here around 1961, completed the book *Racism: A Philosophical Perspective*.

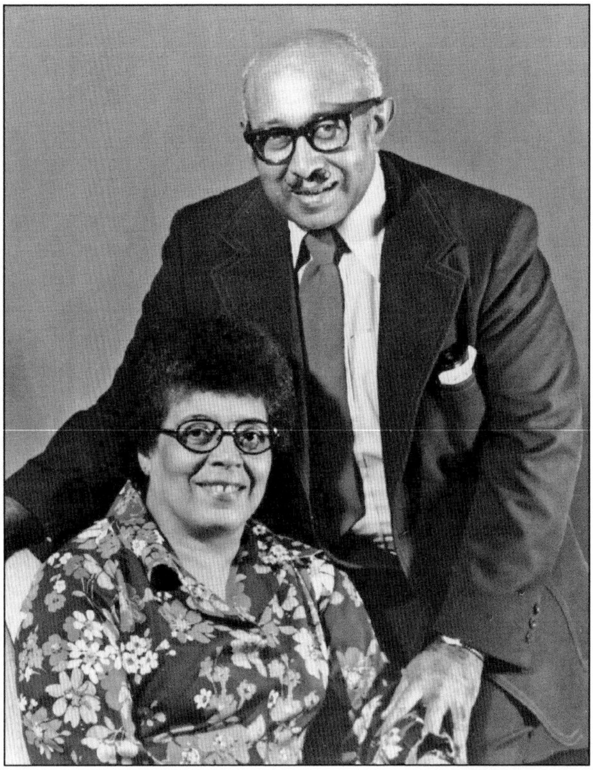

On May 16, 1979, Frances (Nichols) Scott became the first black woman attorney in Spokane. Scott is shown with her husband, Vernon, a chiropractor. She is the mother of two children, Diane Scott Mackey and Kelly Vernon Scott. Scott and 34 other graduates of Gonzaga University Law School were sworn in as members of the Washington State Bar Association. The photograph is from around 1960.

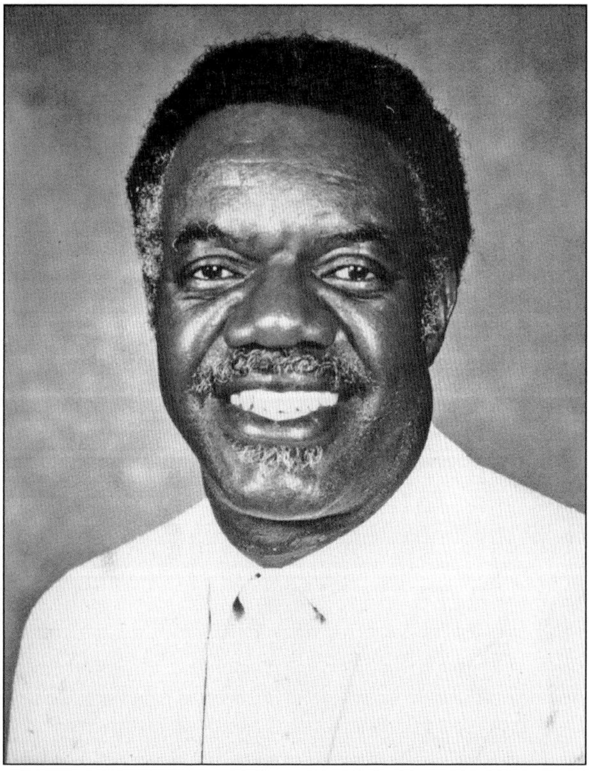

Manuel Brown, shown here about 1980, came to Washington in 1960 with his wife Emelda and their family. He was stationed at Fairchild Air Force Base. Brown retired from the military in 1971 and went to work for the Washington Water Power Company a year later. Brown was the first black foreman with WWP (now Avista). The Brown family are members of Calvary Baptist Church.

Spokane native Dr. Mona Lake Jones is the "poet laureate" of Seattle. She has produced poetry books (*The Color of Culture I* and *The Color of Culture II*), tapes, and CDs. She has traveled extensively, speaking to educational institutions, civic groups, and conventions. She is the daughter of Sylvester and Pauline Lake, the wife of Joe Jones, and the mother of Brent and Dana. The photograph is from the 1990s.

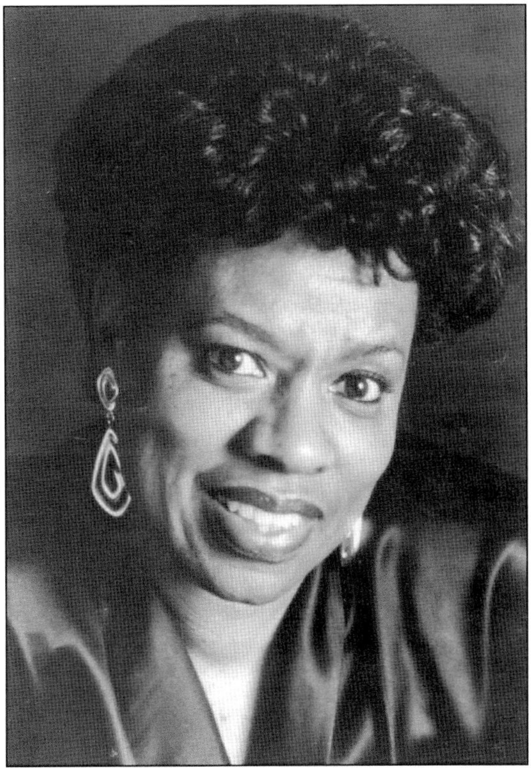

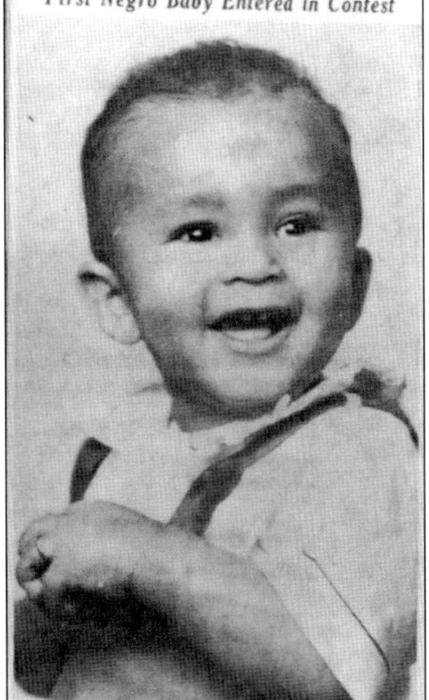

First Negro Baby Entered in Contest

For the first time in 14 years of Chronicle Baby Spokane contests, a Negro baby has been entered. This happy little fellow, Terry Jon Johnson, is the son of Mr. and Mrs. Oliver R. Johnson, N4408 Post. He is eight months old, has six teeth, weighs 20½ pounds and stands alone. His father is widely known locally as one of the Johnson Brothers trio, Negro spiritual singers. Master Terry Jon is going to be a doctor, if Mr. Johnson has his way, he says.

The first Negro in the *Spokane Daily Chronicle*'s baby contest was Terry Jon Johnson, son of Mr. and Mrs. Oliver Johnson, shown here around 1940. This photo takes me back to the "memories of my mind" of African Americans in Spokane; people who shaped my life, and whom I remember with affection: the Nashes, Hopkins, Mims, Amy Carter, the Sepolens, Fishers, Duncans, Edmonds, Carters, Potters, Odessa Mash, the Dorseys, and Ross and Gertrude Mapps. (The whole African American community mourned when the Mapps' son Selassie drowned in the Spokane River. We were all so close.)

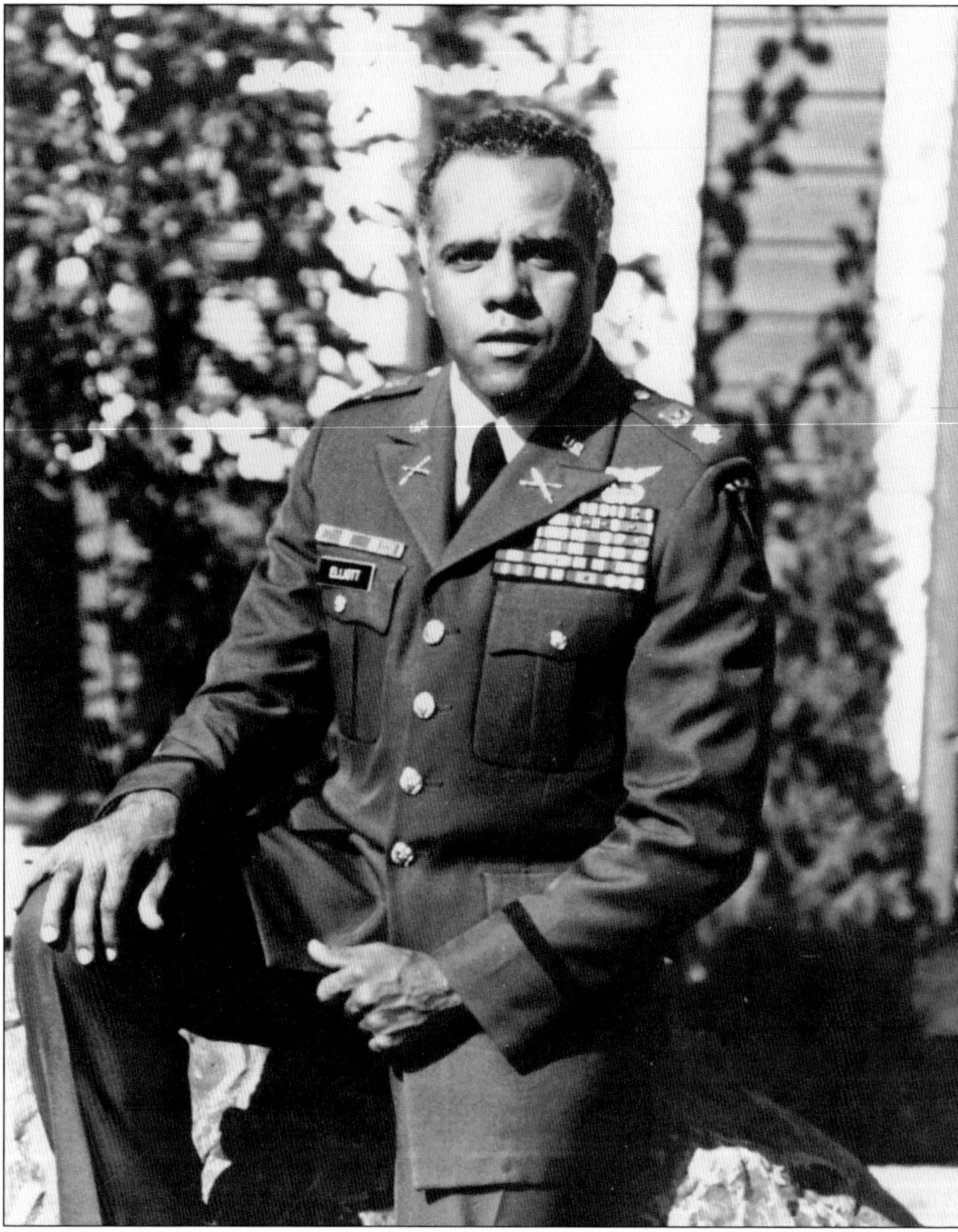

James E. "Bo" Elliott was born November 21, 1945, in Spokane. He was the oldest of six children of Mildred and Clifford Elliott. James graduated from St. Anthony's grade school in 1960 and Gonzaga Prep in 1964, where he played varsity football, basketball, and track. He also was senior class president. Elliott attended the University of San Francisco, where he was a sports editor for the school paper. He received a bachelor's degree in journalism from Eastern Washington College and a master's degree in public administration from Penn State University. Elliott served in the army for more than 30 years, including three tours in Vietnam as a helicopter pilot. He received many medals, including a Silver Star, two Bronze Stars, three Purple Hearts, and two Distinguished Flying Crosses. James Elliott passed away January 24, 2004, leaving behind numerous survivors, including his mother. He was buried at Arlington National Cemetery on February 25, 2004.

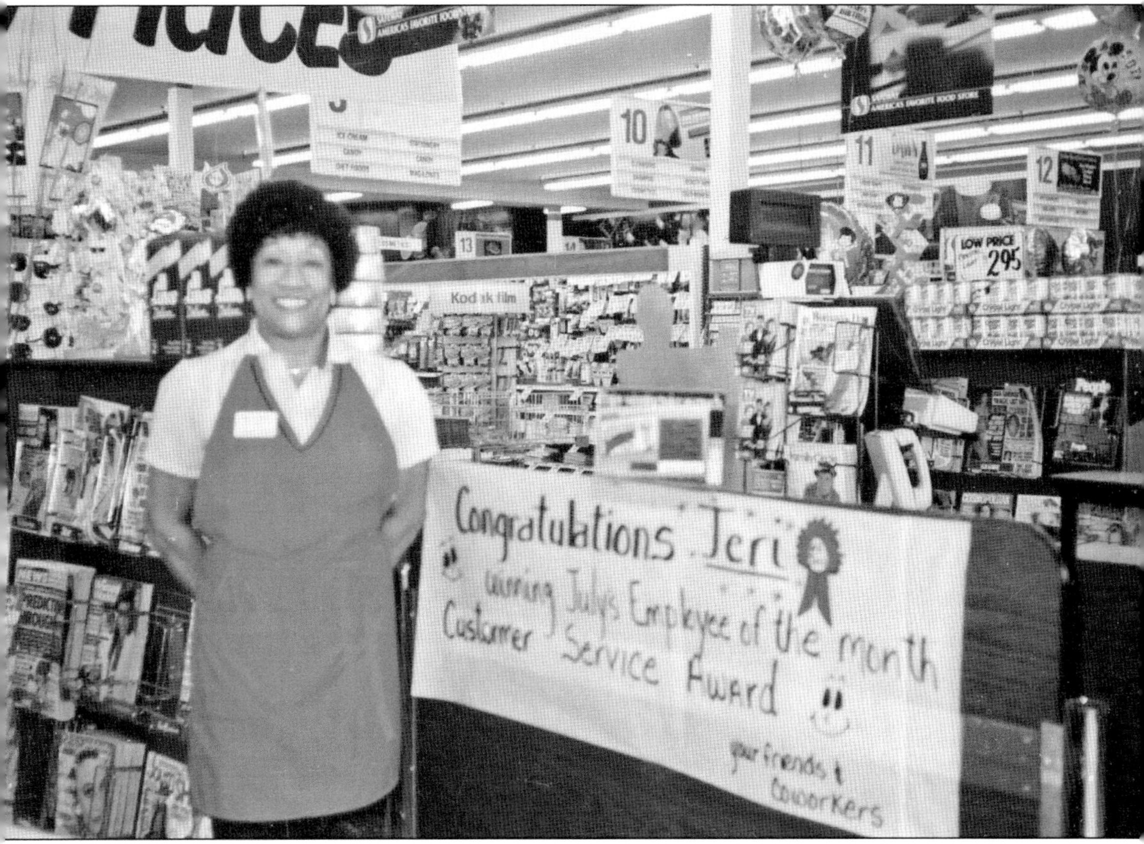

Jerrelene Hill attended Hamilton Elementary School and graduated from Rogers High School in 1950. She is the daughter of Abner (Breckenridge) and Hester Hill. In October 1950 Jerrelene married Sam Williamson, who owned a company called The Floor Doctor that he inherited from his uncle. When their youngest of five children was school age, Jerrelene applied for a job at the Bell Telephone Company. As she left the office, she saw the receptionist tear up her application and throw it in the wastebasket. In 1965 she was hired as a checker at Safeway stores, becoming the first African American to work for a Spokane supermarket as a checker. Jerrelene, pictured here around 1979, worked for Safeway for 27 years, retiring in 1992, but she has not forgotten the day she waited on a man of about 50 who told her, "I wish I had a baby that looked like you. I would take it out and drown it." Jerrelene recalls, "I was stunned. I turned back to my work, but the tears were stinging my eyes."

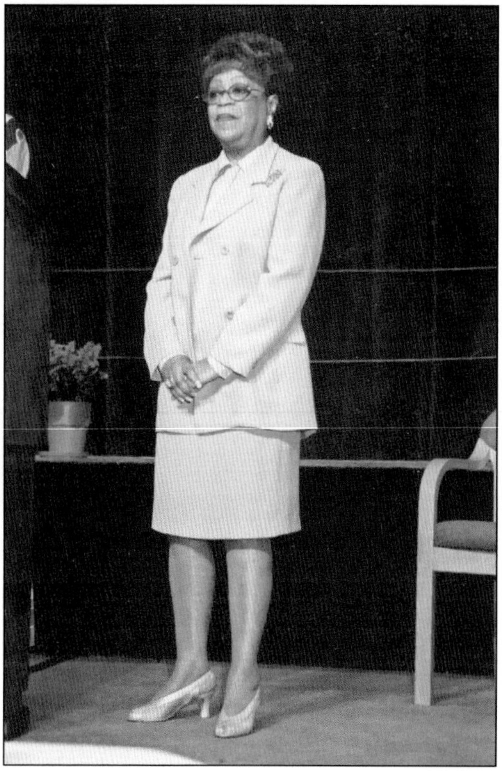

V. Anne Smith, born in Bluefield, West Virginia, came to Spokane in 1968 with her husband Jim and their son. V. Anne found work at Washington Trust Bank. Her husband, after retiring from the military, earned a master's degree and then was personnel director for the City of Spokane. V. Anne, shown here around 2000, has been president of the Spokane branch of the NAACP for several years.

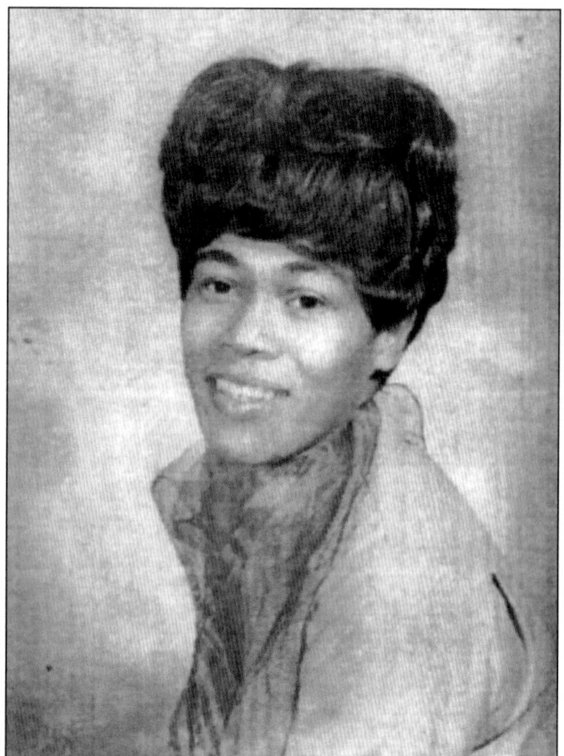

Eileen Kelly Thomas was born July 22, 1936, in New York City. She came to Spokane in 1962 and married Cask Thomas Sr. She was the first black and the first woman to be an animal control officer. Eileen Thomas was given much recognition, including being honored by President Clinton in 1966 for her work as president of the Spokane NAACP. She passed away March 19, 2007.

Rev. Percy ("Happy") Watkins gives a rendition of the "I Have a Dream" speech each year in Spokane on Dr. Martin Luther King Jr. Day. Audiences stand and cheer at the end. Ivan Bush, equal opportunity officer for Spokane School District, and Reverend Watkins, pastor of New Hope Baptist Church, were among the founders of the commemoration and march in Spokane in 1984. This photograph is from 1989.

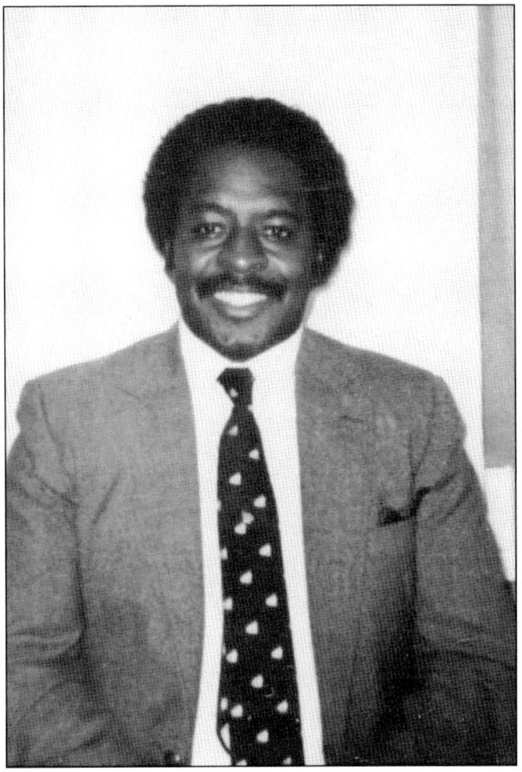

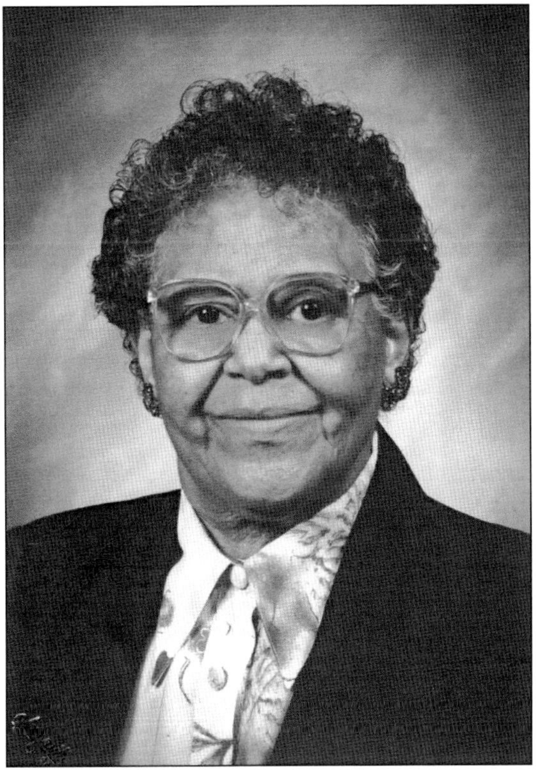

Ruth N. Nichols's education includes a master of arts degree in rehabilitation and counseling psychology from the University of Oregon and a bachelor's degree in sociology from Holy Names College. Pictured here in the 1990s, she was an official delegate to the White House Conference on Aging and a member of the Spokane Chapter of Delta Sigma Theta Sorority. Her special interest is a children's school in Montego Bay, Jamaica.

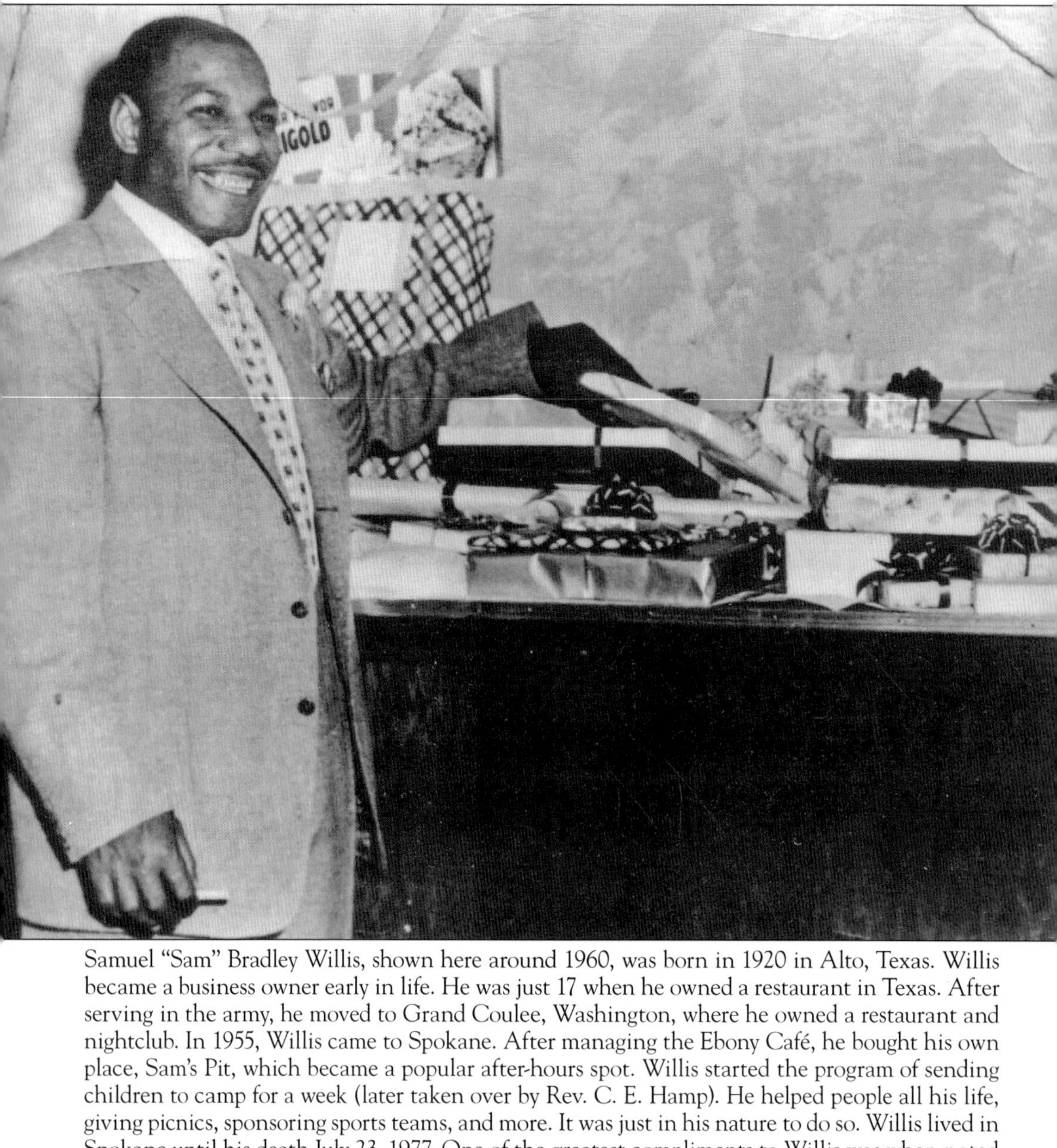

Samuel "Sam" Bradley Willis, shown here around 1960, was born in 1920 in Alto, Texas. Willis became a business owner early in life. He was just 17 when he owned a restaurant in Texas. After serving in the army, he moved to Grand Coulee, Washington, where he owned a restaurant and nightclub. In 1955, Willis came to Spokane. After managing the Ebony Café, he bought his own place, Sam's Pit, which became a popular after-hours spot. Willis started the program of sending children to camp for a week (later taken over by Rev. C. E. Hamp). He helped people all his life, giving picnics, sponsoring sports teams, and more. It was just in his nature to do so. Willis lived in Spokane until his death July 23, 1977. One of the greatest compliments to Willis was when noted attorney Carl Maxey called him "a saint sinner kind of a dude." (Courtesy of May and Ray Hill.)

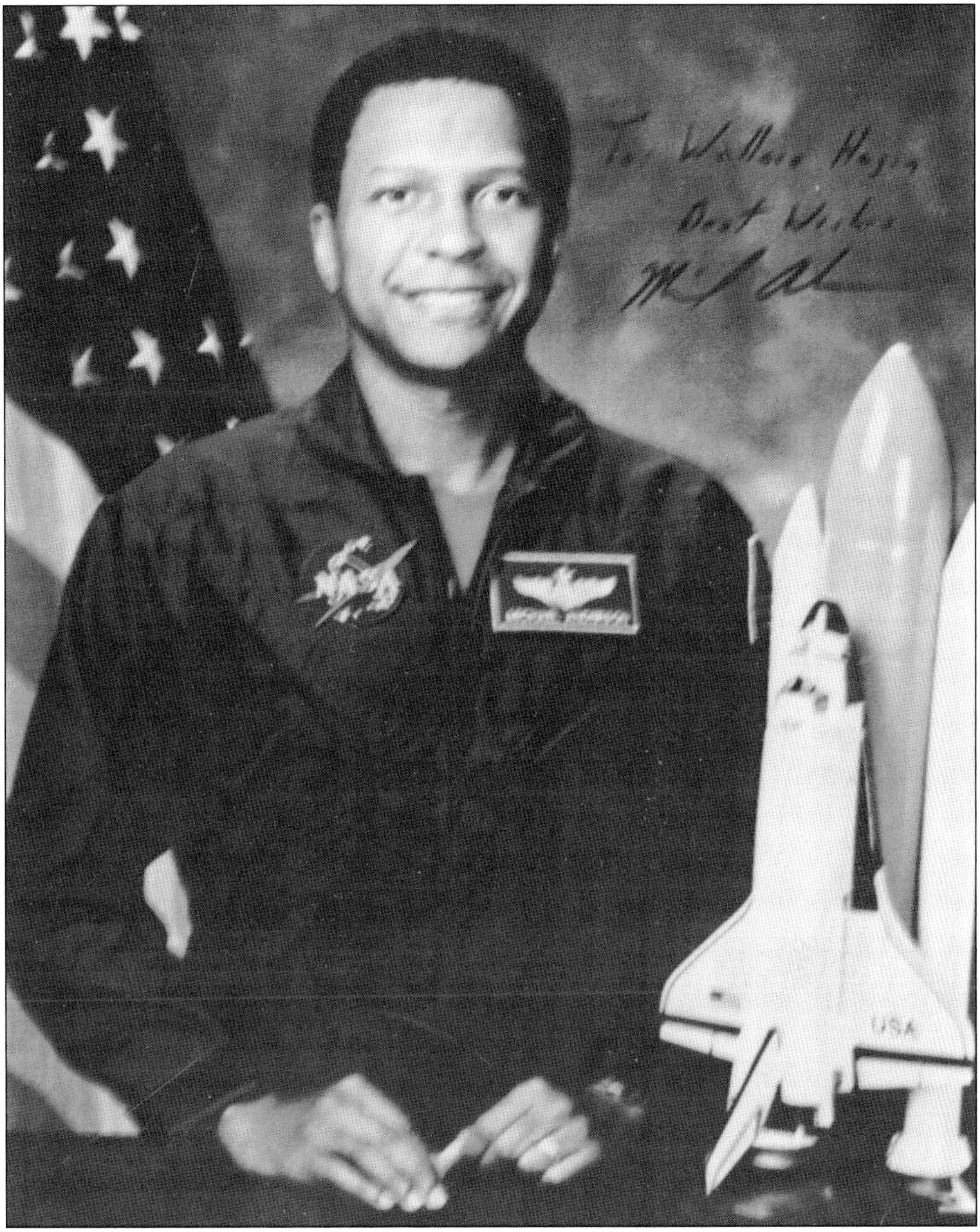

Michael P. Anderson was born December 25, 1959, in Plattsburgh, New York; however, he always considered Spokane, Washington, to be his home. Anderson graduated from Cheney High School in Cheney, Washington, in 1977. He earned a bachelor of science degree in physics/astronomy from the University of Washington in 1981 and a master of science degree in physics from Creighton University in 1990. When Anderson graduated from the University of Washington in 1981, he was commissioned a second lieutenant. He was selected by NASA in December 1994 and reported to the Johnson Space Center in March 1995. Anderson died February 1, 2003, over the southern United States when space shuttle *Columbia* and her crew perished during re-entry. He is survived by his wife Sandy and their two children. Anderson is the son of Barbara and Bobby Anderson of Spokane. This c. 2001 photograph is autographed to Wallace ("Wally") Hagin.

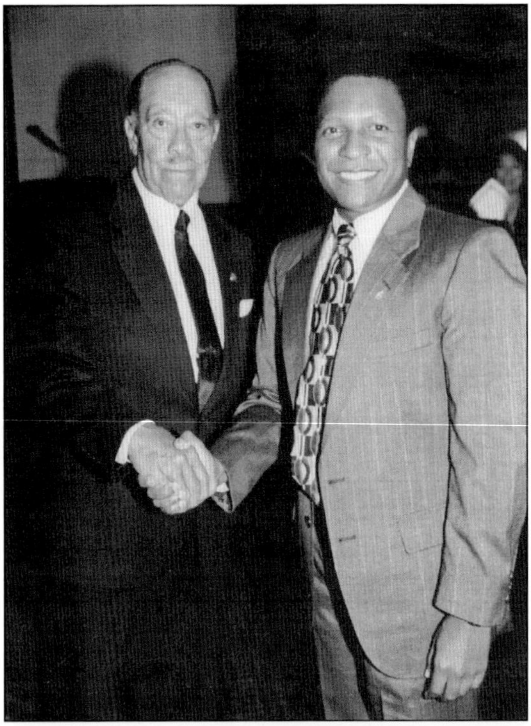

This rare *c.* 2000 photograph is of Wally Hagin, left, and Michael P. Anderson at a banquet in their honor. They were, respectively, the first black licensed pilot in the state of Washington and Spokane's first black astronaut. Hagin was very proud of this photograph and wanted to share it with everyone. He gave it to the Spokane Northwest Black Pioneers for its collection.

Emperor Haile Selassie, heir to a dynasty that traced its origins to the 13th century and from there, by tradition, back to King Solomon and the Queen of Sheba, came to Spokane on his tour of this country in 1954. This photograph shows him at a reception at the Ridpath Hotel. Sylvia and Mona Lake, local young women, attended the affair.

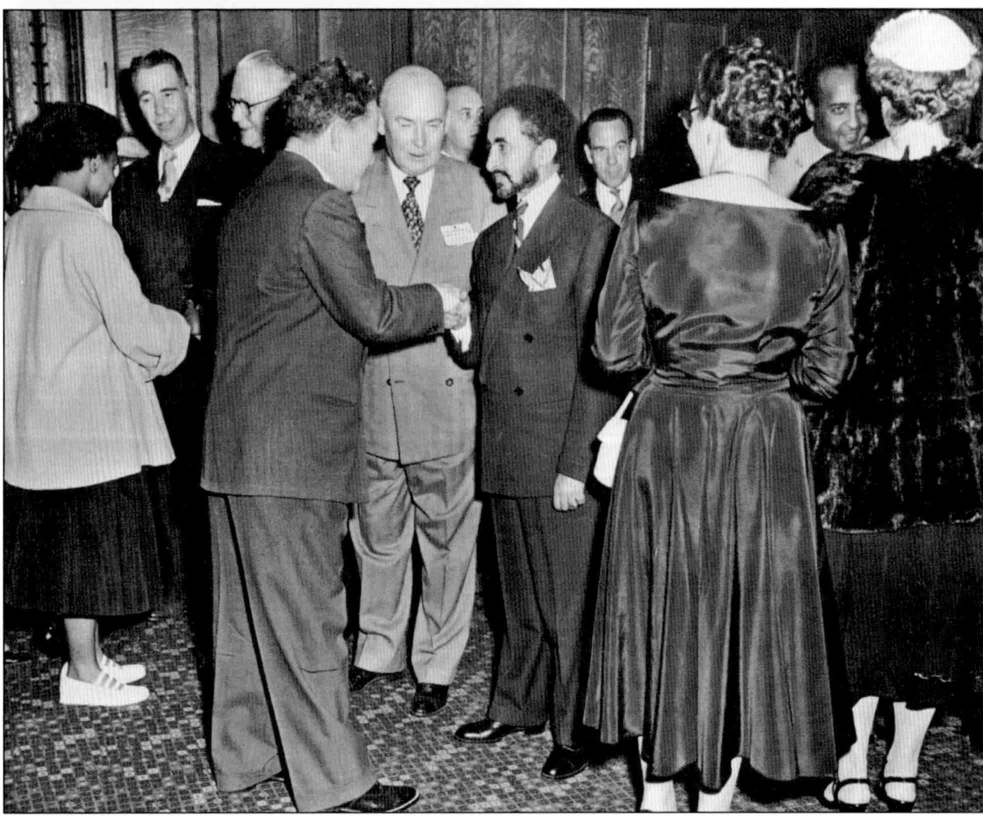

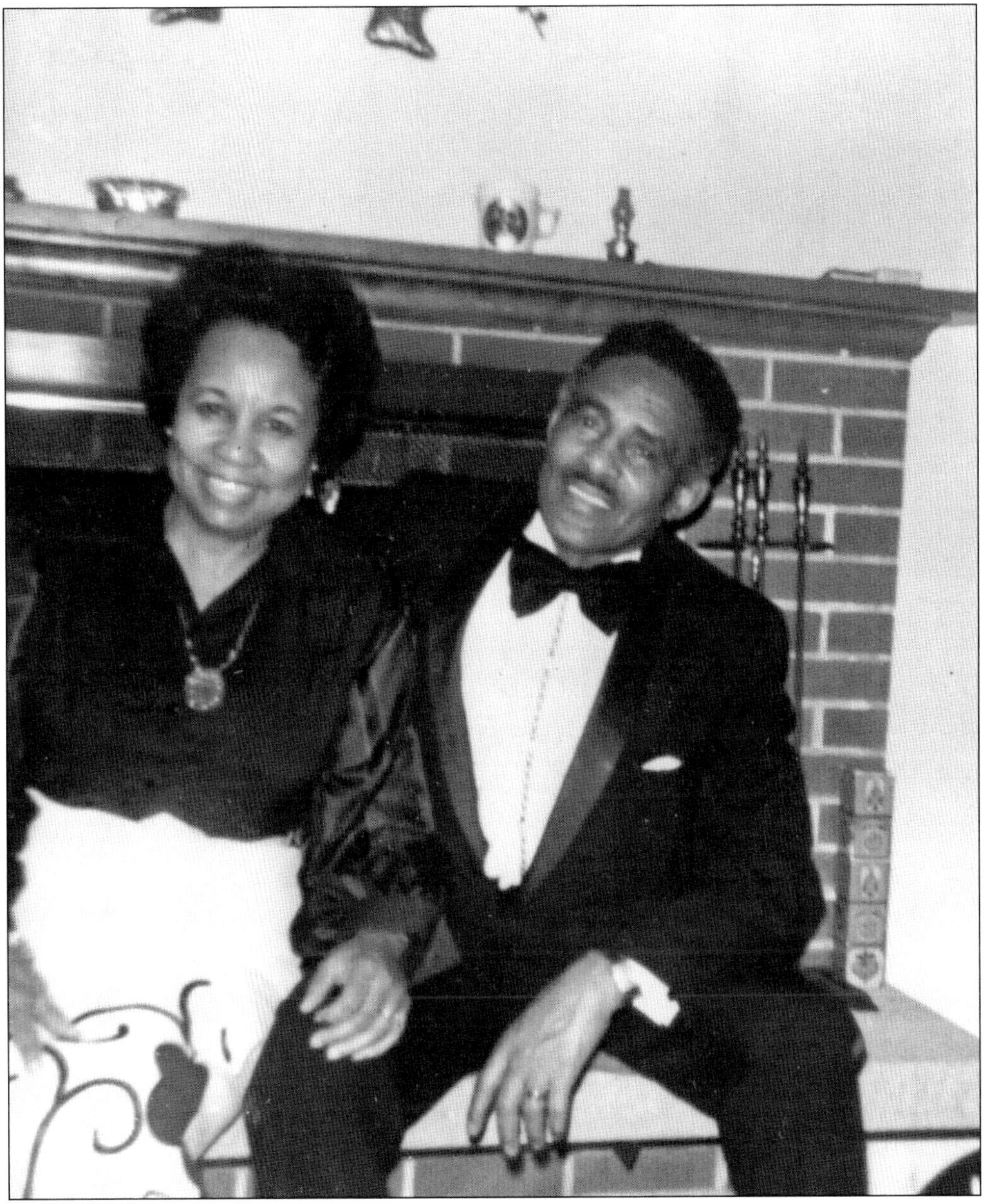

Sylvester and Pauline Lake came to Spokane from Coulee Dam, Washington, where he had worked on the Grand Coulee Dam Project. Having been an expert heavy equipment operator, he got a job working at the Kaiser Aluminum plant in Spokane. Later, through diligence and hard work, he became the first black foreman for the Kaiser Aluminum plant. The Lake family settled into the Spokane community and became very involved in community and civic affairs. They and their two daughters, Sylvia and Mona, were longtime members of Calvary Baptist Church. The Lakes were the first husband and wife to serve as grand master and grand worthy matron of the Prince Hall Masons and Order of the Eastern Stars at the same time. Sylvester Lake, an excellent orator, was known as Candy Man for the pocketful of treats he was always ready to share. He passed away January 21, 2006. Pauline Lake passed away December 6, 2007. This photograph is from about 1960.

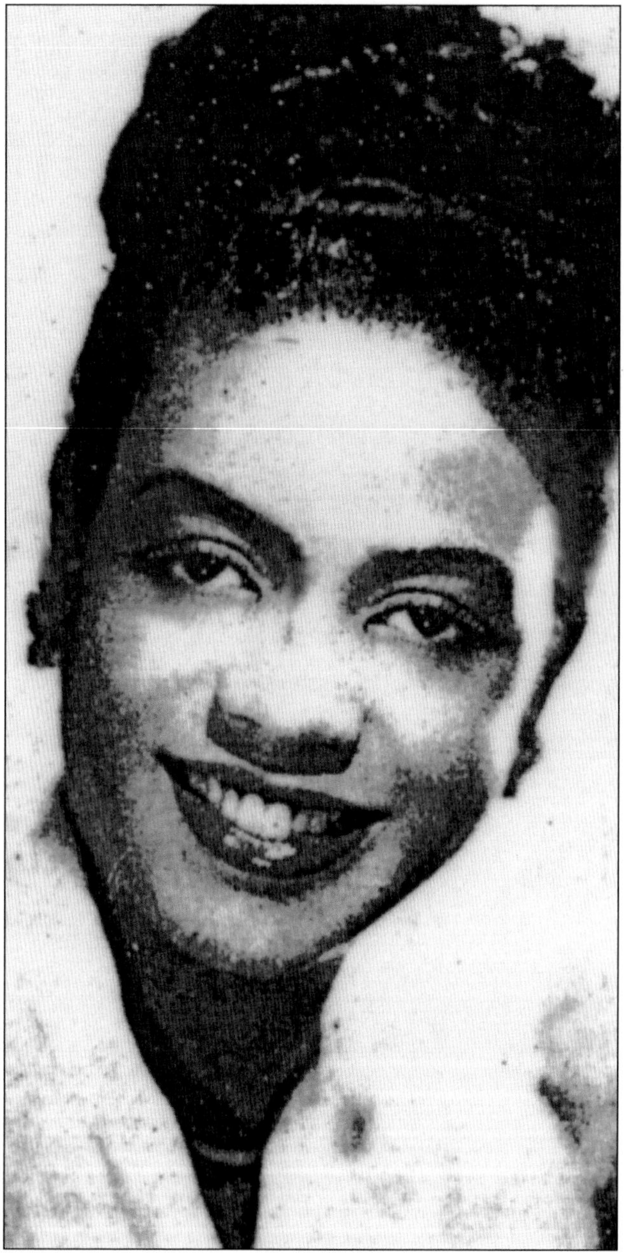

Hazel Scott, a gifted pianist, singer, and actress, came to Spokane in February 1949. Shown here around 1946, she was the wife of Adam Clayton Powell Jr., the outspoken U.S. representative from Harlem, New York. While traveling to Spokane for a concert, she stopped in Pasco, Washington, and was refused service at a local eating place because of her race. She and her husband sued the owners of the restaurant for $50,000 in damages. The trial was held in Spokane, where the owners of the restaurant denied that she was a victim of racism but claimed that she was belligerent in her actions and demeanor. However, in the testimony of Blanche Utz, one of the owners, she admitted that the restaurant's policy included not serving "Negroes." After much deliberation, the Powells won the case. (This account is from the book *Hazel Scott: A Career Curtailed,* by Prof. Dwayne Mack of Berea College, Kentucky.)

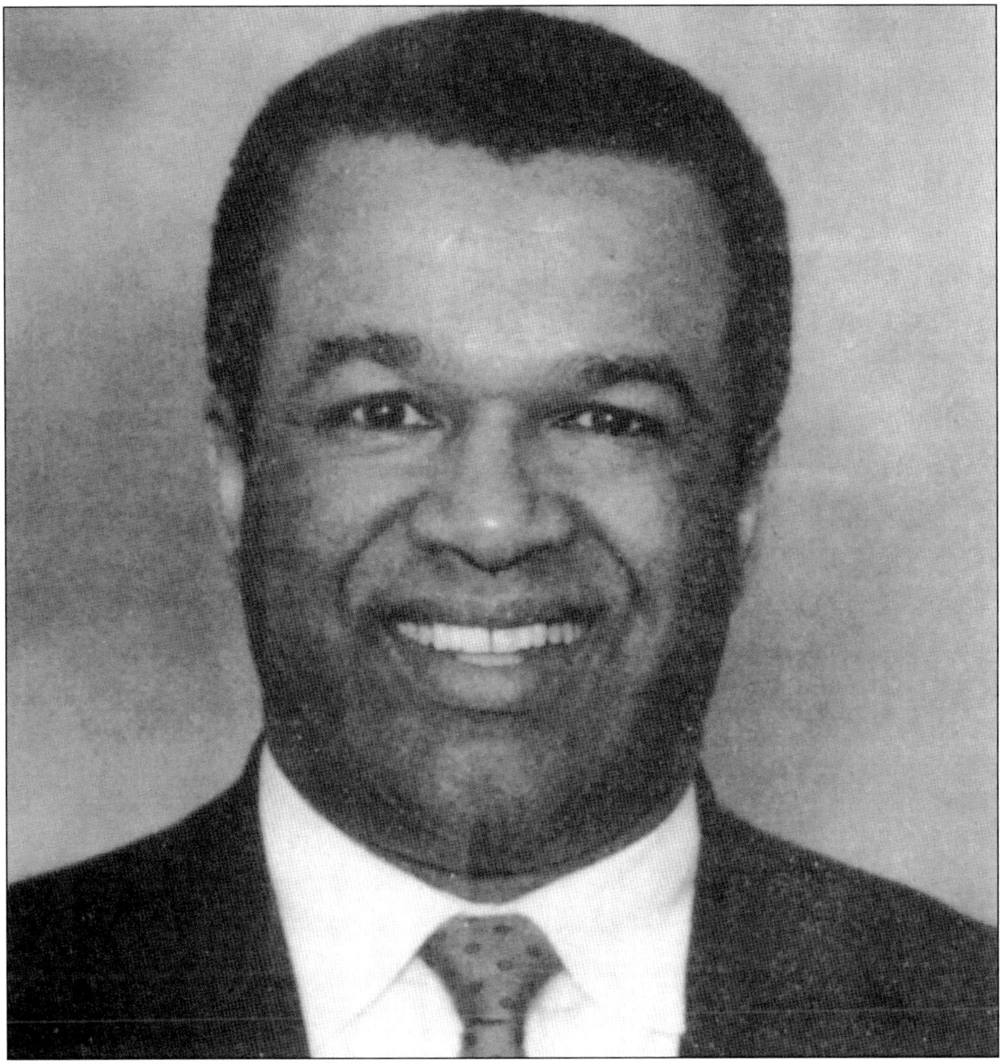

Ronald Cordell Sims was born July 5, 1948, to Rev. James Sims Sr. and Lydia T. Sims. He graduated from Lewis and Clark High School in Spokane and attended Central Washington University in Ellensburg, where he was student body president and earned a bachelor of arts degree in psychology. After graduation, he worked in the office of the Washington state attorney general and for the Federal Trade Commission for the offenders' program of the City of Seattle. He was appointed as King County executive when Gary Locke was elected governor in 1996, and then Sims won elections in 2001 and 2005. In 2009, Ron Sims was appointed deputy secretary of the U.S. Department of Housing and Urban Development in President Obama's administration. He and his wife Cayan Topacio have three sons, Douglas, Daniel, and Aaron. This photograph is from May 17, 1990.

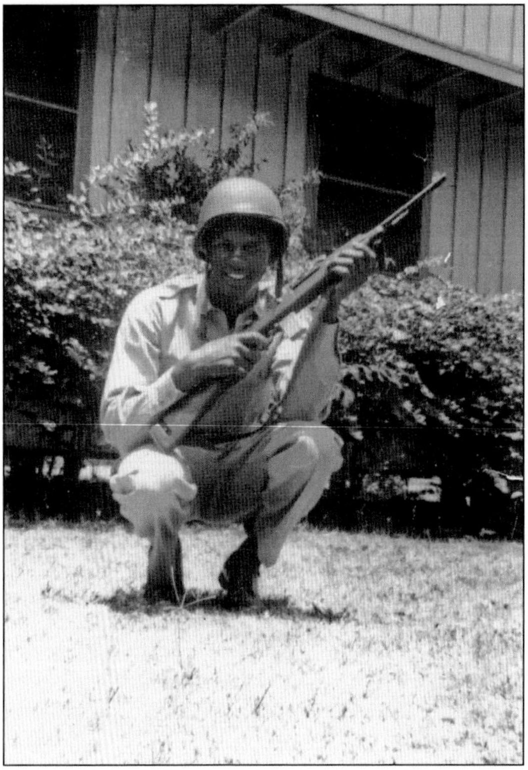

Maurice McFarlin, born in 1930 and shown around 1945, was in the Army Air Force and the reserves. Stationed in Spokane, he married Mary Emma Hill in 1952. Their children are Maurice Jr., Muriel, and Cheryl. Maurice Sr. was the first black postal carrier in Spokane and continued that work for 23 years in his native Chicago. He died in 1977. (Courtesy of Muriel, Cheryl, and Maurice McFarlin Jr.)

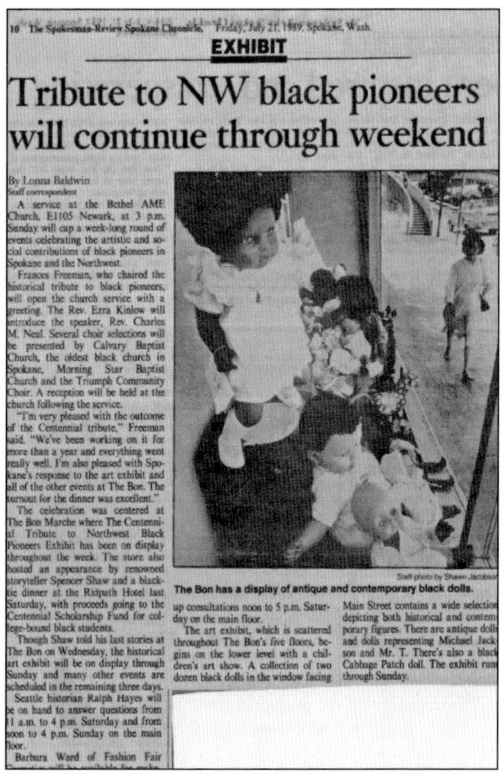

10 The Spokesman-Review Spokane Chronicle, Friday, July 21, 1989, Spokane, Wash.

EXHIBIT

Tribute to NW black pioneers will continue through weekend

By Lonna Baldwin
Staff correspondent

A service at the Bethel AME Church, E1105 Newark, at 3 p.m. Sunday will cap a week-long round of events celebrating the artistic and social contributions of black pioneers in Spokane and the Northwest.

Frances Freeman, who chaired the historical tribute to black pioneers, will open the church service with a greeting. The Rev. Ezra Kinlow will introduce the speaker, Rev. Charles M. Neal. Several choir selections will be presented by Calvary Baptist Church, the oldest black church in Spokane, Morning Star Baptist Church and the Triumph Community Choir. A reception will be held at the church following the service.

"I'm very pleased with the outcome of the Centennial tribute," Freeman said. "We've been working on it for more than a year and everything went really well. I'm also pleased with Spokane's response to the art exhibit and all of the other events at The Bon. The turnout for the dinner was excellent."

The celebration was centered at The Bon Marche where The Centennial Tribute to Northwest Black Pioneers Exhibit has been on display throughout the week. The store also hosted an appearance by renowned storyteller Spencer Shaw and a black-tie dinner at the Ridpath Hotel last Saturday, with proceeds going to the Centennial Scholarship Fund for college-bound black students.

Though Shaw told his last stories at The Bon on Wednesday, the historical art exhibit will be on display through Sunday and many other events are scheduled in the remaining three days.

Seattle historian Ralph Hayes will be on hand to answer questions from 11 a.m. to 4 p.m. Saturday and from noon to 4 p.m. Sunday on the main floor.

Barbara Ward of Fashion Fair

Staff photo by Shawn Jacobson

The Bon has a display of antique and contemporary black dolls.

up consultations noon to 5 p.m. Saturday on the main floor.

The art exhibit, which is scattered throughout The Bon's five floors, begins on the lower level with a children's art show. A collection of two dozen black dolls in the window facing Main Street contains a wide selection depicting both historical and contemporary figures. There are antique dolls and dolls representing Michael Jackson and Mr. T. There's also a black Cabbage Patch doll. The exhibit runs through Sunday.

This newspaper article about the Centennial Tribute to Northwest Black Pioneers, dated Friday, July 21, 1989, shows a few of the 100 black dolls that were featured in the display window at the Bon Marche (Macy's) store in downtown Spokane. Each floor had displays and photographs of the exhibits from Spokane, Seattle, and Tacoma. "Soul food" was served in the store restaurant. (Staff correspondent Lonna Baldwin, copyright 1989. Printed with permission of the *Spokesman Review*.)

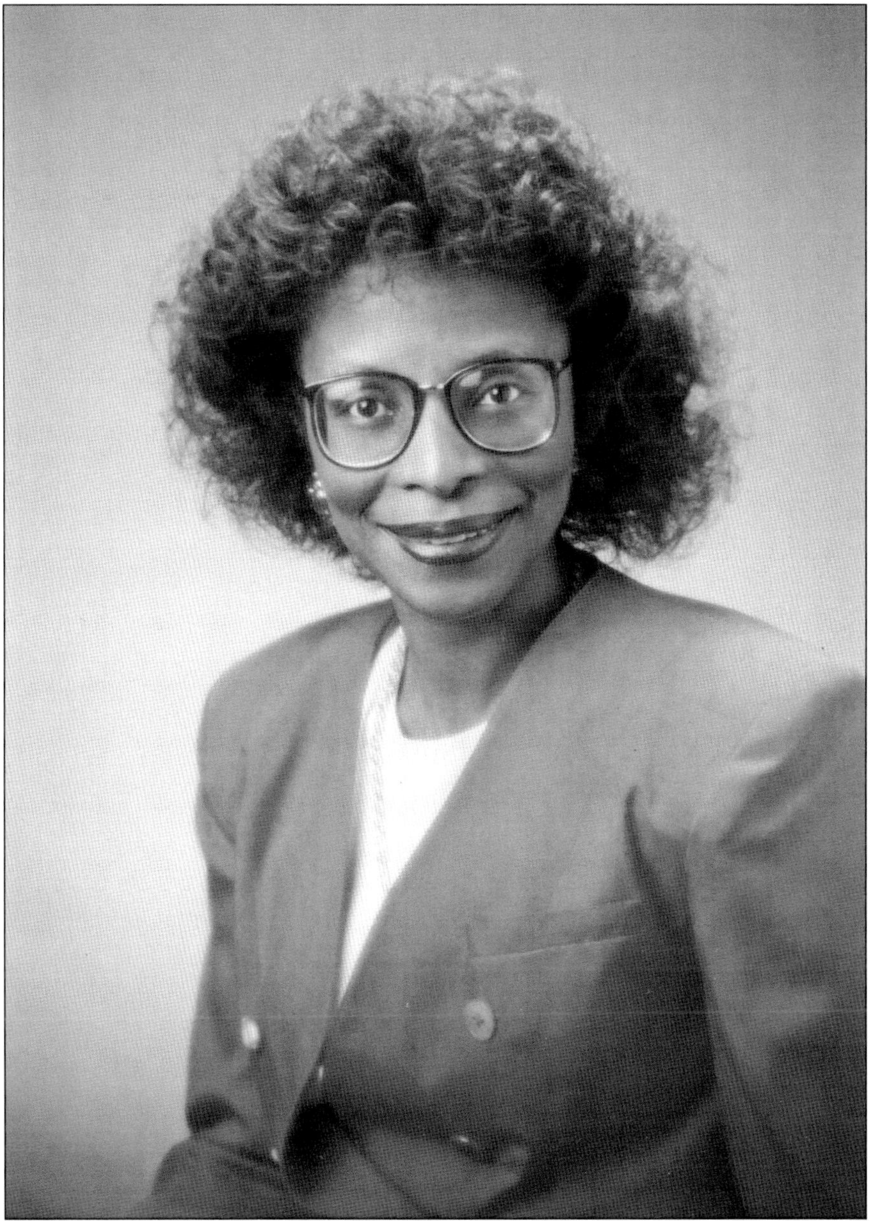

Roberta and Nate Greene owned one of the state of Washington's largest minority-owned businesses, Empire Ford, 423 West Third Avenue, for 21 years until it closed in 2009. Roberta Greene served two terms on the Spokane City Council, as well as on the Community Colleges of Spokane board of trustees, the Workforce Training and Education Coordinating Council, the Spokane Lilac Festival, and the United Way. She is a longtime member of Bethel AME Church, and at this writing, she is a member of the Washington Dental Service board of directors. Nate Greene has been involved in various professional and community based groups and organizations, including the Spokane Area Chamber of Commerce, the state Economic Development Finance Authority, and the Spokane Public Facilities District. He also has been active in fund-raising for the alumni association of Talladega College in Alabama. The Greenes have one son, Steven. This photograph of Roberta is from about 2001.

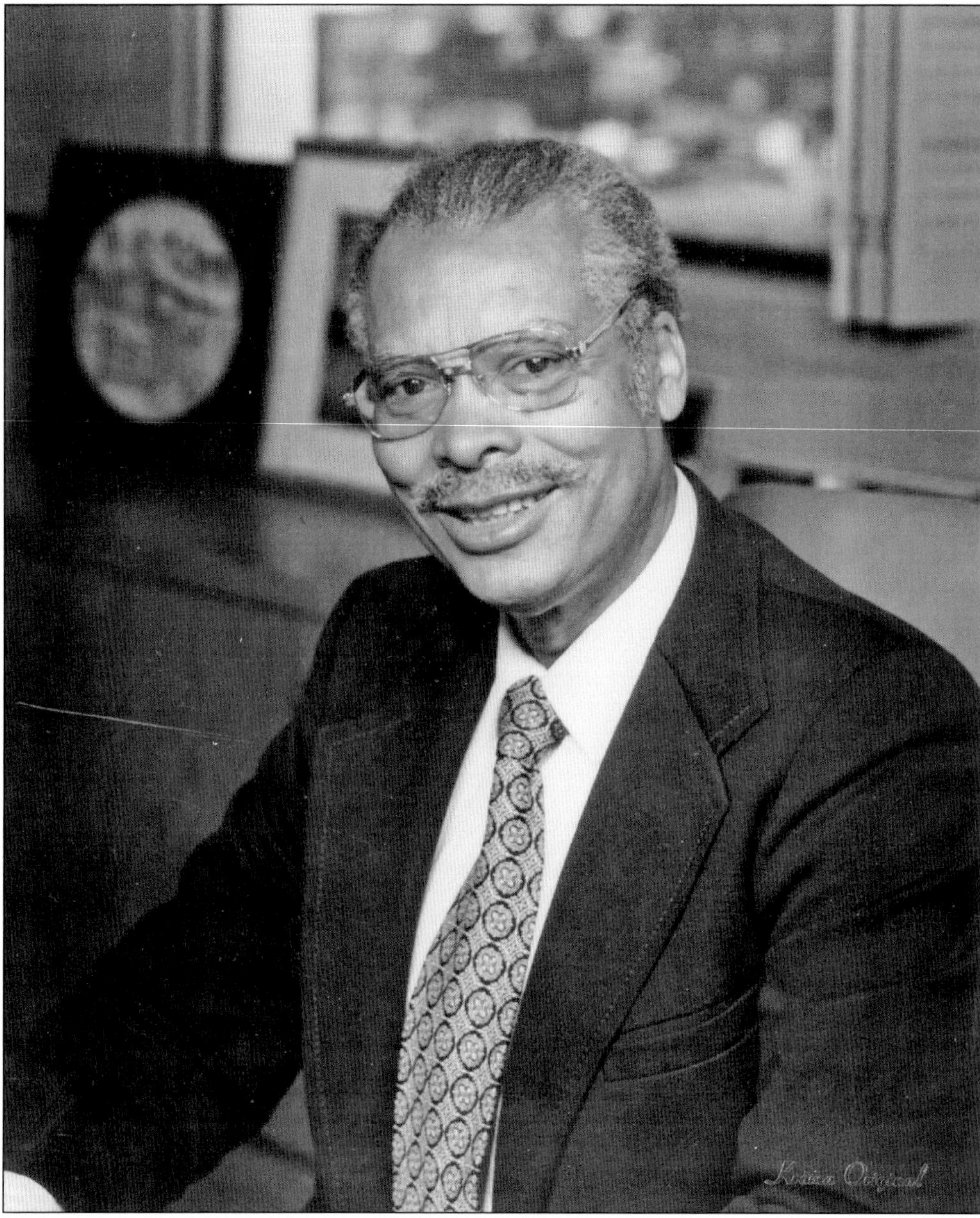

This photograph is of beloved Spokane mayor James E. Chase. Born March 29, 1914, in Wharton, Texas, he was the youngest of seven children. He attended an all-black high school in Ballenger, Texas, although he never received a high school diploma. He and his childhood friend Elmo Dalbert, along with another friend, Harry Blackwell, rode a freight train to Spokane. Once Chase arrived in Spokane, he met Clarence Freeman, and they helped to form the Negro Active League. Chase and Dalbert opened a very successful auto body repair shop. Chase married Eleanor Barrow, and they had one son. His political career began when he won a seat on the Spokane City Council in 1975. He ran for mayor in 1981 and won, becoming the city's first black mayor. His victory was celebrated with a gala ball at the Davenport Hotel as people of all races and all walks of life gathered in the middle of a snowstorm to wish him well. James Chase passed away on May 19, 1987, having made his mark on the city he loved.

ABOUT THE ORGANIZATION

Spokane Northwest Black Pioneers is an organization that was started in July 1988. The organization originally was called A Centennial Tribute to Northwest Black Pioneers. This centennial tribute was sponsored by the Bon Marche department stores to be held in conjunction with the celebration of the 100th centennial of the state of Washington.

In Spokane, black pioneers and others, along with John DeGues and his staff at the Bon Marche, had meetings to plan the celebration. Clarence and Frances Freeman were cochairs for the event.

The Spokane Black Pioneer Committee collected photographs and artifacts to be used in the display. The photographs that were collected from local black citizens and others were taken to Wirsche's photograph studio and copied for the exhibit. Then the originals were returned to the owners. The photographs were captioned by the members, with the help of Nancy Compau of the Spokane Public Library's Northwest Room. The committee met at the Bon Marche from July 18, 1988, until the actual exhibit, from July 15 through July 23, 1989.

The exhibit opened to the public July 16, 1989. The night before, there was a black-tie affair at the Ridpath Hotel for the committee and guests. There also was a special showing of the exhibit. A display was placed on each floor of the Bon Marche department store in downtown Spokane, and each window of the store also had a special display. A soul food menu was offered to patrons in the store's restaurant.

Included with the Spokane exhibit were exhibits from black pioneers in Seattle and Tacoma. All of these exhibits became part of a display that traveled around the state of Washington.

All of the monies collected from the events (T-shirt and booklet sales, restaurant income, and so on) were used for scholarships presented to black students. With this purpose in mind, Spokane Northwest Black Pioneers continues to exhibit its photographs at schools, colleges, churches, civic organizations, businesses, and social gatherings.

Spokane Northwest Black Pioneers' proceeds from sales of this book will be used for scholarships for African American students and to preserve the collection.

—Jerrelene Williamson, President
Spokane Northwest Black Pioneers
cambridge32@comcast.net